D0096401

Anatomy and Physiology

by
Phillip E. Pack, Ph.D.

INCORPORATED

LINCOLN, NEBRASKA 68501

Acknowledgments

I want to thank William C. Matthai, Ph.D., for his valuable suggestions and correction. My sincere thanks to Michele Spence of Cliffs Notes for her always insightful suggestions, careful editing, and endless patience. A thank you to my teachers, colleagues, and students for their challenging questions and stimulating discussions. My sincere gratitude to my wife, Mary McGinnis, for her critical reading and valuable suggestions.

To Mary and Megan

Cover photograph by David Gaz/ The Image Bank

FIRST EDITION

ISBN 0-8220-5301-2

CONTENTS

CONTENTS

CONTENTS

CONTENTS

CONTENTS

CONTENTS

CONTENTS

Anatomy is the study of the *structure* and relationship between body parts. **Physiology** is the study of the *function* of body parts and the body as a whole. Some specializations within each of these sciences follow.

- **Gross (macroscopic) anatomy** is the study of body parts visible to the naked eye, such as the heart or bones.

- **Histology** is the study of tissues at the microscopic level.

- **Cytology** is the study of cells at the microscopic level.

- **Neurophysiology** is the study of how the nervous system functions.

Organization of Living Systems

Living systems can be described from various perspectives, from the very broad (looking at the entire earth) to the very minute (individual atoms). Each perspective provides information about how or why a living system functions.

1. At the **chemical level,** atoms, molecules (combinations of atoms), and the chemical bonds between atoms provide the framework upon which all living activity is based.

2. The **cell** is the smallest unit of life. **Organelles** within the cell are specialized bodies performing specific cellular functions. Cells themselves may be specialized. Thus, there are nerve cells, bone cells, and muscle cells.

3. A **tissue** is a group of similar cells performing a common function. Muscle tissue, for example, consists of muscle cells.

4. An **organ** is a group of different kinds of tissues working together to perform a particular activity. The heart is an organ composed of muscle, nerve, connective, and epithelial tissues.

5. An **organ system** is two or more organs working together to accomplish a particular task. The digestive system, for example, involves the coordinated activities of many organs, including the mouth, stomach, small and large intestines, pancreas, and liver.

6. An **organism** is a system possessing the characteristics of living things—the ability to obtain and process energy, the ability to respond to environmental changes, and the ability to reproduce.

Homeostasis

A characteristic of all living systems is **homeostasis,** or the maintenance of stable, internal conditions within specific limits. In many cases, stable conditions are maintained by **negative feedback.**

In negative feedback, a sensing mechanism (a **receptor**) detects a change in conditions beyond specific limits. A control center, or **integrator** (often the brain), evaluates the change and activates a second mechanism (an **effector**) to correct the condition. Conditions are constantly monitored by receptors and evaluated by the control center. When the control center determines that conditions have returned to normal, corrective action is discontinued. Thus, in *negative* feedback, the variant condition is canceled, or negated, so that conditions are returned to normal. Compare this with **positive feedback,** in which an action intensifies a condition so that it is driven farther beyond normal limits. Such positive feedback is uncommon but does occur during childbirth (labor contractions), lactation (where milk production increases in response to an increase in nursing), and sexual orgasm.

The regulation of glucose concentration in the blood illustrates how homeostasis is maintained by negative feedback. After a meal, the absorption of glucose (a sugar) from the digestive tract increases the amount of glucose in the blood. In response, specialized cells in the pancreas secrete the hormone insulin, which circulates through the blood and stimulates liver and muscle cells to absorb the glucose. Once blood glucose levels return to normal, insulin secretion stops. Later, perhaps after heavy exercise, blood glucose levels may drop because muscle cells absorb glucose from the blood and use it as a source of energy for muscle contraction. In response to falling blood glucose levels, another group of specialized pancreatic cells secretes a second hormone, glucagon. Glucagon stimulates the liver to release its stored glucose into the blood. When blood glucose levels return to normal, glucagon secretion stops.

Anatomical Terminology

In order to identify areas of the body accurately, clearly defined anatomical terms are used. These terms refer to the body in the **anatomical position**—standing erect, facing forward, arms down at the side, with the palms turned forward. In this position, the following terms apply.

1. *Directional terms* are used to describe the relative position of one body part to another. These terms are listed in Table 1.

2. *Body planes and sections* are used to describe how the body or an organ is divided into two parts.

   - **Sagittal planes** divide a body or organ vertically into a right and left part. If the right and left parts are *equal,* the plane is the **midsagittal plane;** if *unequal,* the plane is a **parasagittal plane.**

   - A **frontal (coronal) plane** divides the body or organ vertically into a front and rear part.

Term	Definition	Example
Superior	Above another structure.	The heart is superior to the stomach.
Inferior	Below another structure.	The stomach is inferior to the heart.
Anterior (or ventral)	Toward the front of the body.	The navel is anterior to the spine.
Posterior (or dorsal)	Toward the back of the body.	The spine is posterior to the navel.
Medial	Toward the midline of the body. (The midline divides the body into equal right and left sides.)	The nose is medial to the eyes.
Lateral	Away from the midline of the body (or toward the side of the body).	The ears are lateral to the nose.
Ipsilateral	On the same side of the body.	The spleen and descending colon are ipsilateral.
Contralateral	On opposite sides of the body.	The ascending and descending colons are contralateral.
Intermediate	Between two structures.	The knee is intermediate between the thigh and leg.
Proximal	Closer to the point of attachment of a limb.	The elbow is proximal to the wrist.
Distal	Farther from the point of attachment of a limb.	The foot is distal to the knee.
Superficial	Toward the surface of the body.	The skin is superficial to the muscle.
Deep	Away from the surface of the body.	The skeleton is deep to the skin.

■ Table 1 ■

- A **horizontal** (**transverse**) **plane** divides the body or organ horizontally into a top and bottom part.

3. *Body cavities* are enclosed areas that house organs. These cavities are organized into two groups, as follows.

   ■ The **dorsal** (back) **body cavity** includes the **cranial cavity** (which contains the brain) and the **vertebral cavity** (which contains the spinal cord).

   ■ The **ventral** (front) **body cavity** includes the **thoracic cavity** (which contains the lungs, each in its own **pleural cavity**, and the heart, in the **pericardial cavity**) and the **abdomino-pelvic cavity** (which contains the digestive organs in the **abdominal cavity** and the bladder and reproductive organs in the **pelvic cavity**).

4. *Regional terms* identify specific areas of the body. In some cases, a descriptive word is used to identify the location. For example, the **axial region** refers to the main axis of the body—the head, neck, and trunk. The **appendicular region** refers to the appendages—the arms and legs. Other regional terms use a body part to identify a particular region of the body. For example, the nasal region refers to the nose. Figure 1 lists the major regional terms.

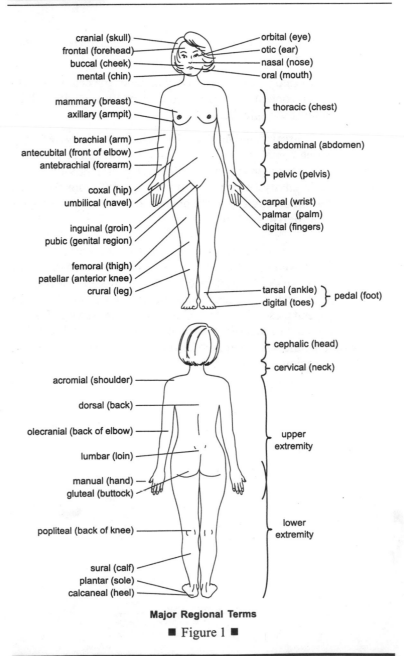

cranial (skull)
frontal (forehead)
buccal (cheek)
mental (chin)

orbital (eye)
otic (ear)
nasal (nose)
oral (mouth)

mammary (breast)
axillary (armpit)

thoracic (chest)

brachial (arm)
antecubital (front of elbow)
antebrachial (forearm)

abdominal (abdomen)

pelvic (pelvis)

coxal (hip)
umbilical (navel)

carpal (wrist)
palmar (palm)
digital (fingers)

inguinal (groin)
pubic (genital region)

femoral (thigh)
patellar (anterior knee)
crural (leg)

tarsal (ankle)
digital (toes)

pedal (foot)

cephalic (head)

cervical (neck)

acromial (shoulder)

dorsal (back)

olecranial (back of elbow)

lumbar (loin)

upper extremity

manual (hand)
gluteal (buttock)

popliteal (back of knee)

lower extremity

sural (calf)
plantar (sole)
calcaneal (heel)

Major Regional Terms

■ Figure 1 ■

Atoms, Molecules, Ions, and Bonds

Matter is anything that takes up space and has mass. Matter consists of **elements** that possess unique physical and chemical properties. The smallest quantity of an element that still possesses the characteristics of that element is an **atom.** Atoms are represented by chemical symbols of one or two letters, such as C (carbon), Ca (calcium), H (hydrogen), O (oxygen), N (nitrogen), and P (phosphorus). Atoms chemically bond together to form **molecules,** and the relative numbers of atoms in a molecule are given as subscripts in its **chemical formula** (O_2, H_2O, $C_6H_{12}O_6$). When the atoms in a molecule are different, the molecule is a **compound** (H_2O and $C_6H_{12}O_6$, but not O_2).

The atoms of every element consist of a nucleus of positively charged **protons** and neutrally charged **neutrons.** Negatively charged **electrons** are arranged outside the nucleus. The atoms of each element differ by their number of protons, neutrons, and electrons. For example, hydrogen has one proton, one electron, and no neutrons, while carbon has six protons, six neutrons, and six electrons. The number and arrangement of electrons of an atom determine the kinds of chemical bonds that it forms and how it reacts with other atoms to form molecules. There are three kinds of **chemical bonds.**

1. **Ionic** bonds form between two atoms when one or more electrons are completely transferred from one atom to the other. The atom that gains electrons has an overall negative charge, and the atom that donates electrons has an overall positive charge. Because of their positive or negative charges, these atoms are **ions.** The attraction of the positive ion to the negative ion constitutes the ionic bond. Sodium (Na) and chlorine (Cl) form ions (Na^+ and Cl^-), which attract one another to form the ionic bond in a sodium chloride (NaCl) molecule. A plus or minus sign following a chemical symbol indicates an

ion with a positive or negative charge that results from the loss or gain of one or more electrons, respectively. Numbers preceding the charges indicate ions whose charges are greater than one (Ca^{2+}, PO_3^{2-}).

2. **Covalent** bonds form when electrons are shared between atoms. That is, neither atom completely retains possession of the electrons (as happens with atoms that form ionic bonds). A **single covalent** bond is formed when two electrons are shared (one from each atom). A **double** or **triple** covalent bond is formed when four or six electrons are shared, respectively. When the two atoms sharing electrons are exactly the same, as in a molecule of oxygen gas (two oxygen atoms to form O_2), the electrons are shared equally and the bond is a **nonpolar covalent** bond. When the atoms are different, such as in a molecule of water (H_2O), the larger nucleus of the oxygen atom exerts a stronger pull on the shared electrons than does the single proton that makes up either hydrogen nucleus. In this case, a **polar covalent** bond is formed because the unequal distribution of the electrons creates areas within the molecule that have either a negative or positive charge (or pole) (Figure 2a).

3. **Hydrogen** bonds are weak bonds that form between the positively charged hydrogen atom in one covalently bonded molecule and the negatively charged area of another covalently bonded molecule. Water, for example, forms hydrogen bonds between water molecules. Since the atoms in water form a polar covalent bond, the positive area in H_2O around the hydrogen proton attracts the negative areas in an adjacent H_2O molecule. This attraction forms the hydrogen bond (Figure 2b).

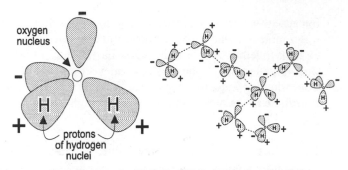

(a) A Water Molecule Showing Polarity Created by Covalent Bonds   **(b) Hydrogen Bonding Between Water Molecules**

■ Figure 2 ■

Inorganic Compounds

Inorganic compounds are typically compounds *without* carbon atoms. Water, O_2, and NaCl are examples of inorganic compounds.

Water is the most abundant substance in the body. Its abundance is due partly to its unique chemical properties, properties created by the influence of its hydrogen bonds. These properties include the following.

1. Water is an excellent **solvent.** Ionic substances are soluble in water (they dissolve) because the poles of the polar water molecules pull them apart, forming ions. Polar covalent substances are also water soluble because they share the same hydrogen bonding with water as water shares with itself. For this reason, polar covalent substances are called **hydrophilic** (water loving). Because they lack charged poles, nonpolar covalent substances do not dissolve in water and are called **hydrophobic** (water fearing).

2. Because water molecules are held together by hydrogen bonds, water molecules have a high degree of **cohesion,** or the ability to stick together. As a result, water has strong **surface tension.** This tension, in turn, gives water strong **capillary action,** allowing water to creep up narrow tubing. These qualities contribute to the movement of water through animal capillaries.

3. The temperature of water is very stable. You must add a relatively large amount of energy to warm (and boil) it and remove a large amount of energy to cool (and freeze) it. So when sweat evaporates from your forehead, a large amount of heat is taken with it and you are cooled.

Organic Molecules

Organic compounds are those that have carbon atoms. In living systems, large organic molecules, called **macromolecules,** may consist of hundreds or thousands of atoms. Most macromolecules are **polymers,** molecules that consist of a single unit (monomer) repeated many times.

Four of carbon's six electrons are available to form bonds with other atoms. Thus, you will always see four lines connecting a carbon atom to other atoms, each line representing a pair of shared electrons (one electron from carbon and one from another atom). Complex molecules can be formed by stringing carbon atoms together in a straight line or by connecting carbons together to form rings. The presence of nitrogen, oxygen, and other atoms adds additional variety to these carbon molecules.

Four important classes of organic molecules—carbohydrates, lipids, proteins, and nucleic acids—are discussed below.

Carbohydrates

Carbohydrates are classified into three groups according to the number of sugar (or saccharide) molecules present.

1. A **monosaccharide** is the simplest kind of carbohydrate. It is a single sugar molecule, such as fructose or glucose (Figure 3). Sugar molecules have the formula $(CH_2O)_n$, where n is any number from 3 to 8. For glucose, n is 6, and its formula is $C_6H_{12}O_6$. The formula for fructose is also $C_6H_{12}O_6$, but as you can see in Figure 3, the placement of the carbon atoms is different. Very small changes in the position of certain atoms, such as those that distinguish glucose and fructose, may dramatically change the chemistry of a molecule.

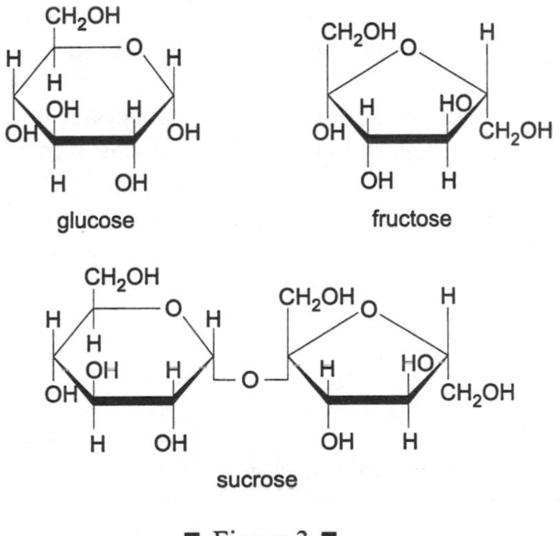

■ Figure 3 ■

2. A **disaccharide** consists of two linked sugar molecules. Glucose and fructose, for example, link to form sucrose.

3. A **polysaccharide** consists of a series of connected monosaccharides. Thus, a polysaccharide is a polymer because it con-

sists of repeating units of a monosaccharide. **Starch** is a polysaccharide made up of a thousand or more glucose molecules and is used in plants for energy storage. A similar polysaccharide, **glycogen,** is used in animals for the same purpose.

Lipids

Lipids are a class of substances that are insoluble in water (and other polar solvents) but are soluble in nonpolar substances (like ether or chloroform). There are three major groups of lipids.

1. **Triglycerides** include fats, oils, and waxes. They consist of three **fatty acids** attached to a **glycerol** molecule (Figure 4). Fatty acids are hydrocarbons (chains of covalently bonded carbons and hydrogens) with a carboxyl group (–COOH) at one end of the chain. A **saturated** fatty acid has a single covalent bond between each pair of carbon atoms, and each carbon has two hydrogens bonded to it. You can remember this fact by thinking that each carbon is "saturated" with hydrogen. An **unsaturated** fatty acid occurs when a double covalent bond replaces a single covalent bond and two hydrogen atoms (Figure 4). **Polyunsaturated** fatty acids have many of these double bonds.

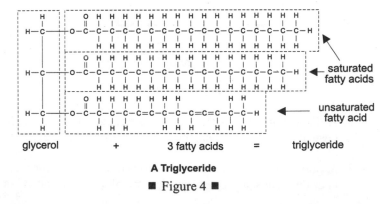

A Triglyceride

■ Figure 4 ■

2. **Phospholipids** look just like lipids except that one of the fatty acid chains is replaced by a phosphate group ($-PO_3^{2-}$) (Figure 5). Additional chemical groups (indicated by R in Figure 5) are usually attached to the phosphate group. Since the fatty acid "tails" of phospholipids are nonpolar and hydrophobic and the glycerol and phosphate "heads" are polar and hydrophilic, phospholipids are often found oriented in sandwichlike formations with the hydrophobic tails grouped together on the inside of the sandwich and the hydrophilic heads oriented toward the outside. Such formations of phospholipids provide the structural foundation of cell membranes.

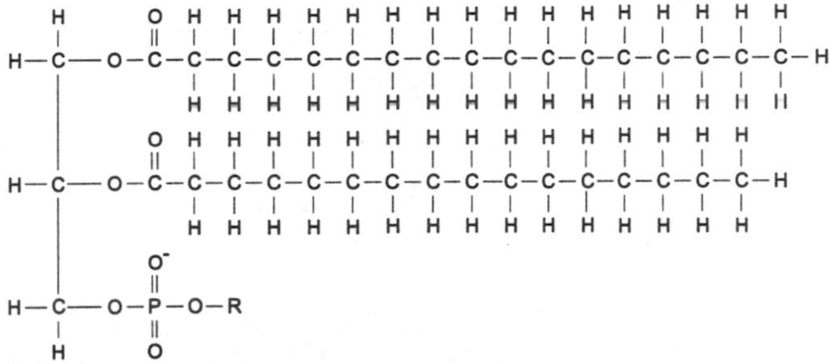

A Phospholipid

■ Figure 5 ■

3. **Steroids** are characterized by a backbone of four linked carbon rings (Figure 6). Examples of steroids include cholesterol (a component of cell membranes) and certain hormones, including testosterone and estrogen.

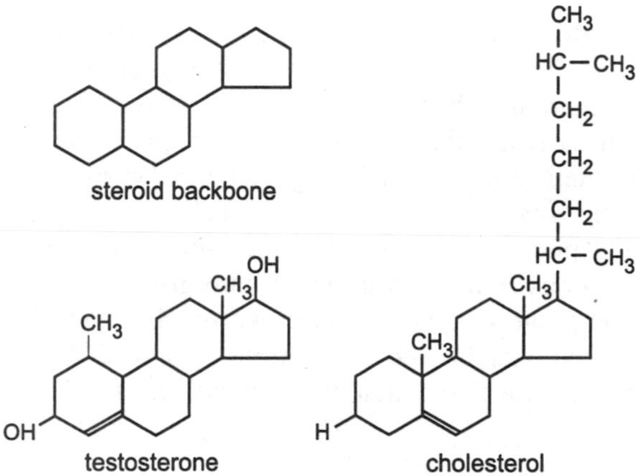

■ Figure 6 ■

Proteins

Proteins represent a class of molecules that have varied functions. Eggs, muscles, antibodies, silk, fingernails, and many hormones are partially or entirely proteins. Although the functions of proteins are diverse, their structures are similar. All proteins are polymers of **amino acids;** that is, they consist of a chain of amino acids covalently bonded. The bonds between the amino acids are called **peptide bonds,** and the chain is a **polypeptide,** or **peptide.** One protein differs from another by the number and arrangement of the 20 different amino acids. Each amino acid consists of a central carbon bonded to an amino group (–NH$_2$), a carboxyl group (–COOH), and a hydrogen atom (Figure 7). The fourth bond of the central carbon is shown with the letter R, which indicates an atom or group of atoms that varies from one kind of amino acid to another. For the simplest amino acid, glycine, the R is a hydrogen atom. For serine, R is CH$_2$OH. For other amino acids, R may contain sulfur (as in cysteine) or a carbon ring (as in phenylalanine).

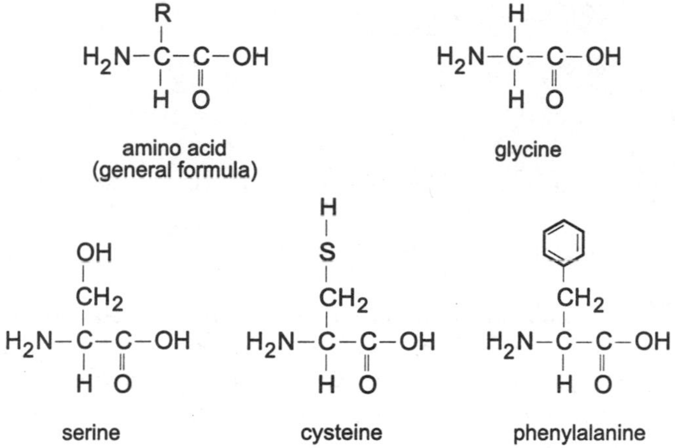

Figure 7

There are four levels that describe the structure of a protein:

1. The **primary structure** of a protein describes the order of amino acids. Using three letters to represent each amino acid, the primary structure for the protein antidiuretic hormone (ADH) can be written as cys-tyr-phe-glu-asn-cys-pro-arg-gly.

2. The **secondary structure** of a protein is a three-dimensional shape that results from hydrogen bonding between amino acids. The bonding produces a spiral (**alpha helix**) or a folded plane that looks much like the pleats on a skirt (**beta pleated sheet**).

3. The **tertiary structure** of a protein includes additional three-dimensional shaping that results from interactions among R groups. For example, hydrophobic R groups tend to clump toward the inside of the protein, while hydrophilic R groups clump toward the outside of the protein. Additional three-dimensional shaping occurs when the amino acid cysteine bonds to another cysteine across a disulfide bond. This causes the protein to twist around the bond (Figure 8).

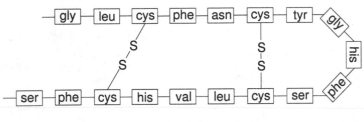

■ Figure 8 ■

4. The **quaternary structure** describes a protein that is assembled from two or more separate peptide chains. The protein hemoglobin, for example, consists of four peptide chains that are held together by hydrogen bonding, interactions among R groups, and disulfide bonds.

Nucleic Acids

The genetic information of a cell is stored in molecules of **deoxyribonucleic acid (DNA)**. The DNA, in turn, passes its genetic instructions to **ribonucleic acid (RNA)** for directing various metabolic activities of the cell.

DNA is a polymer of **nucleotides** (Figure 9). A DNA nucleotide consists of three parts—a **nitrogen base,** a five-carbon sugar called

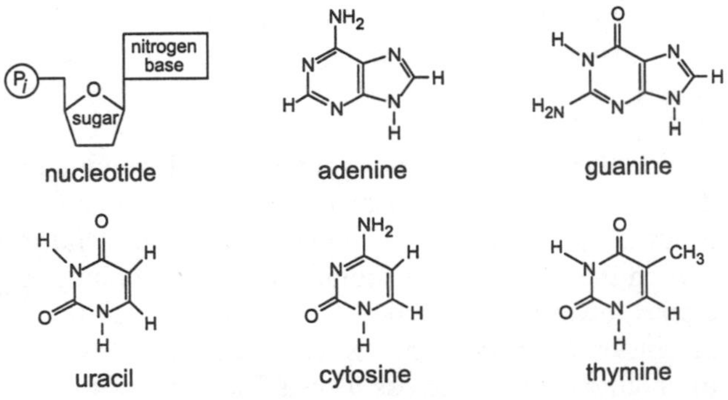

nucleotide

adenine

guanine

uracil

cytosine

thymine

■ Figure 9 ■

deoxyribose, and a **phosphate group.** There are four DNA nucleotides, each with one of the four nitrogen bases (adenine, thymine, cytosine, and guanine). The first letter of each of these four bases is often used to symbolize the respective nucleotide (A for adenine nucleotide, for example).

Figure 10 shows how two strands of nucleotides, paired by weak hydrogen bonds between the bases, form a double-stranded DNA. When bonded in this way, DNA forms a two-stranded spiral, or double helix. *Note that adenine always bonds with thymine and cytosine always bonds with guanine.*

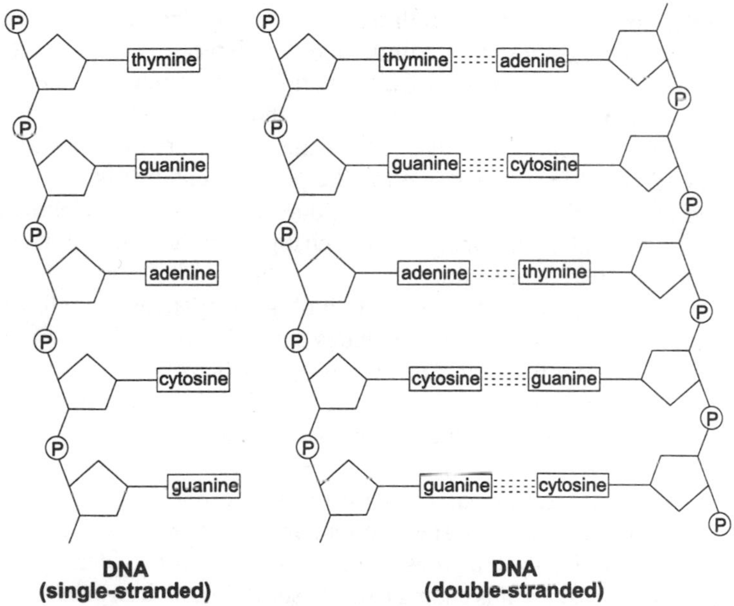

DNA
(single-stranded)

DNA
(double-stranded)

■ Figure 10 ■

RNA differs from DNA in the following ways.

1. The sugar in the nucleotides that make an RNA molecule is **ribose,** not deoxyribose as it is in DNA.

2. The thymine nucleotide does not occur in RNA. It is replaced by **uracil.** When pairing of bases occurs in RNA, uracil (instead of thymine) pairs with adenine.

3. RNA is usually single-stranded and does not form a double helix as does DNA.

Chemical Reactions in Metabolic Processes

In order for a **chemical reaction** to take place, the reacting molecules (or atoms) must first collide and then have sufficient energy (**activation energy**) to trigger the formation of new bonds. Although many reactions can occur spontaneously, the presence of a **catalyst** accelerates the rate of the reaction because it lowers the activation energy required for the reaction to take place. A catalyst is any substance that accelerates a reaction but does not undergo a chemical change itself. Since the catalyst is not changed by the reaction, it can be used over and over again.

Chemical reactions that occur in biological systems are referred to as **metabolism.** Metabolism includes the breakdown of substances (**catabolism**), the formation of new products (**synthesis** or **anabolism**), or the transferring of energy from one substance to another. Metabolic processes have the following characteristics in common:

1. **Enzymes** act as catalysts for metabolic reactions. Enzymes are proteins that are specific for particular reactions. The standard suffix for enzymes is "ase," so it is easy to identify enzymes that use this ending (though some do not). The substances on which the enzyme acts is called the **substrate.** For example, the enzyme amylase catalyzes the breakdown of the substrate amylose (starch) to produce the product glucose.

The **induced-fit model** describes how enzymes work. Within the protein (the enzyme), there is an **active site** with which the reactants readily interact because of the shape, polarity, or other characteristics of the active site. The interaction of the reactants (substrate) and the enzyme causes the enzyme to change shape. The new position places the substrate molecules in a position favorable to their reaction and accelerates the formation of the product.

2. **ATP (adenosine triphosphate)** is a common source of activation energy for metabolic reactions. In Figure 11, the wavy lines between the last two phosphate groups of the ATP molecule indicate high-energy bonds. When ATP supplies energy to a reaction, it is usually the energy in the last bond that is delivered to the reaction. In the process of giving up this energy, the last phosphate bond is broken and the ATP molecule is converted to ADP (adenosine diphosphate) and a phosphate group (indicated by P_i). In contrast, new ATP molecules are assembled by phosphorylation when ADP combines with a phosphate group using energy obtained from some energy-rich molecule (like glucose).

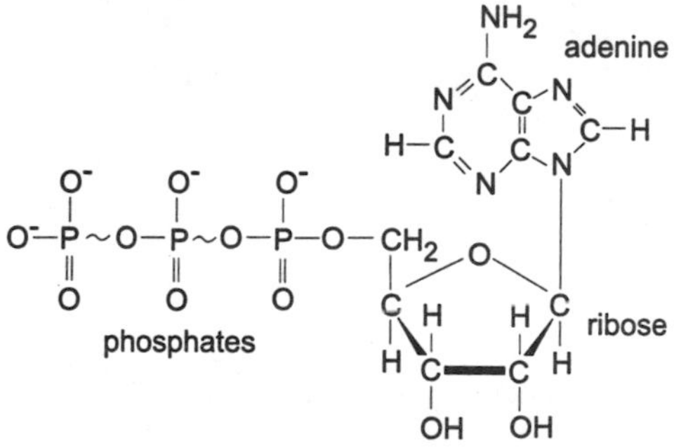

Adenosine Triphosphate (ATP)
■ Figure 11 ■

3. **Cofactors** are nonprotein molecules that assist enzymes. A **holoenzyme** is the union of the cofactor and the enzyme (called an **apoenzyme** when part of a holoenzyme). If cofactors are *organic*, they are called **coenzymes** and usually function to donate or accept some component of a reaction, often electrons. Some vitamins are coenzymes or components of coenzymes. *Inorganic* cofactors are often metal ions, like Fe^{++}.

The Cell and Its Membrane

The **cell** is the basic functional unit of all living things. The **plasma membrane (cell membrane)** bounds the cell and encloses the nucleus and cytoplasm. The **cytoplasm** consists of specialized bodies called organelles suspended in a fluid matrix, the **cytosol,** which consists of water and dissolved substances such as proteins and nutrients.

The Plasma Membrane

The **plasma membrane** separates internal metabolic events from the external environment and controls the movement of materials into and out of the cell. The plasma membrane is a double phospholipid membrane (**lipid bilayer**) with the nonpolar hydrophobic tails pointing toward the inside of the membrane and the polar hydrophilic heads forming the two outer faces (Figure 12).

Proteins and cholesterol molecules are scattered throughout the flexible phospholipid membrane. Proteins may attach loosely to the inner or outer surface of the membrane (**peripheral proteins**), or they may lie across the membrane, extending from inside to outside (**integral proteins**). The mosaic nature of scattered proteins within a flexible matrix of phospholipid molecules describes the **fluid mosaic model** of the cell membrane. Additional features of the plasma membrane follow.

1. The **phospholipid bilayer** is selectively permeable. Only small, uncharged, polar molecules, such as H_2O and CO_2, and hydrophobic molecules—nonpolar molecules like O_2 and lipid-soluble molecules such as hydrocarbons—can freely cross the membrane.

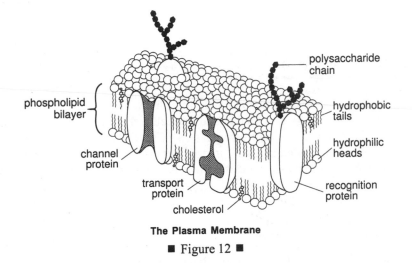

The Plasma Membrane

■ Figure 12 ■

2. **Channel proteins** provide passageways through the membrane for certain hydrophilic (water-soluble) substances such as polar and charged molecules.

3. **Transport proteins** spend energy (ATP) to transfer materials across the membrane. When energy is used for this purpose, the materials are said to be *actively* transported, and the process is called **active transport.**

4. **Recognition proteins** distinguish the identity of neighboring cells. These proteins have oligosaccharide (short polysaccharide) chains attached to their surfaces extending out from the cell.

5. **Adhesion proteins** attach cells to neighboring cells or provide anchors for the internal filaments and tubules that give stability to the cell.

6. **Receptor proteins** provide binding sites for hormones or other trigger molecules. In response to the hormone or trigger molecule, a specific cell response is activated.

7. **Electron transfer proteins** are involved in transferring electrons from one molecule to another during chemical reactions.

The Nucleus and Other Organelles

Organelles are bodies within the cytoplasm that serve to physically separate the various metabolic reactions that occur within cells. They include the following (Figure 13).

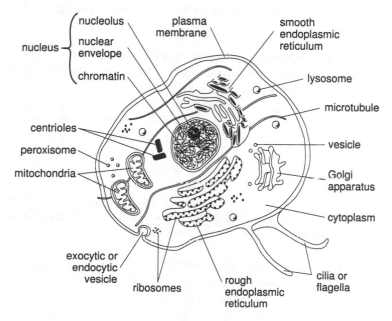

■ Figure 13 ■

1. The **nucleus** is bounded by the **nuclear envelope,** a phospholipid bilayer similar to the plasma membrane. The nucleus contains DNA (deoxyribonucleic acid), the hereditary information of the cell. Normally, the DNA is spread out within the nucleus as a threadlike matrix called **chromatin.** When the cell begins to divide, the chromatin condenses into rod-shaped bodies called **chromosomes,** each of which, before dividing, is made up of two long DNA molecules and various histone molecules. The histones serve to organize the lengthy DNA, coiling it into bundles called **nucleosomes.** Also visible within the nucleus are one or more **nucleoli,** each consisting of DNA in the process of manufacturing the components of **ribosomes.** Ribosomes are shipped to the cytoplasm where they assemble amino acids into proteins. The nucleus also serves as the site for the separation of chromosomes during cell division.

2. The **endoplasmic reticulum,** or **ER,** consists of stacks of flattened sacs involved in the production of various materials. In cross section, they appear as a series of mazelike channels, often closely associated with the nucleus. When ribosomes are present, the ER (called **rough ER**) attaches polysaccharide groups to polypeptides as they are assembled by the ribosomes. **Smooth ER,** without ribosomes, is responsible for various activities, including the synthesis of lipids and hormones, especially in cells that produce these substances for export from the cell. In liver cells, smooth ER is involved in the breakdown of toxins, drugs, and toxic by-products from cellular reactions.

3. A **Golgi apparatus** (**Golgi complex** or **Golgi body**) is a group of flattened sacs arranged like a stack of bowls. They function to modify and package proteins and lipids into **vesicles,** small, spherically shaped sacs that bud from the ends of a Golgi apparatus. Vesicles often migrate to and merge with the plasma membrane, releasing their contents to the outside of the cell.

4. **Lysosomes** are vesicles from a Golgi apparatus that contain digestive enzymes. They break down food, cellular debris, and foreign invaders such as bacteria.

5. **Mitochondria** carry out aerobic respiration, a process in which energy (in the form of ATP) is obtained from carbohydrates.

6. **Microtubules, intermediate filaments,** and **microfilaments** are three protein fibers of decreasing diameter, respectively. All are involved in establishing the shape of or in coordinating movements of the **cytoskeleton,** the internal structure of the cytoplasm.

   - **Microtubules** are made of the protein **tubulin** and provide support and motility for cellular activities. They are found in the **spindle apparatus** (which guides the movement of chromosomes during cell division) and in flagella and cilia (described below), structures that project from the plasma membrane to provide motility to the cell.

   - **Intermediate filaments** provide support for maintaining the shape of the cell.

   - **Microfilaments** are made of the protein **actin** and are involved in cell motility. They are found in muscle cells and in cells that move by changing shape, such as phagocytes (white blood cells that wander throughout the body attacking bacteria and other foreign invaders).

7. **Flagella** and **cilia** are structures that protrude from the cell membrane and make wavelike movements. Flagella and cilia are classified by their lengths and by their numbers per cell: flagella are long and few; cilia are short and many. A single flagellum propels sperm, while the numerous cilia that line the respiratory tract sweep away debris. Structurally, both flagella and cilia consist of microtubules arranged in a "9 + 2" array, that is, nine pairs (doublets) of microtubules arranged in a circle surrounding a pair of microtubules (Figure 14).

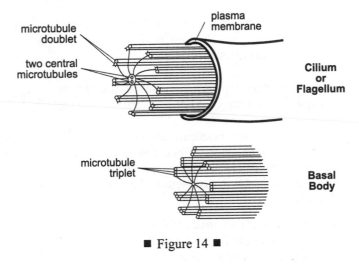

■ Figure 14 ■

8. **Centrioles** and **basal bodies** act as **microtubule organizing centers (MTOCs)**. A pair of centrioles (enclosed in a **centrosome**) located outside the nuclear envelope gives rise to the microtubules that make up the spindle apparatus used during cell division. Basal bodies are at the base of each flagellum and cilium and appear to organize their development. Both centrioles and basal bodies are made up of nine triplets arranged in a circle (Figure 14).

9. **Peroxisomes** are organelles that break down various substances. During the breakdown process, O_2 combines with hydrogen to form toxic hydrogen peroxide (H_2O_2), which in turn is converted to H_2O. Peroxisomes are common in liver and kidney cells, where they break down toxic substances.

Cell Junctions

The plasma membranes of adjacent cells are usually separated by extracellular fluids that transport nutrients and wastes to and from the blood stream. In certain tissues, however, the membranes of adjacent cells may join and form a junction. Three kinds of **cell junctions** are recognized, as follows (Figure 15).

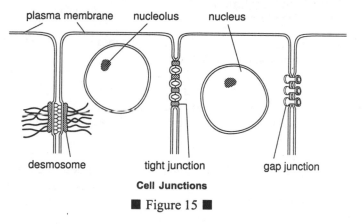

Cell Junctions

■ Figure 15 ■

1. **Desmosomes** are protein attachments between adjacent cells. Inside the plasma membrane, a desmosome bears a disk-shaped structure from which protein fibers extend into the cytoplasm. Desmosomes act like spot welds to hold together tissues that undergo considerable stress (such as skin or heart muscle).

2. **Tight junctions** are tightly stitched seams between cells. The junction completely encircles each cell, preventing the movement of material between the cells. Tight junctions are characteristic of cells lining the digestive tract, where materials are required to pass through cells (rather than intercellular spaces) to penetrate the blood stream.

3. **Gap junctions** are narrow tunnels between cells that consist of proteins called **connexons.** The proteins allow only the passage of ions and small molecules. In this manner, gap junctions allow communication between cells through the exchange of materials or through the transmission of electrical impulses.

Movement of Substances

The following terms are used to describe the movement of substances between cells and into and out of a cell.

1. The movement of substances may occur across a **selectively permeable membrane** (such as the plasma membrane). A selectively permeable membrane allows only specific substances to pass.

2. The substance whose movement is being described may be *water* (the *solvent*), or it may be the substance dissolved in the water (the *solute*).

3. Movement of substances may occur from higher to lower concentrations (*down* the concentration gradient) or the reverse (*up* or *against* the gradient).

4. Solute concentrations between two areas may be compared. A solute, relative to another region, may be **hypertonic** (a higher concentration of *solutes*), **hypotonic** (a lower concentration of *solutes*), or **isotonic** (an equal concentration of *solutes*).

5. The movement of substances may be *passive* or *active.* Active movement requires the expenditure of energy and usually occurs up a gradient.

Passive Transport Processes

Passive transport processes describe the movement of substances from regions of higher to lower concentrations (*down* a concentration gradient) and do not require expenditure of energy.

1. **Bulk flow** is the collective movement of substances in the same direction in response to a force, such as pressure. Blood moving through a blood vessel is an example of bulk flow.

2. **Simple diffusion,** or **diffusion,** is the *net* movement of substances from an area of higher concentration to an area of lower concentration. This movement occurs as a result of the random and constant motion characteristic of all molecules (atoms or ions), motion that is independent from the motion of other molecules. Since, at any one time, some molecules may be moving against the gradient and some molecules may be moving down the gradient (remember, the motion is random), the word "net" is used to indicate the overall, eventual result of the movement. If a concentration gradient exists, then the molecules (which are constantly moving) will eventually become evenly distributed (a state of **equilibrium**).

3. **Osmosis** is the diffusion of *water* molecules across a selectively permeable membrane. When water moves into a body by osmosis, hydrostatic pressure (**osmotic pressure**) may build up inside the body.

4. **Dialysis** is the diffusion of *solutes* across a selectively permeable membrane. The term dialysis is usually used when different solutes are separated by a selectively permeable membrane.

5. **Facilitated diffusion** is the diffusion of *solutes* through channel proteins in the plasma membrane. Note that *water* can pass through the plasma membrane without the aid of specialized proteins.

Active Transport Processes

Active transport is the movement of *solutes against* a gradient and requires the expenditure of *energy* (usually ATP). Active transport is achieved through one of the following two mechanisms.

1. *Transport proteins* in the plasma membrane transfer solutes such as small ions (Na^+, K^+, Cl^-, H^+), amino acids, and monosaccharides across the membrane.

2. *Vesicles* or other bodies in the cytoplasm move macromolecules or large particles across the plasma membrane. Types of **vesicular transport** are described below.

   ■ **Exocytosis** describes the process of vesicles fusing with the plasma membrane and releasing their contents to the outside of the cell. This process is common when a cell produces substances for export.

   ■ **Endocytosis** describes the capture of a substance outside the cell when the plasma membrane merges to engulf it. The substance subsequently enters the cytoplasm enclosed in a vesicle. There are three kinds of endocytosis.

   Phagocytosis ("cellular eating") occurs when *undissolved* material enters the cell. The plasma membrane wraps around the solid material and engulfs it, forming a phagocytic vesicle. Phagocytic cells (such as certain white blood cells) attack and engulf bacteria in this manner.

   Pinocytosis ("cellular drinking") occurs when *dissolved* substances enter the cell. The plasma membrane folds inward to form a channel allowing the liquid to enter. Subsequently, the plasma membrane closes off the channel, encircling the liquid inside a pinocytic vesicle.

   Receptor-mediated endocytosis occurs when *specific molecules* in the fluid surrounding the cell bond to specialized receptors in the plasma membrane. As in pinocytosis, the plasma membrane folds inward and the formation of a vesicle follows. Certain hormones are able to target specific cells by receptor-mediated endocytosis.

Cell Division

Cell division consists of two phases, **nuclear division** followed by **cytokinesis.** Nuclear division divides the genetic material in the nucleus, while cytokinesis divides the cytoplasm. There are two kinds of nuclear division—mitosis and meiosis. Mitosis divides the nucleus so that both daughter cells are genetically identical. In contrast, meiosis is a reduction division, producing daughter cells that contain half the genetic information of the parent cell.

The first step in either mitosis or meiosis begins with the condensation of the genetic material, **chromatin,** into tightly coiled bodies, the **chromosomes.** Each chromosome is made of two identical halves called **sister chromatids**, which are joined at the **centromere.** Each chromatid consists of a single, tightly coiled molecule of DNA. **Somatic cells** (all body cells except eggs and sperm) are **diploid cells** because each cell contains two copies of every chromosome. A pair of such chromosomes is called a **homologous pair.** In a homologous pair of chromosomes, one homologue originates from the maternal parent, the other from the paternal parent. There are 46 chromosomes, 23 homologous pairs, consisting of a total of 92 chromatids.

When a cell is not dividing, the chromatin is enclosed within a clearly defined nuclear envelope, one or more nucleoli are visible within the nucleus, and two centrosomes (each containing two centrioles) lie adjacent to one another outside the nuclear envelope. These features are characteristic of **interphase,** the nondividing but metabolically active period of the **cell cycle** (Figure 16). When cell division begins, these features change, as described below.

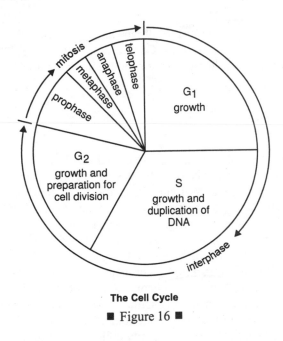

The Cell Cycle

■ Figure 16 ■

Mitosis

There are four phases in **mitosis** (adjective, **mitotic**): **prophase, metaphase, anaphase,** and **telophase** (Figure 17).

1. During **prophase,** the nucleoli disappear, the chromatin condenses into chromosomes, the nuclear envelope breaks down, and the **mitotic spindle** is assembled. The development of the mitotic spindle begins as the centrosomes move apart to opposite ends (poles) of the nucleus. As they move apart, microtubules develop from each centrosome, increasing in length by the addition of tubulin units. Microtubules from each centrosome connect to specialized regions in the centromere called **kinetochores.** Microtubules tug on the kinetochores, moving the chromosomes back and forth, toward one pole, then the other. In addition to these microtubules, the spindle also includes other microtubules from each centrosome that overlap

at the center of the spindle and do not attach to the chromosomes.

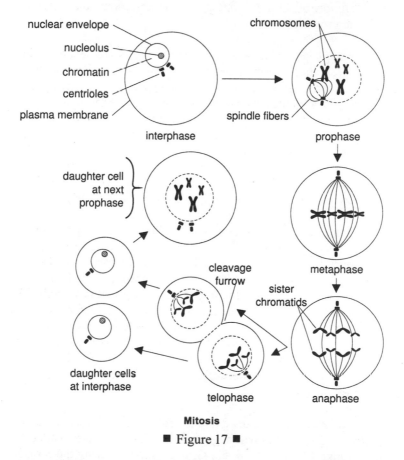

Mitosis
■ Figure 17 ■

2. **Metaphase** begins when the chromosomes are distributed across the **metaphase plate,** a plane lying between the two poles of the spindle. Metaphase ends when the microtubules, still attached to the kinetochores, pull each chromosome apart into two chromatids. Each chromatid is complete with a cen-

tromere and kinetochores. Once separated from its sister chromatid, each chromatid is called a chromosome. (To count the number of chromosomes at any one time, count the number of centromeres.)

3. **Anaphase** begins after the chromosomes are separated into chromatids. During anaphase, the microtubules connected to the chromatids (now chromosomes) shorten, effectively pulling the chromosomes to opposite poles. Overlapping microtubules originating from opposite centrosomes but not attached to chromosomes interact to push the poles farther apart. At the end of anaphase, each pole has a complete set of chromosomes, the same number of chromosomes as the original cell. (Since it consists of only one chromatid, each chromosome contains only a single copy of the DNA molecule.)

4. **Telophase** concludes the nuclear division. During this phase, a nuclear envelope develops around each pole, forming two nuclei. The chromosomes within each of these nuclei disperse into chromatin, and the nucleoli reappear. Simultaneously, **cytokinesis** occurs, dividing the cytoplasm into two cells. Microfilaments form a ring inside the plasma membrane between the two newly forming nuclei. As the microfilaments shorten, they act like purse strings to pull the plasma membrane into the center, dividing the cell into two daughter cells. The groove that forms as the purse strings are tightened is called a **cleavage furrow.**

Once mitosis is completed and interphase begins, the cell begins a period of growth. Growth begins during the first phase, called G_1, and continues through the S and G_2 phases. Also during the S phase the second DNA molecule for each chromosome is synthesized. As a result of this DNA replication, each chromosome gains a second chromatid. During the G_2 period of growth, materials for the next mitotic division are prepared. The time span from one cell division through G_1, S, and G_2 is called a **cell cycle** (Figure 16).

A cell that begins mitosis in the diploid state, that is, with two copies of every chromosome, will end mitosis with two copies of every chromosome. However, each of these chromosomes will consist of only one chromatid, or one DNA molecule. During interphase, the second DNA molecule is replicated from the first, so that when the next mitotic division begins, each chromosome will, again, consist of two chromatids.

Meiosis

Meiosis (adjective, **meiotic**) is very similar to mitosis. The major distinction is that meiosis consists of two groups of divisions, meiosis I and meiosis II (Figure 18). In meiosis I, homologous chromosomes pair at the metaphase plate, and then the homologues migrate to opposite poles. In meiosis II, chromosomes spread across the metaphase plate, and sister chromatids separate and migrate to opposite poles. Thus, meiosis II is analogous to mitosis. A summary of each meiotic stage follows.

1. **Prophase I** begins like prophase of mitosis. The nucleolus disappears, chromatin condenses into chromosomes, the nuclear envelope breaks down, and the spindle apparatus develops. Once the chromosomes are condensed, however, their behavior differs from that in mitosis. During prophase I, homologous chromosomes pair, a process called **synapsis.** These pairs of homologous chromosomes are called **tetrads** (a group of four chromatids) or **bivalents.** During synapsis, corresponding regions along nonsister chromatids form close associations called **chiasmata** (singular, **chiasma**). Chiasmata are sites where genetic material is exchanged between nonsister homologous chromatids, a process called **crossing over.** The result contributes to a mixing of genetic material from both parents, a process called **genetic recombination.**

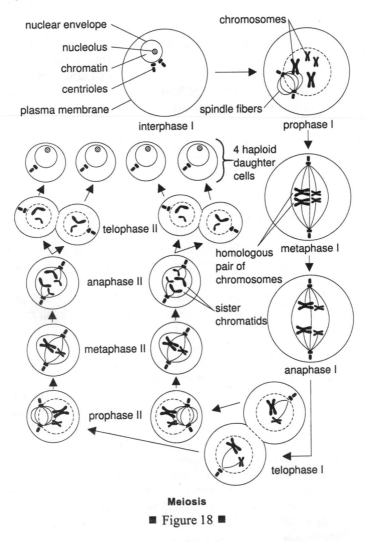

Meiosis
■ Figure 18 ■

2. At **metaphase I,** homologous pairs of chromosomes are spread across the metaphase plate. Microtubules extending from one pole are attached to kinetochores of one member of each ho-

mologous pair. Microtubules from the other pole are connected to the second member of each homologous pair.

3. **Anaphase I** begins when homologues within tetrads uncouple as they are pulled to opposite poles.

4. In **telophase I,** the chromosomes have reached their respective poles, and a nuclear membrane develops around them. Note that each pole will form a new nucleus that will have half the number of chromosomes, but each chromosome will contain two chromatids. Since daughter nuclei will have half the number of chromosomes, cells that they eventually form will be **haploid.**

5. **Cytokinesis** occurs forming two daughter cells. A brief interphase may follow, but no replication of chromosomes occurs. Instead, part II of meiosis begins in both daughter nuclei.

6. In **prophase II,** the nuclear envelope disappears and the spindle develops. There are no chiasmata and no crossing over of genetic material as in prophase I.

7. In **metaphase II,** the chromosomes align singly on the metaphase plate (not in tetrads as in metaphase I). Single alignment of chromosomes is exactly what happens in mitosis—except, now there is only half the number of chromosomes.

8. **Anaphase II** begins as each chromosome is pulled apart into two chromatids by the microtubules of the spindle apparatus. The chromatids (now chromosomes) migrate to their respective poles. Again, this is exactly what happens in mitosis—except, now there is only half the number of chromosomes.

9. In **telophase II,** the nuclear envelope reappears at each pole and cytokinesis occurs. The end result of meiosis is four haploid cells. Each cell contains half the number of chromosomes, and each chromosome consists of only one chromatid.

Meiosis ends with four haploid daughter cells, each with half the number of chromosomes (one chromosome from each homologous pair). These are **gametes,** that is, eggs and sperm. The fusing of an egg and a sperm, **fertilization (syngamy)**, gives rise to a diploid cell, the **zygote.** The single-celled zygote then divides by *mitosis* to produce a multicellular embryo, fetus, and after nine months, a new-born infant. Note that one copy of each chromosome pair in the zygote originates from one parent, and the second copy from the other parent. Thus, a pair of homologous chromosomes in the diploid zygote represents both maternal and paternal heritage.

DNA Replication

During the S phase of interphase of the cell cycle, a second chromatid is assembled. The second chromatid contains a copy of the DNA molecule found in the first chromatid. The copying process, called **DNA replication,** involves separating ("unzipping") the DNA molecule into two strands, each of which serves as a template to assemble a new, complementary strand. The result is two identical double-stranded molecules of DNA. Each of these double-stranded molecules of DNA consists of a single strand of old DNA (the template strand) and a single strand of new, replicated DNA (the complementary strand).

Two difficulties must be resolved during replication. First, DNA polymerase, the enzyme that regulates the attachment of new nucleotides to the growing complement strand, can perform this task in only one direction on a DNA strand. The two strands that make up the double helix, however, are oriented in opposite directions (antiparallel). On one strand, the DNA polymerase can operate continuously *toward* the **replication fork** as the DNA double helix is unzipped. The new DNA strand generated in this manner is called the **leading complementary strand.** Since the nucleotides of the second template strand are oriented in the opposite direction, DNA polymerase must operate *away* from the replication fork. As a result, replication of the second strand occurs in short segments. As the replication fork advances, the DNA polymerase must repeatedly return to the replication fork to begin replication of a short segment of DNA. The short segments are connected by the enzyme DNA ligase. The new DNA strand generated here is called the **lagging complementary strand.**

The second difficulty that is resolved during replication is that DNA polymerase cannot itself *initiate* replication. Instead, the enzyme RNA primase initiates each replication using RNA (*not* DNA) nucleotides. After a short RNA nucleotide segment is generated, DNA polymerase takes over with DNA nucleotides. The initial RNA nucleotides are later replaced with the appropriate DNA nucleotides.

The details of DNA replication are summarized below. Numbers correspond to events illustrated in Figure 19.

1. The enzyme **helicase** unwinds the DNA helix, producing a Y-shaped **replication fork.**

2. **RNA primase** initiates DNA replication by producing short segments of RNA nucleotides (called **RNA primers**). (See 2A and 2B in Figure 19.)

3. **DNA polymerase** attaches to the RNA primers and begins adding DNA nucleotides to the complement strand. (In Figure 19, the RNA primase is present only on the lagging strand.)

4. The **leading complementary strand** is assembled continuously as the double-helix DNA uncoils.

5. The **lagging complementary strand** is assembled in short segments, which are subsequently joined by **DNA ligase.** (See 5A, 5B, and 5C in Figure 19.)

6. The RNA primers are replaced by DNA nucleotides.

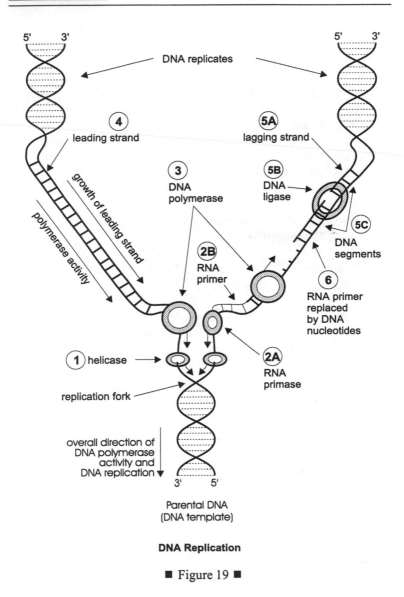

DNA Replication

■ Figure 19 ■

Mutations

The replication process of DNA is extremely accurate. However, errors occur when nucleotide bases between DNA strands are occasionally paired incorrectly. In addition, errors in DNA molecules may arise as a result of exposure to radiation (such as ultraviolet or x-ray) or various reactive chemicals. When errors occur, repair mechanisms are available to make corrections.

If a DNA error is not repaired, it becomes a **mutation.** A mutation is any sequence of nucleotides in a DNA molecule that does not exactly match the original DNA molecule from which it was copied. Mutations include an incorrect nucleotide (**substitution**), a missing nucleotide (**deletion**), or an additional nucleotide not present in the original DNA molecule (**insertion**). When an insertion mutation occurs, it causes all the subsequent nucleotides to be displaced one position, producing a **frameshift mutation.** Radiation or chemicals that cause mutations are called **mutagens. Carcinogens** are mutagens that activate uncontrolled cell growth (cancer).

Protein Synthesis

The DNA in chromosomes contains genetic instructions that regulate development, growth, and the metabolic activities of cells. The DNA instructions determine whether a cell will be that of a pea plant, a human, or some other organism, as well as establish specific characteristics of the cell in that organism. For example, the DNA in a cell may establish that it is a human cell. If, during development, it becomes a cell in the iris of an eye, the DNA will direct other information appropriate for its location in the organism, such as the production of brown, blue, or other pigmentation. DNA controls the cell in this manner because it contains codes for polypeptides. Many polypeptides are enzymes that regulate chemical reactions, and these chemical reactions influence the resulting characteristics of the cell. Thus, from the molecular viewpoint, *traits are the end products of metabolic processes regulated by enzymes.* A gene is defined as the DNA segment that codes for a particular enzyme or other polypeptide (**one-gene-one-polypeptide hypothesis**).

The process that describes how enzymes and other proteins are made from DNA is called **protein synthesis.** There are three steps in protein synthesis—**transcription, RNA processing,** and **translation.** In transcription, RNA molecules are created by using the DNA molecule as a template. After transcription, RNA processing modifies the RNA molecule with deletions and additions. In translation, the processed RNA molecules are used to assemble amino acids into a polypeptide.

There are three kinds of RNA molecules produced during transcription, as follows.

1. **Messenger RNA (mRNA)** is a single strand of RNA that provides the template used for sequencing amino acids into a polypeptide. A triplet group of three adjacent nucleotides on the mRNA, called a **codon,** codes for one specific amino acid. Since there are 64 possible ways that four nucleotides can be arranged in triplet combinations ($4 \times 4 \times 4 = 64$), there are 64 possible codons. The **genetic code** is a table of information that provides the "decoding" for each codon. That is, it identifies the amino acid specified by each of the possible 64 codon combinations. For example, the codon composed of the three nucleotides cytosine-guanine-adenine (CGA) codes for the amino acid arginine.

2. **Transfer RNA (tRNA)** is a short RNA molecule (consisting of about 80 nucleotides) that is used for transporting amino acids to their proper places on the mRNA template. Interactions among various parts of the tRNA molecule result in base-pairings between nucleotides, folding the tRNA in such a way that it forms a three-dimensional molecule. (In two dimensions, a tRNA resembles the three leaflets of a clover leaf.) One end of the tRNA attaches to an amino acid. Another por-

tion of the tRNA, specified by a triplet combination of nucleotides, is the **anticodon.** During translation, the anticodon of the tRNA base pairs with the codon of the mRNA.

3. **Ribosomal RNA (rRNA)** molecules are the building blocks of ribosomes. The nucleolus is an assemblage of DNA actively being transcribed into rRNA. Within the nucleolus, various proteins imported from the cytosol are assembled with rRNA to form large and small ribosome subunits. Together, the two subunits form a ribosome which coordinates the activities of the mRNA and tRNA during translation. Ribosomes have three binding sites—one for the mRNA, one for a tRNA that carries a growing polypeptide chain, and one for a second tRNA that delivers the next amino acid that will be inserted into the growing polypeptide chain.

The details of transcription, RNA processing, and protein synthesis are summarized below (Figures 20 and 21).

1. During transcription, the **RNA polymerase** attaches to **promoter** regions on the DNA and begins to unzip the DNA into two strands. (See 1 in Figure 20.)

2. As the RNA polymerase unzips the DNA, it assembles new nucleotides using one strand of the DNA as a template. In contrast to the process of DNA replication, the new nucleotides are RNA nucleotides, and only one DNA strand is transcribed. (See 2 in Figure 20.)

3. Transcription continues until the RNA polymerase reaches a special sequence of nucleotides that serves as a termination point. The RNA polymerase and the newly created RNA molecule are released. This newly created RNA molecule may be mRNA, tRNA, or rRNA (depending on which DNA segment is transcribed). (See 3 in Figure 20.)

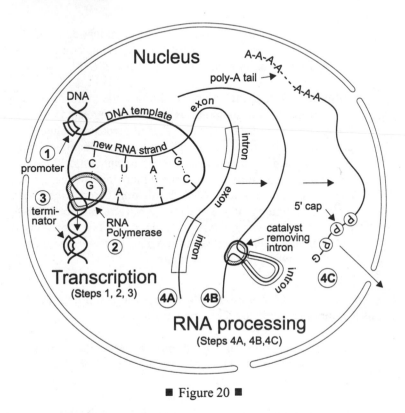

■ Figure 20 ■

4. During RNA processing, newly created mRNA molecules undergo two kinds of alterations. In the first modification, noncoding *in*tervening sequences called **introns** are removed, leaving only **exons**, sequences that *ex*press a code for a polypeptide. A second modification adds two special sequences—a **5' cap** to one end of the mRNA and a **poly-A tail** to the other end. (See 4A, 4B, and 4C in Figure 20.)

5. The mRNA, tRNA, and ribosomal subunits are transported across the nuclear envelope and into the cytoplasm. In the cytoplasm, amino acids attach to one end of the tRNAs. (See 5A, 5B, and 5C in Figure 21.)

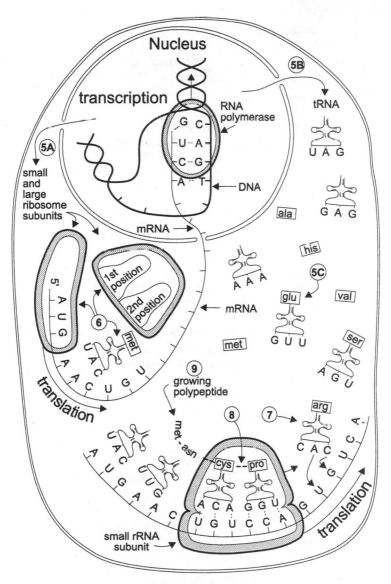

Protein Synthesis

■ Figure 21 ■

6. **Translation** begins when the small and large ribosomal subunits attach to one end of the mRNA. Also, a tRNA (with anticodon UAC) carrying the amino acid methionine attaches to the mRNA (at the "start" codon AUG) within the ribosome. (See 6 in Figure 21.)

7. A second tRNA, also bearing an amino acid, arrives and fills a second tRNA position. The codon on the mRNA determines which tRNA (and thus, which amino acid) fills the second position. (Step 7 in Figure 21 shows an incoming tRNA approaching a yet to be vacated position.)

8. The amino acid of the first tRNA attaches to the amino acid of the second tRNA, forming a pair of amino acids. Then, the first tRNA is released. The ribosome moves over one codon position, thereby putting the second tRNA in the first position and vacating the second position. (Step 8 in Figure 21 shows this process after several tRNAs have delivered amino acids.)

9. A new tRNA (with its amino acid) fills the vacant position. Now, the *two* amino acids being held by the tRNA in the first position are transferred to the amino acid of the newly arrived tRNA, forming a polypeptide chain of three amino acids. Again, the tRNA in the first position is released, the ribosome moves over one codon position, and the second tRNA position is vacant.

10. The process continues, as new tRNAs bring more amino acids. As each new tRNA arrives, the polypeptide chain is elongated by one new amino acid, growing in sequence and length as dictated by the codons on the mRNA. (See 9 in Figure 21.) Eventually, a "stop" codon is encountered and the ribosome subunits and polypeptide are released.

Once the polypeptide is released, interactions among the amino acids give it its special three-dimensional shape. Subsequent processing by the endoplasmic reticulum or a Golgi body may make final modifications before the protein functions as a structural element or as an enzyme.

Histology is the study of tissues at the microscopic level. **Tissues are groups of similar cells performing a common function.** There are four categories of tissues:

1. Epithelial tissue

2. Connective tissue

3. Nervous tissue

4. Muscle tissue

Epithelial Tissue

Epithelial tissue, or **epithelium,** has the following general characteristics.

1. Epithelium consists of closely packed, flat cells. There is little intercellular material.

2. The tissue is avascular, or without blood vessels. Nutrient and waste exchange occurs through neighboring connective tissues by diffusion.

3. The upper surface of epithelium is free, or exposed to the outside of the body or to an internal body cavity. The basal surface rests on connective tissue. A thin, extracellular layer called the **basement membrane** forms between the epithelial and connective tissue.

4. Cell division in epithelium occurs readily to replace damaged cells.

There are two kinds of epithelial tissues:

1. *Covering and lining* epithelium covers the outside surfaces of the body and lines internal organs.

2. *Glandular* epithelium secretes hormones or other products.

Epithelium That Covers or Lines

Epithelial tissues that cover or line surfaces are classified by *cell shape* and by the *number* of cell layers. The following terms are used to describe these features.

1. *Cell shape:*

   - **Squamous** cells are flat. The nucleus, located near the upper surface, has the appearance of a "fried egg."

   - **Cuboidal** cells are cube or hexagon shaped with a central, circular nucleus. These cells produce secretions (sweat, for example) or absorb substances (digested foods, for example).

   - **Columnar** cells are tall with an oval nucleus near the basement membrane. These thick cells serve to protect underlying tissues or may function to absorb substances. Some have **microvilli**, minute surface extensions, to increase surface area for absorbing substances, while others may have **cilia** that help move substances over their surface (such as mucus through the respiratory tract).

   - **Transitional** cells range from flat to tall cells that can extend or compress in response to body movement.

2. *Number of cell layers:*

- **Simple** describes a single layer of cells.

- **Stratified** describes epithelium consisting of multiple layers.

- **Pseudostratified** describes a single layer of cells of different sizes, giving the appearance of being multilayered.

Names of epithelial tissues include a description of both their shape and their number of cell layers. The presence of cilia may also be identified in their names. For example, *simple squamous* describes epithelium consisting of a single layer of flat cells. *Pseudostratified columnar ciliated* epithelium describes a single layer of tall, ciliated cells of more than one size. *Stratified* epithelium is named after the shape of the outermost cell layer. Thus, *stratified squamous* epithelium has outermost layers of squamous cells, even though some inner layers consist of cuboidal or columnar cells. These and other epithelial tissues are illustrated in Figure 22.

Glandular Epithelium

Glandular epithelium forms two kinds of glands:

1. **Endocrine glands** secrete **hormones** directly into the bloodstream. For example, the thyroid gland secretes the hormone thyroxin into the bloodstream, where it is distributed throughout the body, stimulating an increase in the metabolic rate of body cells.

2. **Exocrine glands** secrete their substances into tubes, or **ducts,** which carry the secretions to the epithelial surface. Examples of secretions include sweat, saliva, milk, stomach acid, and digestive enzymes.

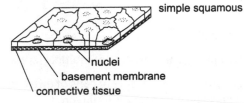

simple squamous

Cells: single-layered

Nuclei: centrally located

Functions: diffusion, filtration, secretion

nuclei

basement membrane

connective tissue

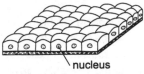

simple cuboidal

Cells: single-layered

Nuclei: centrally located and spherical

Functions: absorption, secretion

nucleus

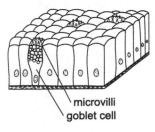

simple columnar

Cells: single-layered

Nuclei: basal and oval

Functions: absorption, secretion

(May bear cilia and contain goblet cells with microvilli)

microvilli

goblet cell

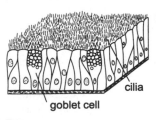

pseudostratified

Cells: single-layered, differing in heights

Nuclei: at various positions

Functions: absorption

(May bear cilia and contain goblet cells)

cilia

goblet cell

Epithelial Tissues

■ Figure 22a ■

Cells: several layers of
squamous cells on
cuboidal and/or
columnar cells

Nuclei: centrally located

Functions: protection

stratified squamous

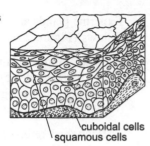

cuboidal cells
squamous cells

Cells: two layers

Nuclei: centrally located
and spherical

Functions: protection

stratified cuboidal

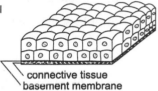

connective tissue
basement membrane

Cells: single lay of
columnar cells on
several layers of
cuboidal (or many
sided) cells

Nuclei: basal and oval

Functions: protection,
secretion

stratified columnar

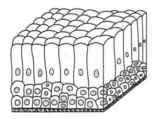

Cells: squamous to
cuboidal depending
on degree of stretch

Nuclei: centrally located

Functions: distention
(occurs only in
bladder, ureter, and
urethra)

transitional
epithelium

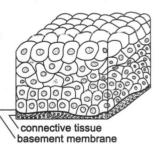

connective tissue
basement membrane

Epithelial Tissues
■ Figure 22b ■

Exocrine glands are classified according to their *structure,* as follows (Figure 23).

- **Unicellular** or **multicellular** describes a single-celled gland or a gland made of many cells, respectively. A multicellular gland consists of a group of secretory cells and a duct through which the secretions pass as they exit the gland.

- **Branched** refers to a branching arrangement of *secretory* cells in the gland.

- **Simple** or **compound** refers to whether the *duct* of the gland (not the *secretory* portion) does not branch or branches, respectively.

- **Tubular** describes a gland whose secretory cells form a tube, while **alveolar** (or **acinar**) describes secretory cells that form a bulblike sac.

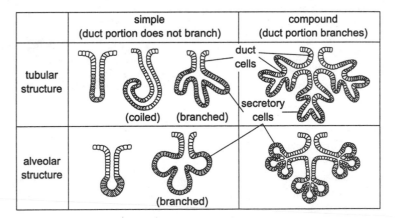

Exocrine Glands
■ Figure 23 ■

Exocrine glands are also classified according to their *function*, as follows (Figure 24).

- In **merocrine glands,** secretions pass through the cell membranes of the secretory cells.

- In **apocrine glands**, a portion of the cell containing secretions is released as it separates from the rest of the cell.

- In **holocrine glands**, entire secretory cells disintegrate and are released along with their contents.

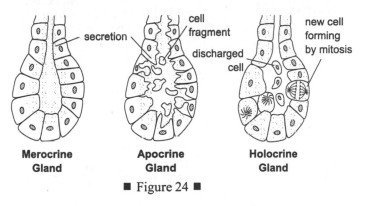

Merocrine Gland   **Apocrine Gland**   **Holocrine Gland**

■ Figure 24 ■

Connective Tissue

A summary of the various kinds of **connective tissues** is given in Table 2 and Figure 25. Some general characteristics of connective tissues follow.

1. *Nerve supply.* Most connective tissues have a nerve supply (as does epithelial tissue).

2. *Blood supply.* There is a wide range of vascularity among connective tissues, although most are well vascularized (unlike epithelial tissues, which are all avascular).

3. *Structure.* Connective tissue consists of scattered cells immersed in an intercellular material called the **matrix.** The matrix consists of **fibers** and **ground substance.** The kinds and amounts

Tissue Type		Cells Present	Fibers Present	Matrix Characteristics
Loose Connective Tissue	areolar	fibroblasts macrophages adipocytes mast cells plasma cells	collagen elastic reticular	loosely arranged fibers in gelatinous ground substance
	adipose	adipocytes	reticular collagen	closely packed cells with a small amount of gelatinous ground substance; stores fat
	reticular	reticular cells	reticular	loosely arranged fibers in gelatinous ground substance
Dense Connective Tissue	dense regular	fibroblasts	collagen (some elastic)	*parallel*-arranged bundles of fibers with few cells and little ground substance; great tensile strength
	dense irregular			*irregularly* arranged bundles of fibers with few cells and little ground substance; high tensile strength
Cartilage	hyaline (gristle)	chondrocytes	collagen (some elastic)	limited ground substance; dense, semisolid matrix
	fibrocartilage			limited ground substance; intermediate between hyaline cartilage and dense connective tissue
	elastic		elastic	limited ground substance; flexible but firm matrix
Bone (osseous tissue)	compact (dense)	osteoblasts osteocytes	collagen	rigid, calcified ground substance with osteons (canal systems)
	spongy (cancellous)			rigid, calcified ground substance (no osteons)
Blood & Lymph (vascular tissue)	blood	erythrocytes leukocytes thrombocytes	"fibers" are soluble proteins that form during clotting	"matrix" is liquid blood plasma
	lymph	leukocytes		

■ Table 2 ■

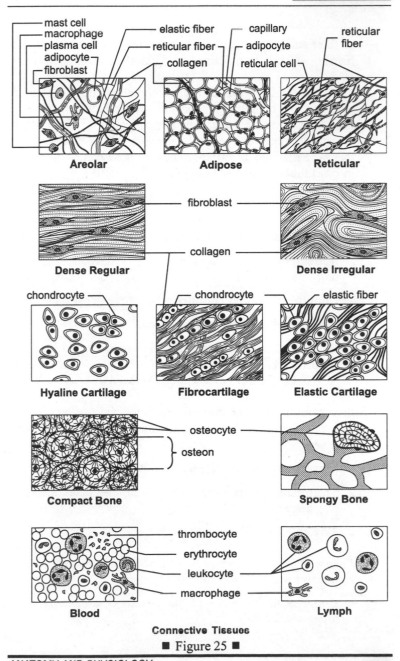

mast cell
macrophage
plasma cell
adipocyte
fibroblast

elastic fiber
reticular fiber
collagen

capillary
adipocyte
reticular cell

reticular fiber

Areolar

Adipose

Reticular

fibroblast

collagen

Dense Regular

Dense Irregular

chondrocyte

chondrocyte

elastic fiber

Hyaline Cartilage

Fibrocartilage

Elastic Cartilage

osteocyte

osteon

Compact Bone

Spongy Bone

thrombocyte
erythrocyte
leukocyte
macrophage

Blood

Lymph

Connective Tissues

■ Figure 25 ■

of fiber and ground substance determine the character of the matrix, which in turn defines the kind of connective tissue.

4. *Cell types.* Fundamental cell types, characteristic of each kind of connective tissue, are responsible for producing the matrix. Immature forms of these cells (whose names end in *blast*) secrete the fibers and ground substance of the matrix. Cells that have matured, or differentiated, (whose names often end in *cyte*) function mostly to maintain the matrix.

- **Fibroblasts** are common in both loose and dense connective tissues.

- **Adipocytes,** or fat cells, occur in loose connective tissue.

- **Reticular cells** resemble fibroblasts but have long, cellular processes (extensions). They occur in loose connective tissue.

- **Chondroblasts** and **chondrocytes** occur in cartilage.

- **Osteoblasts** and **osteocytes** occur in bone.

- **Hemocytoblasts** occur in the bone marrow and produce **erythrocytes** (red blood cells), **leukocytes** (white blood cells), and **thrombocytes** (blood platelets).

In addition to the fundamental cell types, various leukocytes migrate from the bone marrow to connective tissues and provide various body defense activities.

- **Macrophages** engulf foreign and dead cells.

- **Mast cells** secrete histamine, which stimulates immune responses.

- **Plasma cells** produce antibodies.

5. *Fibers.* Matrix fibers are proteins that provide support for the connective tissue. There are three types:

- **Collagen fibers,** made of the protein *collagen*, are both tough and flexible.

- **Elastic fibers,** made of the protein *elastin*, are strong and stretchable.

- **Reticular fibers,** made of thin collagen fibers with a glycoprotein coating, branch frequently to form a netlike (reticulate) pattern.

6. *Ground substance.* Ground substance may be fluid, gel, or solid, and, except for blood, is secreted by the cells of the connective tissue.

   - **Cell adhesion proteins** hold the connective tissue together.

   - **Proteoglycans** provide the firmness of the ground substance. Hyaluronic sulfate and chondroitin sulfate are two examples.

7. *Classification.* There are five general categories of **mature connective tissue:**

   - **Loose connective tissue** has abundant cells among few or loosely arranged fibers and a sparse to abundant gelatinous ground substance.

   - **Dense connective tissue** has few cells among a dense network of fibers with little ground substance.

   - **Cartilage** has cells distributed among fibers in a firm jellylike ground substance. Cartilage is tough but flexible, avascular, and without nerves.

   - **Bone** has cells distributed among abundant fibers in a solid ground substance containing minerals, mostly calcium phosphate. Bone is organized in units, called **osteons (Haversian system).** Each osteon consists of a central canal **(Haversian canal),** which contains blood vessels and nerves, surrounded by concentric rings **(lamellae)** of hard matrix and collagen fibers. Between the lamellae are cavities **(lacunae)** which contain bone cells **(osteocytes).** Canals **(canaliculi)** radiate from the central canal and allow nutrient and waste exchange with the osteocytes.

- **Blood** is composed of various blood cells and cell fragments (platelets) distributed in a fluid matrix called blood plasma.

8. *Tissue origin.* All mature connective tissues originate from **embryonic connective tissue.** There are two kinds of embryonic connective tissues:

- **Mesenchyme** is the origin of all mature connective tissues.

- **Mucous connective tissue** is a temporary tissue formed during embryonic development.

Epithelial Membranes

An **epithelial membrane** is a combination of epithelial and connective tissues working together to perform a specific function. As such, it acts as an organ. There are four principal types of epithelial membranes, as follows.

1. **Serous membranes** line interior organs and cavities. The serous membranes that line the heart, lungs, and abdominal cavities and organs are called the **pericardium, pleura,** and **peritoneum,** respectively.

2. **Mucous membranes** line body cavities that open to the outside of the body. These include the nasal cavity and the digestive, respiratory, and urogenital tracts.

3. **Synovial membranes** line the cavities at bone joints.

4. The **cutaneous membrane** is the skin.

Nervous Tissue

Nervous tissue consists of two kinds of nerve cells.

1. **Neurons** are the basic structural unit of the nervous system. Each cell consists of the following parts (Figure 26).

   - The **cell body** contains the nucleus and other cellular organelles.

   - The **dendrites** are typically short, slender extensions of the cell body that *receive* stimuli.

   - The **axon** is typically a long, slender extension of the cell body that *sends* stimuli.

2. **Neuroglia,** or **glial cells,** provide support functions for the neurons, such as insulation or anchoring neurons to blood vessels.

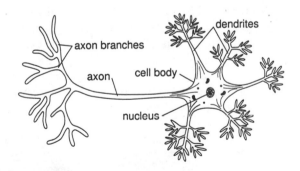

A Neuron
■ Figure 26 ■

Muscle Tissue

There are three kinds of **muscle tissues** (Figure 27).

1. **Skeletal muscle** consists of long cylindrical cells that, under a microscope, appear striated with bands perpendicular to the length of the cell. The many nuclei in each cell (**multinucleated** cells) are located near the outside along the plasma membrane. Skeletal muscle is attached to bones and causes movements of the body. Because it is under our conscious control, it is also called **voluntary muscle.**

2. **Cardiac muscle,** like skeletal muscle, is striated. However, cardiac muscle cells have a single, centrally located nucleus, and the muscle fibers branch often. Where two cardiac muscle cells meet, they form an **intercalated disc** containing gap junctions, which bridge the two cells.

3. **Smooth muscle** consists of cells with a single, centrally located nucleus. The cells are elongated with tapered ends and do not appear striated. Smooth muscle lines the walls of blood vessels and certain organs such as the digestive and urogenital tracts, where it serves to advance the movement of substances. Smooth muscle is called **involuntary muscle** because it is not under direct conscious control.

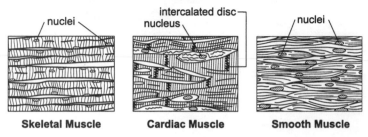

Skeletal Muscle   Cardiac Muscle   Smooth Muscle

■ Figure 27 ■

The **skin,** or **integument,** is considered an organ because it consists of two tissues—epithelial and connective. In addition, accessory organs, such as glands, hair, and nails, are present, making the skin and accessory organs, together, the integumentary *system.* A section of skin with various accessory organs is shown in Figure 28.

The skin consists of two layers, the **epidermis** and the underlying **dermis.** Although technically not part of the skin, the **hypodermis (subcutaneous layer,** or **superficial fascia)** lies beneath the dermis.

The Epidermis

The **epidermis** consists of stratified squamous epithelium. Four cell types are present.

1. **Keratinocytes** produce keratin, a protein that hardens and waterproofs the skin. Mature keratinocytes at the skin surface are dead and filled almost entirely with keratin.

2. **Melanocytes** produce melanin, a pigment that protects cells from ultraviolet radiation. Melanin from the melanocytes is transferred to the keratinocytes.

3. **Langerhans cells** are phagocytic macrophages that interact with white blood cells during an immune response.

4. **Merkel cells** occur deep in the epidermis at the epidermal-dermal boundary. They form Merkel discs, which in association with nerve endings, serve a sensory function.

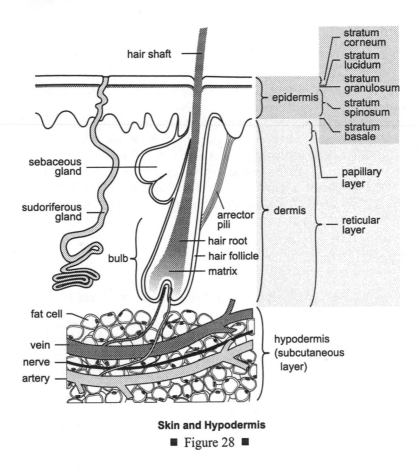

Skin and Hypodermis

■ Figure 28 ■

Five layers make up the epidermis.

1. The **stratum corneum** contains many layers of dead, anucleate keratinocytes completely filled with keratin. The outermost layers are constantly shed.

2. The **stratum lucidum** contains two to three layers of anucleate cells. This layer is usually apparent only in thick skin (palms of hands and soles of feet).

3. The **stratum granulosum** contains two to four layers of cells held together by desmosomes. These cells contain **keratohyaline granules,** which contribute to the formation of keratin in the upper layers of the epidermis.

4. The **stratum spinosum** contains eight to ten layers of cells connected by demosomes. These cells are moderately active in mitosis.

5. The **stratum basale** contains a single layer of columnar cells actively dividing by mitosis to produce cells that migrate into the upper epidermal layers and ultimately to the surface of the skin.

The Dermis

The second layer of the skin, **the dermis,** consists of various connective tissues. As connective tissue, it contains fibroblasts and macrophages within a gelatinous matrix containing collagen, elastic, and reticular fibers. This structure provides strength, extensibility (the ability to be stretched), and elasticity (the ability to return to its original form).

The dermis consists of two layers, as follows.

1. The **papillary layer** is a thin, outer layer with fingerlike projections called **dermal papillae** that protrude into the epidermis. In the hands and feet, the dermal papillae generate **epidermal ridges** (sweat from the epidermal ridges leaves fingerprints).

2. The **reticular layer** is a thick layer, below the papillary layer, that makes up most of the dermis.

The Hypodermis

The **hypodermis** (**subcutaneous layer,** or **superficial fascia**) lies between the dermis and underlying tissues and organs. It consists of mostly adipose tissue and is the storage site of most body fat. It serves to fasten the skin to the underlying surface, provide thermal insulation, and absorb shocks from impacts to the skin.

Accessory Organs of the Skin

The following **accessory organs (skin derivatives)** are embedded in the skin.

1. **Hair** is composed of the following structures.

   - The **hair shaft** is the portion of the hair that is visible on the surface of the skin.

   - The **hair root** is the portion of the hair that penetrates the skin (epidermis and dermis).

   - The **hair follicle** is the sheath that surrounds the hair in the skin.

   - The **bulb** is the base of the hair follicle.

   - The **matrix** is the bottom of the hair follicle (located within the bulb). Here, cells are actively dividing, producing new hair cells. As these cells differentiate, they produce keratin and absorb melanin from nearby melanocytes. As younger cells are produced below them, the more mature cells are pushed upward, where they eventually die. The keratin they leave behind contributes to the growth of the hair. The color of the hair is determined by the pigments absorbed from the melanocytes.

- The **arrector pili** is a smooth muscle that is attached to the hair follicle. When the muscle contracts, the hair becomes erect; in humans, "goose bumps" are produced.

2. **Nails** are keratinized epithelial cells. The semilunar lighter region of the nail, the **lunula,** is the area of new nail growth. Below the lunula, the nail **matrix** is actively producing nail cells which contribute to the growth of the nail.

3. **Sudoriferous (sweat) glands** secrete sweat. Sweat consists of water with various salts and other substances. There are four kinds of sudoriferous glands.

   - **Eccrine glands** occur under most skin surfaces and secrete a watery solution through **pores** (openings at the skin surface), which serves to cool the skin as it evaporates.

   - **Apocrine glands** occur under skin surfaces of the armpits and pubic regions and, beginning with puberty, secrete a solution in response to stress or sexual excitement. The solution, more viscous than that secreted by eccrine glands, is secreted into hair follicles.

   - **Ceruminous glands** secrete **cerumen** (earwax) into the external ear canal. The wax helps to impede the entrance of foreign bodies.

   - **Mammary glands** produce milk that is secreted through the nipples of the breasts.

4. **Sebaceous (oil) glands** secrete **sebum,** an oily substance, into hair follicles or sometimes through skin surface pores. Sebum inhibits bacterial growth and helps prevent drying of hair and skin. An accumulation of sebum in the duct of a sebaceous gland produces whiteheads, blackheads (if the sebum oxidizes), and acne (if the sebum becomes infected by bacteria).

Skin Physiology

The skin performs a variety of functions.

1. *Protection* is provided against biological invasion, physical damage, and ultraviolet radiation.

2. *Sensation* for touch, pain, and heat is provided by nerve endings.

3. *Thermoregulation* is supported through sweating and regulation of blood flow through the skin.

4. *Metabolism* of vitamin D occurs in the skin.

5. *Storage* of blood that can be shunted to other parts of the body when needed takes place in the skin.

6. *Excretion* of salts and a small amount of wastes (ammonia and urea) occurs with the production of sweat.

The **skeletal system** consists of bones, cartilage, and the membranes that line the bones. Each bone is an organ that includes connective tissue (bone, blood, cartilage, adipose tissue, and fibrous connective tissue), nervous tissues, and muscle and epithelial tissues (within the blood vessels).

Functions of Bones

1. *Support.* Bones provide a framework for the attachment of muscles and other tissues.

2. *Protection.* Bones such as the skull and rib cage protect internal organs from injury.

3. *Movement.* Bones enable body movements by acting as levers and points of attachment for muscles.

4. *Mineral storage.* Bones serve as a reservoir for calcium and phosphorus, essential minerals for various cellular activities throughout the body.

5. *Blood cell production.* The production of blood cells, or **hematopoiesis,** occurs in the red marrow found within the cavities of certain bones.

6. *Energy storage.* Lipids (fats) stored in adipose cells of the yellow marrow serve as an energy reservoir.

Types of Bones

1. **Long bones** are longer than they are wide. The length of the bone, or **shaft,** widens at the extremities (ends).

2. **Short bones** are cubelike, about as long as they are wide.

3. **Flat bones,** such as ribs or skull bones, are thin or flattened.

4. **Irregular bones,** such as vertebrae, facial bones, and hip bones, have specific shapes unlike those above.

The following two bone types are usually classified separately.

1. **Sesamoid,** or **round, bones,** such as the kneecap, are found embedded within certain tendons.

2. **Sutural,** or **Wormian, bones** occur between the sutures (joints) of the cranial bones of the skull.

Bone Structure

There are two kinds of **bone tissue** (Figure 29):

1. **Compact bone** is the hard material that makes up the shaft of long bones and the outside surfaces of other bones. Compact bone consists of cylindrical units called **osteons (Haversian systems)**. Each osteon contains concentric **lamellae** (layers) of hard, calcified matrix with **osteocytes** (bone cells) lodged in **lacunae** (spaces) between the lamellae. Smaller canals, or **canaliculi,** radiate outward from a **central canal (Haversian canal)** which contains blood vessels and nerve fibers. Osteocytes within an osteon are connected to each other and to the central canal by fine cellular extensions. Through these cellu-

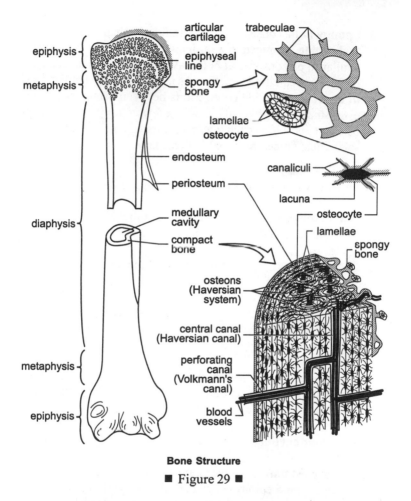

Bone Structure
■ Figure 29 ■

lar extensions, nutrients and wastes are exchanged between the osteocytes and the blood vessels. **Perforating canals (Volkmann's canals)** provide channels that allow the blood vessels that run through the central canals to connect to the blood vessels in the **periosteum** that surrounds the bone.

2. **Spongy bone** consists of thin, irregularly shaped plates called
trabeculae, arranged in a latticelike network. Trabeculae are
similar to osteons in that both have osteocytes in lacunae that
lie between calcified lamellae. As in osteons, canaliculi present
in trabeculae provide connections between osteocytes. However, since each trabecula is only a few cell layers thick, each
osteocyte is able to exchange nutrients with nearby blood vessels. Thus, no central canal is necessary.

The main features of a **long bone** follow (Figure 29).

1. The **diaphysis,** or shaft, is the long, tubular portion of long
bones. It is composed of compact bone tissue.

2. The **epiphysis** (plural, **epiphyses**) is the expanded end of a
long bone.

3. The **metaphysis** is the area where the diaphysis meets the
epiphysis. It includes the **epiphyseal line,** a remnant of cartilage from growing bones.

4. The **medullary cavity,** or **marrow cavity,** is the open area
within the diaphysis. The adipose tissue inside the cavity stores
lipids and forms the yellow marrow.

5. **Articular cartilage** covers the *epiphysis* where joints occur.

6. The **periosteum** is the membrane covering the *outside of the
diaphysis* (and epiphyses where articular cartilage is absent).
It contains osteoblasts (bone-forming cells), osteoclasts (bone-
destroying cells), nerve fibers, and blood and lymphatic vessels. Ligaments and tendons attach to the periosteum.

7. The **endosteum** is the membrane that lines the *marrow cavity.*

The main features of **short, flat,** and **irregular bones** follow.

1. In short and irregular bones, spongy bone tissue is encircled by a thin layer of compact bone tissue.

2. In flat bones, the spongy bone tissue is sandwiched between two layers of compact bone tissue. The spongy bone tissue is called the **diploë.**

3. Periosteum covers the outside layer of compact bone tissue.

4. Endosteum covers the trabeculae that fill the inside of the bone.

5. In certain bones (ribs, vertebrae, hip bones, sternum), the spaces between the trabeculae contain red marrow, which is active in hematopoiesis.

Bone Development

The skeleton arises from fibrous membranes and hyaline cartilage during the first month of embryonic development. These tissues are replaced with bone by two different bone-building, or **ossification,** processes.

The first process, called **intramembranous ossification,** occurs when *fibrous membranes* are replaced by bone tissue. The process, occurring only in certain flat bones, is summarized in two basic steps, as follows.

1. Spongy bone tissue begins to develop at sites within the membranes called **centers of ossification.**

2. Red bone marrow forms within the spongy bone tissue, followed by the formation of compact bone on the outside.

The second ossification process, called **endochondral ossification,** occurs when *hyaline cartilage* is replaced by bone tissue. The process, occurring in most bones of the body, follows the steps listed below.

1. At a **primary ossification center,** in the center of a cartilage model, hyaline cartilage breaks down, forming a cavity.

2. A **periosteal bud,** consisting of osteoblasts, osteoclasts, red marrow, nerves, and blood and lymph vessels, invades the cavity. The osteoblasts produce spongy bone tissue.

3. A **medullary cavity** forms as osteoclasts break down the newly produced spongy bone tissue. The medullary cavity expands as it follows the spread of the primary ossification center to the ends of the bone.

4. Compact bone tissue replaces cartilage on the outside of the bone.

5. In long bones, **secondary ossification centers** form in the epiphyses. As in the shaft, a periosteal bud develops. However, the spongy bone tissue that subsequently develops is not replaced by a medullary cavity.

6. **Articular cartilage** is formed from cartilage remaining on the outside of the epiphyses.

7. The **epiphyseal plate** is formed from cartilage remaining between the expanding primary and secondary ossification centers.

Bone Growth

Bones elongate as chondrocytes in the cartilage of the epiphyseal plate divide. These cell divisions produce new cartilage within the epiphyseal plate bordering the epiphyses. At the other end of the epiphyseal plate, bordering the diaphysis, older cartilage is broken down by invading osteoclasts and is eventually replaced by the expanding medullary cavity.

Bone Homeostasis

Remodeling is the process of creating new bone and removing old bone. It occurs constantly in growing children as well as in adults in the following situations.

- Remodeling occurs when bones grow, redistributing bone tissue to maintain the shape and structure of the bone.

- Remodeling occurs in response to new stresses applied to a bone, increasing bone strength by adding new bone tissue where appropriate.

- Remodeling occurs when calcium stored in the bones is removed for metabolic processes in other parts of the body. Similarly, remodeling occurs when excess calcium is returned to the bone reservoir.

- Remodeling occurs during the repair of broken bones.

Surface Features of Bones

The surfaces of bones bear projections, depressions, ridges, and various other features. A **process** (projection) on one bone may fit with a depression on a second bone to form a joint. Another process allows for the attachment of a muscle or ligament. Grooves and openings provide passageways for blood vessels or nerves. A list of the various processes and other surface features appears in Table 3.

Group	Term	Definition
General	Process	Projection or prominence on a bone
Processes that help form joints	Condyle	Large, rounded articular process
	Facet	Smooth, flat surface
	Head	Enlarged portion at an end of a bone
	Ramus	Branch or extension of a bone
Processes that provide for the attachment of muscles and ligaments	Crest	Narrow ridge
	Epicondyle	Process on or above a condyle
	Linea (line)	Narrow ridge (less prominent than a crest)
	Spine (spinous process)	Sharp or pointed process
	Trochanter	Large, irregularly shaped process (found only on the femur)
	Tubercle	Small, knoblike process
	Tuberosity	Large, knoblike process
Depressions or openings (may provide passageways for blood vessels and nerves)	Fissure	Narrow opening
	Foramen	Round opening
	Fossa	Shallow depression
	Fovea	Pitlike depression
	Fontanel	Membrane-covered spaces between skull bones
	Meatus	Tubelike passage
	Sinus	Interior cavity
	Sulcus (or groove)	Long, narrow depression

■ Table 3 ■

Organization of the Skeleton

The bones of the body are categorized into two groups, the **axial skeleton** and the **appendicular skeleton.** The bones of the axial skeleton revolve around the vertical *axis* of the skeleton, while the bones of the appendicular skeleton make up the limbs that have been *appended* to the axial skeleton. A list of the bones in the axial and appendicular skeletons is given in Tables 4 and 5, respectively. Major bones of both skeletons are shown in Figure 30.

Bone Group	General Description	Name of Bone	No. of Bones	Additional Information
axial skeleton (80)	cranium (8)	1. frontal	1	
		2. parietal	2	
		3. temporal	2	
		4. sphenoid	1	
		5. ethmoid	1	
		6. occipital	1	
	facial bones (14)	1. mandible	1	lower jawbone
		2. maxilla	2	upper jawbone
		3. zygomatic bone	2	cheek bones
		4. nasal bone	2	
		5. lacrimal bone	2	
		6. palatine	2	
		7. inferior nasal concha	2	
		8. vomer	1	
	hyoid	hyoid	1	
	ear ossicles	malleus, incus, stapes	6	2 each
	vertebral column (26)	cervical vertebrae	7	$C_1 - C_7$
		thoracic vertebrae	12	$T_1 - T_{12}$
		lumbar vertebrae	5	$L_1 - L_5$
		sacrum	1	5 fused $S_1 - S_5$
		coccyx	1	4 fused
	thorax (thoracic cage or bony thorax)	sternum	1	
		true ribs (7 pair)	14	vertebrosternal
		false ribs (3 pair)	6	vertebrochondral
		false ribs (floating ribs)	4	vertebral ribs

■ Table 4 ■

Bone Group	General Description	Name of Bone	No. of Bones	Notes
appendicular skeleton (126 bones)	pectoral girdle (shoulder girdle)	clavicle	2	collarbone
		scapula	2	shoulder blade
	upper limb (60)	humerus	2	1 per arm
		ulna	2	1 per forearm
		radius	2	1 per forearm
		carpals (16)		8 per wrist
		1. scaphoid	2	
		2. trapezium	2	
		3. capitate	2	
		4. trapezoid	2	
		5. lunate	2	
		6. triquetrum	2	
		7. pisiform	2	
		8. hamate	2	
		metacarpals	10	5 in each palm
		phalanges	28	3 per digit (pollex has 2)
	pelvic girdle (hip) (2)	coxal bones (os coxae)	2	hip bones
		1. ilium		
		2. ischium		(3 fused pairs)
		3. pubis		
	lower limb (60)	femur	2	
		patella	2	
		tibia	2	
		fibula	2	
		tarsal (14)		
		1. talus	2	
		2. calcaneus	2	
		3. cuboid	2	
		4. navicular	2	
		5. medial cuneiform	2	
		6. interm. cuneiform	2	
		7. lateral cuneiform	2	
		metatarsals	10	5 per foot
		phalanges	28	3 per toe (hallux has 2)

■ Table 5 ■

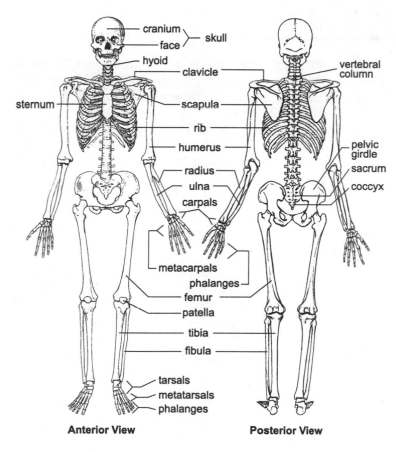

Anterior View **Posterior View**

■ Figure 30 ■

Skull: Cranium and Facial Bones

The skull consists of 8 **cranial bones** and 14 **facial bones.** The bones are listed in Table 4, but note that only 6 types of cranial bones and 8 types of facial bones are listed because some of the bones (as indicated in the table) exist as pairs.

The bones of the skull provide protection for the brain and the organs of vision, taste, hearing, equilibrium, and smell. The bones also provide attachment for muscles that move the head and control facial expressions and chewing.

Specific characteristics of these bones are illustrated in Figures 31 and 32, while some general features of the skull are given below.

- **Sutures** are immovable interlocking joints that join skull bones together (see Figure 32a).

- **Fontanels** are spaces between cranial bones that are filled with fibrous membranes. The spaces provide pliability for the skull when it passes through the birth canal and for brain growth during infancy. Bone growth eventually fills the spaces by age two.

- **Sutural (Wormian)** bones are very small bones that develop within sutures. Their number and location vary.

- The **cranial vault** denotes the top, sides, front, and back of the cranium. The **cranial floor (base)** denotes the bottom of the cranium.

- **Cranial fossae** are three depressions in the floor of the cranium. These fossae, called the anterior, middle, and posterior cranial fossae, provide spaces that accommodate the shape of the brain.

- The **nasal cavity** is formed by cartilage and several bones. Air entering the cavity is warmed and cleansed by mucus lining the cavity.

- **Sinuses (paranasal sinuses)** are mucus-lined cavities inside cranial and facial bones that surround the nasal cavity. The cavities secrete mucus that drains into the nasal cavity. The cavities also act as resonance chambers that enhance vocal (and singing) quality.

Hyoid Bone

Located in the neck, the **hyoid bone** is isolated from all other bones. (See Figure 32a.) It is connected by ligaments to the styloid processes of the temporal bones. Muscles from the tongue, neck, pharynx, and larynx that attach to the hyoid bone contribute to movements involved in swallowing and speech.

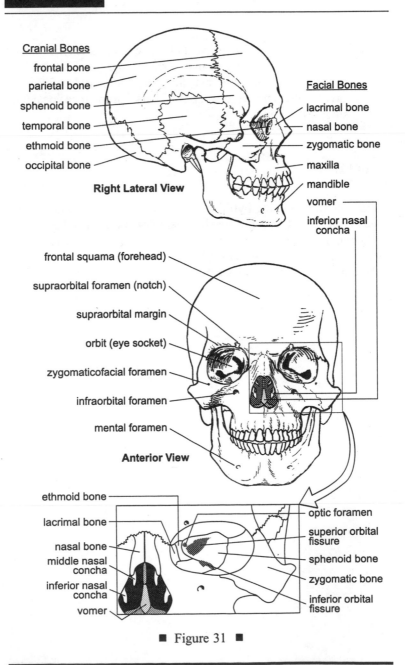

Cranial Bones
- frontal bone
- parietal bone
- sphenoid bone
- temporal bone
- ethmoid bone
- occipital bone

Right Lateral View

Facial Bones
- lacrimal bone
- nasal bone
- zygomatic bone
- maxilla
- mandible
- vomer
- inferior nasal concha

frontal squama (forehead)
supraorbital foramen (notch)
supraorbital margin
orbit (eye socket)
zygomaticofacial foramen
infraorbital foramen
mental foramen

Anterior View

ethmoid bone
lacrimal bone
nasal bone
middle nasal concha
inferior nasal concha
vomer

optic foramen
superior orbital fissure
sphenoid bone
zygomatic bone
inferior orbital fissure

■ Figure 31 ■

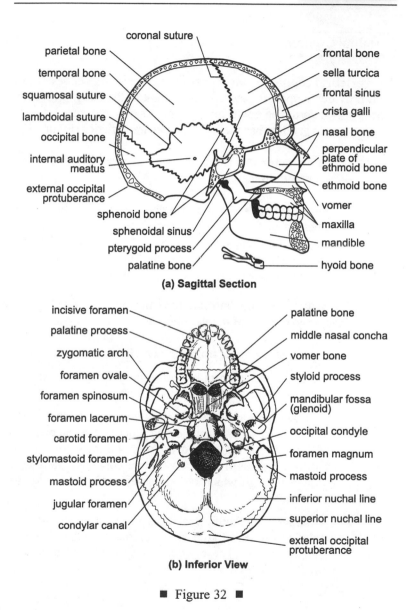

(a) Sagittal Section

- parietal bone
- temporal bone
- squamosal suture
- lambdoidal suture
- occipital bone
- internal auditory meatus
- external occipital protuberance
- sphenoid bone
- sphenoidal sinus
- pterygold process
- palatine bone
- coronal suture
- frontal bone
- sella turcica
- frontal sinus
- crista galli
- nasal bone
- perpendicular plate of ethmoid bone
- ethmoid bone
- vomer
- maxilla
- mandible
- hyoid bone

(b) Inferior View

- incisive foramen
- palatine process
- zygomatic arch
- foramen ovale
- foramen spinosum
- foramen lacerum
- carotid foramen
- stylomastoid foramen
- mastoid process
- jugular foramen
- condylar canal
- palatine bone
- middle nasal concha
- vomer bone
- styloid process
- mandibular fossa (glenoid)
- occipital condyle
- foramen magnum
- mastoid process
- inferior nuchal line
- superior nuchal line
- external occipital protuberance

■ Figure 32 ■

Vertebral Column

The **vertebral column (spine)** consists of 26 vertebrae bones (Table 6). It provides support for the head and trunk of the body, protection for the spinal cord, and connecting points for ribs and muscles.

A typical **vertebra** has the following characteristics (Figure 33):

1. The **body (centrum)** is the disc-shaped, anterior portion that gives strength to the bone.

2. The **vertebral arch** is a bony ring behind the vertebral body. The opening in the ring is the **vertebral foramen,** the passageway for the spinal cord. The **vertebral canal** is the continuous passageway formed by the vertebral foramens of successive vertebrae.

3. The **pedicles** and the **laminae** form the anterior and posterior sides, respectively, of the vertebral arch.

4. Seven processes project from the **vertebral arch:**

   - A **spinous process** projects posteriorly from the vertebral arch. Muscle and ligaments attach here.

   - Two **transverse process**es project from the vertebral arch, one from each side, at each of the junctures of the pedicles and laminae. Muscles and ligaments attach here. Each transverse process of cervical vertebrae contains a transverse foramen through which blood vessels and nerves pass to the brain.

   - Two **superior articular process**es project from the superior side of the vertebral arch, one from each of the pedicles-laminae junction. These processes articulate (form joints) with the vertebra above.

■ Two **inferior articular process**es project from the inferior side of the vertebral arch, one from each of the pedicles-laminae junction. These processes articulate (form joints) with the vertebra below.

5. The **intervertebral foramina** are notches in the anterior and posterior surfaces of each pedicle of the vertebral arch. Adjacent notches of successive vertebrae form a passage for nerves that branch from the spinal cord to outside the vertebral column.

6. **Intervertebral discs** separate adjacent vertebrae. Each disc consists of an outer ring of fibrocartilage (**annulus fibrosus**) surrounding a semifluid cushion (**nucleus pulposus**) that provides elasticity and compressibility.

The vertebral column is divided into four groups, each group contributing to the alternating concave and convex curves of the spine (Figure 33). As the vertebrae progress down the column, their bodies get more massive, enabling them to bear more weight.

The **sacrum** is a triangular bone below the last lumbar vertebra (Figure 33). It is formed by the fusion of five vertebrae (S_1–S_5).

The **coccyx,** formed by four fused vertebrae, is a small triangle-shaped bone that attaches to the bottom of the sacrum (Figure 33).

Vertebra		Body	Spinous Process	Transverse Process	Vertebral Foramen
cervical	C₁ (atlas)	none, bony ring	none	with transverse foramen	large; lightbulb-shaped
	C₂ (axis)	relatively small; with dens (odontoid process)	bifid		large, heart-shaped
	C₃ - C₆	relatively small; oval			large; triangular
	C₇ (vertebra prominens)	relatively small; oval	prominently long; not bifid		
thoracic	T₁ - T₁₀	larger than C₁-C₇, heart-shaped; 2 facets or demi-facets for articulating with rib head	long; points down	with facets for articulating with rib tubercle	circular
	T₁₁ - T₁₂	larger than C₁-C₇, heart-shaped; with 1 demi-facet for articulating with rib head		no facets for rib joint	
lumbar	L₁ - L₅	largest of all vertebrae; kidney-shaped	short, thick; points horizontally		
sacrum	5 fused S₁ - S₅	fusion of 5 vertebrae forms a triangular bone	fuse to become the medial sacral crest	becomes the lateral sacral crest	becomes sacral canal
coccyx	4 fused				

■ Table 6 ■

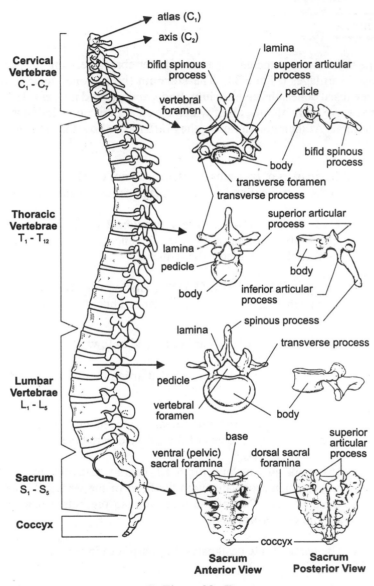

atlas (C₁)

axis (C₂)

Cervical Vertebrae C₁ - C₇

lamina

bifid spinous process

superior articular process

pedicle

vertebral foramen

bifid spinous process

body

transverse foramen

transverse process

Thoracic Vertebrae T₁ - T₁₂

superior articular process

lamina

pedicle

body

body

inferior articular process

spinous process

lamina

transverse process

Lumbar Vertebrae L₁ - L₅

pedicle

body

vertebral foramen

body

base

superior articular process

ventral (pelvic) sacral foramina

dorsal sacral foramina

Sacrum S₁ - S₅

Coccyx

coccyx

Sacrum Anterior View

Sacrum Posterior View

■ Figure 33 ■

Thorax

The **thoracic cage** includes the thoracic vertebrae, sternum, ribs, and costal cartilages (Figure 34). The **sternum** (breastbone) consists of three fused bones: the **manubrium, body,** and **xiphoid process.** There are twelve pairs of **ribs,** all of which attach at their posterior ends to vertebrae. At their anterior ends, they differ as to how they attach, as follows:

1. Seven pairs of **true ribs (vertebrosternal ribs)** attach directly to the sternum with hyaline cartilage called **costal cartilage.**

2. Three pairs of **false ribs (vertebrochondral ribs)** do *not* attach to the sternum. Rather, they connect (with costal cartilage) to the rib directly above them.

3. Two pairs of **false ribs (floating ribs** or **vertebral ribs)** do not attach to anything at their anterior ends.

Important features of a rib are described below.

1. The **head** is the end of the rib that articulates with the vertebral column.

2. The **superior** and **inferior facets** are facets on the head that articulate with the facets of the thoracic vertebrae.

3. The **neck,** just beyond the head, bears a tubercle (rounded process) that articulates with the facet of the vertebral transverse process. Part of the tubercle also presents a place of attachment for ligaments.

4. The **costal angle** designates the sharp turn in the rib.

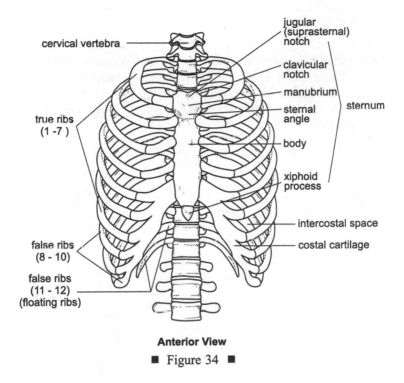

Anterior View

■ Figure 34 ■

5. The **costal groove,** a passageway on the inside of the bending rib, provides for blood vessels and intercostal nerves.

6. The **body (shaft)** is the major part of the rib, that part beyond the costal angle.

7. **Intercostal spaces,** the areas between the ribs, are occupied by the intercostal muscles.

Pectoral Girdle

Each of the two **pectoral (shoulder) girdles** consists of two bones: the S-shaped **clavicle** and the flat, triangular **scapula.** The clavicle articulates with the sternum and the scapula. In turn, the scapula articulates with the humerus of the arm. Figure 35 illustrates details of these bones.

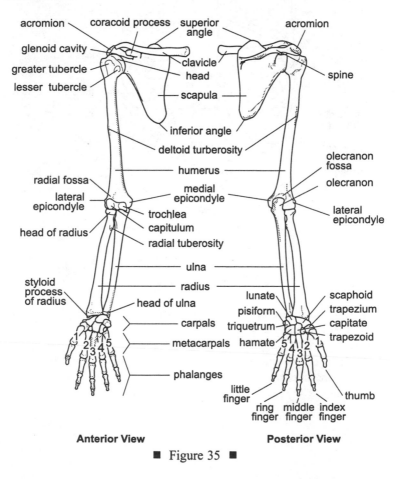

Anterior View   **Posterior View**

■ Figure 35 ■

Upper Limb

The **upper limb** consists of the arm, forearm, and hand. The thirty bones of each upper limb are illustrated in Figure 35.

Pelvic Girdle

The **pelvic (hip) girdle** transfers the weight of the upper body to the legs. It consists of a pair of **coxal bones (os coxae, hip bones)**, each of which contains three fused bones: the **ilium, ischium,** and **pubis.** Together with the sacrum and coccyx, the pelvic girdle forms a bowl-shaped region, the **pelvis,** that protects internal reproductive organs, the urinary bladder, and the lower part of the digestive tract. Features of these bones are given in Figure 36.

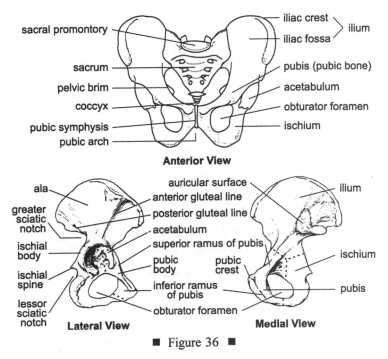

■ Figure 36 ■

Lower Limb

The thigh, leg, and foot constitute the **lower limb.** The bones of the lower limbs are considerably larger and stronger than comparable bones of the upper limbs because the lower limbs must support the entire weight of the body while walking, running, or jumping. Features of the 30 bones of each lower limb are illustrated in Figure 37.

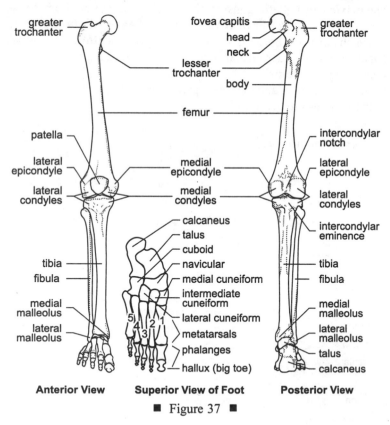

■ Figure 37 ■

A joint (articulation) occurs wherever bones meet. Joints are classified both structurally and functionally, as follows (Table 7).

Structural classification is based on the materials that hold the joint together and whether or not a cavity is present in the joint. There are three structural classes.

1. **Fibrous joints** are held together by fibrous connective tissue. No joint cavity is present. Fibrous joints may be immovable or slightly movable.

2. **Cartilaginous joints** are held together by cartilage (hyaline or fibrocartilage). No joint cavity is present. Cartilaginous joints may be immovable or slightly movable.

3. **Synovial joints** are characterized by a **synovial cavity (joint cavity)** containing synovial fluid. Synovial joints are freely movable and characterize most joints of the body. Other features of a synovial joint follow (Figure 38).

   ■ **Articular cartilage** (hyaline cartilage) covers the end of each bone.

   ■ A **synovial membrane** surrounds the synovial cavity. Its areolar connective tissue secretes a lubricating **synovial fluid** into the synovial cavity.

   ■ A **fibrous capsule** outside the synovial membrane surrounds the joint. It often contains bundles of dense, irregular, connective tissue called **ligaments.** The ligaments provide strength and flexibility to the joint.

   ■ The **articular capsule** is composed of the synovial membrane and fibrous capsule.

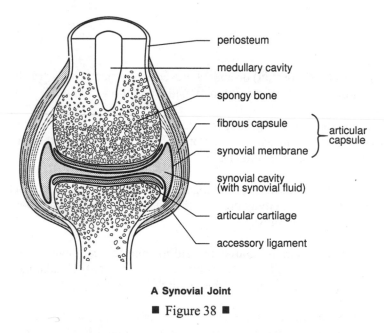

A Synovial Joint

■ Figure 38 ■

- **Accessory ligaments** lie outside the articular capsule (**extracapsular ligaments**) or inside the synovial cavity (**intracapsular ligaments**).

Functional classification is based on the degree to which the joint permits movement. There are three types:

1. A **synarthrosis** joint permits no movement. Structurally, it may be a fibrous or cartilaginous joint.

2. An **amphiarthrosis** joint permits only slight movement. Structurally, it may be a fibrous or cartilaginous joint.

3. A **diarthrosis joint** is a freely movable joint. Structurally, it is always a synovial joint.

The various specific joint types with descriptions and examples are given in Table 7.

Functional Class	Structural Class	Joint Type	Description of Joint	Example
synarthrosis (immovable)	fibrous	suture	interlocking seams	between cranial bones
		gomphosis	peg-and-socket joint	between teeth & sockets
	cartilag-inous	syn-chondrosis	hyaline cartilage joint	between diaphysis & epiphysis in long bones
amphiarthrosis (slightly movable)	fibrous	syn-desmosis	ligament or interosseous membrane	distal joint of tibia & fibula
	cartilag-inous	symphysis	fibrocartilage acts as compressible cushion	Intervertebral discs of vertebral column
diarthrosis (freely movable)	synovial	gliding	two sliding surfaces	between carpals
		hinge	concave surface with convex surface	between humerus & ulna
		pivot	rounded end fits into ring of bone and ligament	between atlas (C_1) & axis (C_2) vertebrae
		condyloid	oval condyle with oval cavity	between metacarpals & phalanges
		saddle	each surface is both concave and convex	between carpus & the first metacarpal
		ball-and-socket	ball-shaped head with cup-shaped socket	between femur & pelvis

■ Table 7 ■

Types of Muscles

There are three types of muscles:

1. **Skeletal muscle** is attached to bones and causes movements of the body. Skeletal muscle is also called **striated muscle** (because of its banding pattern when viewed under a microscope) or **voluntary muscle** (because muscle contraction can be consciously controlled).

2. **Cardiac muscle** is responsible for the rhythmic contractions of the heart. Cardiac muscle is involuntary—it generates its own stimuli to initiate muscle contraction.

3. **Smooth muscle** lines the walls of hollow organs. For example, it lines the walls of blood vessels and of the digestive tract where it serves to advance the movement of substances. Smooth muscle contraction is relatively slow and involuntary.

Connective Tissue Associated with Muscle Tissue

A skeletal muscle consists of numerous muscle cells called **muscle fibers.** Three layers of connective tissues surround these fibers to form a muscle. These and other connective tissues associated with muscles are listed below.

1. The **endomysium** is the connective tissue that surrounds each muscle fiber (cell).

2. The **perimysium** encircles a group of muscle fibers, forming a **fascicle.**

3. The **epimysium** encircles all the fascicles to form a complete muscle.

4. A **tendon** is a *cordlike* extension of the three linings listed above. It extends beyond the muscle tissue to connect the muscle to a bone or to other muscles.

5. An **aponeurosis** is a *flat, broad* extension of the three muscle linings and serves the same function as a tendon.

6. The **deep fascia** surrounds the perimysium and encloses or lines other nearby structures such as blood vessels, nerves, and the body wall.

7. The **superficial fascia** (**hypodermis** or **subcutaneous layer**) lies immediately below the skin. The superficial fascia merges with the deep fascia where muscle surfaces and skin meet.

Structure of Skeletal Muscle

A muscle fiber (cell) has special terminology and distinguishing characteristics, as follows.

1. The **sarcolemma,** or plasma membrane of the muscle cell, is highly invaginated by transverse tubules (T tubules) that permeate the cell.

2. The **sarcoplasm,** or cytoplasm of the muscle cell, contains calcium-storing **sarcoplasmic reticulum,** the specialized endoplasmic reticulum of a muscle cell.

3. Striated muscle cells are *multinucleate.* The nuclei lie along the periphery of the cell, forming swellings visible through the sarcolemma.

4. Nearly the entire volume of the cell is filled with numerous, long **myofibrils.** Myofibrils consist of two types of filaments, as follows (Figure 39).

■ **Thin filaments** consist of two strands of the globular protein **actin** arranged in a double helix. Along the length of the helix are **troponin** and **tropomyosin** molecules that cover special binding sites on the actin.

■ **Thick filaments** consist of groups of the filamentous protein **myosin.** Each myosin filament forms a protruding head at one end. An array of myosin filaments possesses protruding heads at numerous positions at both ends.

Within a myofibril, actin and myosin filaments are parallel and arranged side-by-side. The overlapping filaments produce a repeating pattern that gives skeletal muscle its striated appearance. Each repeating unit of the pattern, called a **sarcomere,** is separated by a border, or **Z disc (Z line)**, to which the actin filaments are attached. The myosin filaments, with their protruding heads, float between the actin, unattached to the Z disc.

Muscle Contraction

Muscle contraction is described by the **sliding-filament model,** as follows.

1. *ATP binds to a myosin head and forms ADP + P_i.* When ATP binds to a myosin head, it is converted to ADP and P_i, which remain attached to the myosin head.

2. *Ca^{2+} exposes the binding sites on the actin filaments.* Ca^{2+} binds to the troponin molecule causing tropomyosin to expose positions on the actin filament for the attachment of myosin heads.

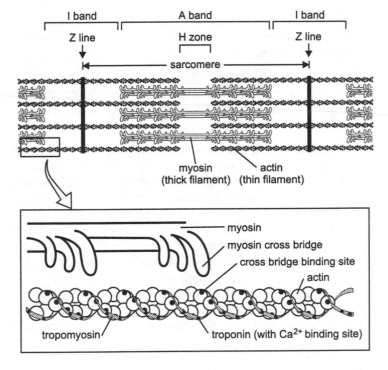

I band   A band   I band

Z line   H zone   Z line

sarcomere

myosin   actin
(thick filament)   (thin filament)

myosin
myosin cross bridge
cross bridge binding site
actin

tropomyosin   troponin (with Ca^{2+} binding site)

■ Figure 39 ■

3. *Cross bridges between myosin heads and actin filaments form.*
   When attachment sites on the actin are exposed, the myosin
   heads bind to actin to form cross bridges.

4. *ADP and P_i are released, and sliding motion of actin results.*
   The attachment of cross bridges between myosin and actin
   causes the release of ADP and P_i. This, in turn, causes a change
   in shape of the myosin head, which generates a sliding movement of the actin toward the center of the sarcomere. This
   pulls the two Z discs together, effectively contracting the muscle
   fiber to produce a **power stroke.**

5. *ATP causes the cross bridges to unbind.* When a new ATP molecule attaches to the myosin head, the cross bridge between the actin and myosin breaks, returning the myosin head to its unattached position.

Without the addition of a new ATP molecule, the cross bridges remain attached to the actin filaments. This is why corpses become stiff with **rigor mortis** (new ATP molecules are unavailable).

Stimulation of Muscle Contraction

Neurons, or nerve cells, are stimulated when the polarity across their plasma membrane changes. The polarity change, called an **action potential,** travels along the neuron until it reaches the end of the neuron. A gap called a **synapse** or **synaptic cleft** separates the neuron from a muscle cell or another neuron. If a neuron stimulates a muscle, then the neuron is a **motor neuron,** and its specialized synapse is called a **neuromuscular junction.** Muscle contraction is stimulated through the following steps.

1. *Action potential generates release of acetylcholine.* When an action potential of a neuron reaches the neuromuscular junction, the neuron secretes the neurotransmitter acetylcholine (ACh), which diffuses across the synaptic cleft.

2. *Action potential is generated on the motor end plate and throughout the T tubules.* Receptors on the motor end plate, a highly folded region of the sarcolemma, initiate an action potential. The action potential travels along the sarcolemma throughout the transverse system of tubules.

3. *Sarcoplasmic reticulum releases Ca^{2+}.* As a result of the action potential throughout the transverse system of tubules, the sarcoplasmic reticulum releases Ca^{2+}.

4. *Myosin cross bridges form.* The Ca^{2+} released by the sarco-plasmic reticulum binds to troponin molecules on the actin helix, prompting tropomyosin molecules to expose binding sites for myosin cross-bridge formation. If ATP is available, muscle contraction begins.

Phases of a Muscle Contraction

A muscle contraction in response to a single, nerve action potential is called a **twitch contraction.** A **myogram,** a graph of muscle strength (**tension**) with time, shows three phases (Figure 40a).

1. The **latent period** is the time required for the release of Ca^{2+}.

2. The **contraction period** represents the time during actual muscle contraction.

3. The **relaxation period** is the time during which Ca^{2+} is re-turned to the sarcoplasmic reticulum by active transport.

4. The **refractory period** is the time immediately following a stimulus during which the muscle fiber will not respond to a second stimulus. For skeletal muscle fibers, this period typi-cally ends during the early part of the contraction period.

Quality of a Muscle Contraction

The following factors contribute to the strength and maximum dura-tion of a muscle contraction.

1. *Frequency of stimuli.* If stimuli are repeatedly applied to a muscle fiber, Ca^{2+} may not be completely transported back into the sarcoplasmic reticulum before the next stimulus oc-

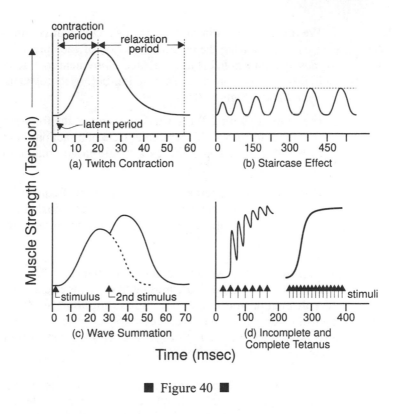

■ Figure 40 ■

curs. Depending upon the frequency of stimuli, Ca^{2+} may accumulate. In turn, the extra Ca^{2+} results in more power strokes and a stronger muscle contraction. Depending upon the frequency of stimuli, several effects are observed.

■ A **staircase effect** (**treppe**) is produced if each successive stimulus occurs *after* the relaxation period of the previous stimulus. Each successive muscle contraction is greater than the previous one, up to some maximum value (Figure 40b). In addition to the accumulation of Ca^{2+}, other factors, such as increases in temperature and changes in pH, may contribute to this "warming up" effect commonly employed by athletes.

- **Wave (temporal) summation** occurs if consecutive stimuli are applied *during* the relaxation period of each preceding muscle contraction. In this case, each subsequent contraction builds upon the previous contraction before its relaxation period ends (Figure 40c).

- **Incomplete (unfused) tetanus** occurs when the frequency of stimuli increases. Successive muscle contractions begin to blend, almost appearing as a single large contraction (Figure 40d).

- **Complete (fused) tetanus** occurs when the frequency of stimuli increases still further. In this case, individual muscle contractions completely fuse to produce one large muscle contraction (Figure 40d).

2. *Strength of stimulus.* Muscle contractions intensify when more motor neurons stimulate more muscle fibers. This effect, called **recruitment** or **multiple motor unit summation,** is also responsible for our fine motor coordination because by continually varying the stimulation of specific muscle fibers, smooth body movements are maintained.

3. *Length of muscle fiber contraction.* Because a muscle is attached to bones, muscle contraction is restricted to lengths that are between 60% and 175% of the length that produces optimal strength. This range of muscle lengths limits myosin cross bridges and actin only to positions where they overlap and thus can generate contractions.

4. *Type of contraction.* Muscle contraction implies that there is movement between myosin cross bridges and actin. However, this movement does not necessarily result in shortening of the muscle. As a result, two kinds of muscle contractions are defined.

   - **Isotonic contractions** occur when muscles change length during a contraction. Picking up a book is an example.

- **Isometric contractions** occur when muscles do not change length during a contraction. When holding a book in midair, muscle fibers produce a force, but no motion is generated.

5. *Type of muscle fiber.* Muscle fibers are classified into two groups.

   - **Slow fibers** contract slowly, have a high endurance, and are red from their rich blood supply. However, they do not produce much strength. These fibers are used for long-distance running.

   - **Fast fibers** contract rapidly, fatigue rapidly, and are white because the blood supply is limited. They generate considerable strength. These fibers are used for short-distance running.

6. *Muscle tone.* In any relaxed skeletal muscle, a small number of contractions continuously occur. Observed as firmness in a muscle, these contractions maintain body posture and increase muscle readiness.

7. *Muscle fatigue.* Muscle fibers stop contracting when inadequate amounts of ATP are available. Lack of oxygen and glycogen and the accumulation of lactic acid (a byproduct of ATP production in the absence of oxygen), together with the lack of ATP, all contribute to muscle fatigue.

Muscle Metabolism

In order for muscles to contract, ATP must be available in the muscle fiber. ATP is available from the following sources.

1. *ATP from within the cell.* ATP available within the muscle fiber can maintain muscle contraction for several seconds.

2. *ATP from creatine phosphate.* Creatine phosphate, a high-energy molecule stored in muscle cells, transfers its high-energy phosphate group to ADP to form ATP. The creatine phosphate in muscle cells is able to generate enough ATP to maintain muscle contraction for about 15 seconds.

3. *ATP from glucose stored within the cell.* Glucose within the cell is stored in the carbohydrate glycogen. Through the metabolic process of **glycogenolysis,** glycogen is broken down to release glucose. ATP is then generated from glucose by cellular respiration.

4. *ATP from glucose and fatty acids obtained from the bloodstream.* When energy requirements are high, glucose from glycogen stored in the liver and fatty acids from fat stored in adipose cells and the liver are released into the bloodstream. Glucose and fatty acids are then absorbed from the bloodstream by muscle cells. ATP is then generated from these energy-rich molecules by cellular respiration.

Cellular respiration is the process by which ATP is obtained from energy-rich molecules. Several major metabolic pathways are involved, some of which require the presence of oxygen. Important pathways are summarized below.

1. In **glycolysis,** glucose is broken down to **pyruvic acid,** and two ATP molecules are generated. Because no oxygen is used during the various metabolic steps of this pathway, glycolysis is called an **anaerobic** process.

2. In **anaerobic respiration,** pyruvic acid (from glycolysis) is converted to **lactic acid.** No ATP is generated and, as its name indicates, no oxygen is required. The importance of this process is that it regenerates certain coenzymes necessary for glycolysis to continue. Thus, *in the absence of oxygen,* anaerobic respiration is indirectly responsible for the production of two ATPs (during glycolysis).

- *Advantages of anaerobic respiration:* Anaerobic respiration is relatively rapid, and it does not require oxygen.

- *Disadvantages of anaerobic respiration:* Anaerobic respiration generates only two ATPs, and lactic acid is produced. Most lactic acid diffuses out of the cell and into the bloodstream and is subsequently absorbed by the liver. Some of the lactic acid remains in the muscle fibers, where it contributes to muscle fatigue. Because both the liver and muscle fibers must convert the lactic acid back to pyruvic acid when oxygen becomes available, anaerobic respiration is said to produce an **oxygen debt.**

3. In **aerobic respiration,** pyruvic acid (from glycolysis) and fatty acids (from the bloodstream) are broken down, producing H_2O and CO_2 (carbon dioxide) and regenerating the coenzymes for glycolysis. A total of 36 ATP molecules is produced (including the two from glycolysis). However, oxygen is required for this pathway.

   - *Advantages of aerobic respiration:* Aerobic respiration generates a large amount of ATP.

   - *Disadvantages of aerobic respiration:* Aerobic respiration is relatively slow and requires oxygen.

When the ATP generated from creatine phosphate is depleted, the immediate requirements of contracting muscle fibers force anaerobic respiration to begin. Anaerobic respiration can supply ATP for about 30 seconds. If muscle contraction continues, aerobic respiration, the slower ATP-producing pathway, begins and produces large amounts of ATP as long as oxygen is available. Eventually, oxygen is depleted and aerobic respiration stops. However, ATP production by anaerobic respiration may still support some further muscle contraction. Ultimately, the accumulation of lactic acid from anaerobic respiration and the depletion of resources (ATP, oxygen, and glycogen) lead to muscle fatigue, and muscle contraction stops.

Structure of Cardiac Muscle

Although it is striated, **cardiac muscle** differs from skeletal muscle in that it is highly branched with cells connected by overlapping projections of the sarcolemma called **intercalated discs.** These discs contain desmosomes and gap junctions. In addition, cardiac muscle is **autorhythmic,** generating its own action potential which spreads rapidly throughout muscle tissue by electrical synapses across the gap junctions.

Structure of Smooth Muscle

Due to its irregular arrangement of actin and myosin filaments, **smooth muscle** does not have the striated appearance of skeletal muscle. In addition, the sarcolemma does not form a system of transverse tubules, and as a result, contraction is controlled and relatively slow, properties appropriate for smooth muscle function.

In addition to the thick myosin and thin actin filaments, smooth muscles also possess noncontracting intermediate filaments. The intermediate fibers attach to **dense bodies** that are scattered through the sarcoplasm and attached to the sarcolemma. During contraction, the movement of myosin and actin is transferred to intermediate fibers which pull on the dense bodies which, in turn, pull the muscle cell together. In this way, the dense bodies function similarly to the Z discs in striated muscle.

The **muscular system** consists of skeletal muscles and their associated connective tissues. It does not include cardiac muscle or smooth muscle, which are associated with the systems in which they are found, such as the cardiovascular, digestive, urinary, or other organ systems.

Skeletal Muscle Actions

A skeletal muscle may attach a bone to another bone (often across a joint) or a bone to another structure, such as skin. When the muscle contracts, one of the structures usually remains stationary, while the other moves. The following terms refer to this characteristic of muscle contraction.

- The **origin** of the muscle is the muscle end that attaches to the stationary structure, usually a bone.

- The **insertion** of the muscle is the muscle end that attaches to the moving structure.

- The **belly** of the muscle is that part of the muscle between the origin and insertion.

A particular body movement is usually influenced by several muscles, as follows.

1. The **prime mover** is the muscle that is most responsible for the movement.

2. **Synergists** are other muscles that assist the prime mover. Synergists may stabilize nearby bones, or refine the movement of the prime mover.

3. **Antagonists** are muscles that cause a movement opposite to that of the prime mover. If the prime mover raises an arm,

then its antagonist pulls the arm down. An antagonist is generally attached to the opposite side of the joint to which the prime mover is attached.

Names of Skeletal Muscles

Skeletal muscles are often named after the following characteristics.

1. *Number of origins.* Biceps, triceps, and quadriceps indicate two, three, and four origins, respectively.

2. *Location of origin or insertion.* The sternocleidomastoid names the sternum ("sterno") and clavicle ("cleido") as its origins and the mastoid process of the temporal bone as its insertion.

3. *Location.* In addition to its origin or insertion, a muscle name may indicate a nearby bone or body region. For example, the temporalis muscle covers the temporal bone.

4. *Shape.* The deltoid (triangular), trapezius (trapezoid), serratus (saw-toothed) and rhomboideus major (rhomboid) muscles have names that describe their shapes.

5. *Direction of muscle fibers.* The terms rectus (parallel), transverse (perpendicular), and oblique (at an angle) in muscle names refer to the direction of the muscle fibers with respect to the midline of the body.

6. *Size.* Maximus (largest), minimus (smallest), longus (longest), and brevis (shortest) are common suffixes added to muscle names.

7. *Action.* Terms such as flexor, extensor, abductor, and adductor are added as prefixes to muscle names to indicate the kind of movement generated by the muscle.

Muscle Size and Arrangement of Muscle Fascicles

The size of a muscle influences its capabilities. When a muscle fiber (cell) contracts, it can shorten to nearly half its relaxed length. The *longer* a muscle fiber, then, the greater *range* of movement it can generate. In contrast, an increase in the *number* of muscle fibers increases the *strength* of the contraction.

Muscle fibers are grouped into **fascicles**, which are, in turn, grouped together to form a muscle. The size (length) and number of fascicles determine the strength and range of movement of a muscle. Common fascicle patterns follow.

1. **Parallel fascicles** have their long axes parallel to each other. Parallel fascicles can be flat, or *straplike*, or they can bulge at their bellies and be spindle shaped, or *fusiform*.

2. **Circular fascicles** are arranged in concentric rings. Muscles with this pattern form *sphincter* muscles that control the opening and closing of orifices.

3. **Pennate fascicles** are short and attach obliquely to a long tendon that extends across the entire muscle. In a *unipennate* pattern, the muscle resembles one half of a feather (the tendon is represented by the shaft of the feather). A *bipennate* pattern resembles a complete feather, with fascicles attached to both sides of a central tendon. A *multipennate* pattern of fascicles resembles three or more feathers attached at their bases.

Major Skeletal Muscles

The major skeletal muscles are described in Tables 8–11 and illustrated in Figures 41–46.

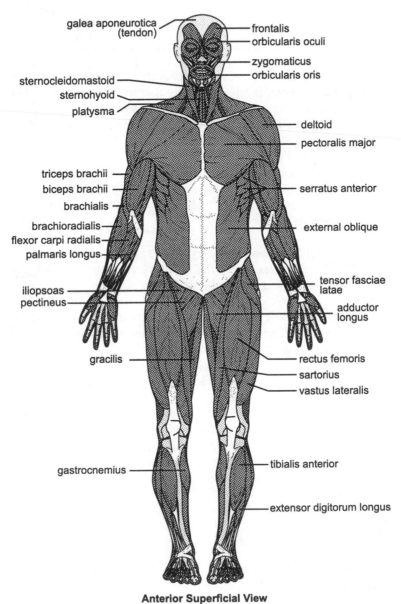

Anterior Superficial View

■ Figure 41 ■

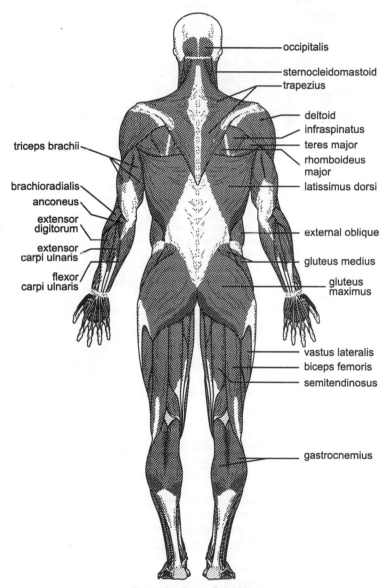

occipitalis

sternocleidomastoid
trapezius

deltoid
infraspinatus
teres major
rhomboideus
major
latissimus dorsi

triceps brachii

brachioradialis
anconeus
extensor
digitorum
extensor
carpi ulnaris
flexor
carpi ulnaris

external oblique

gluteus medius

gluteus
maximus

vastus lateralis
biceps femoris
semitendinosus

gastrocnemius

Posterior Superficial View

■ Figure 42 ■

Muscles of the Head and Neck		
Muscle	Origin/Insertion	Action
epicranius:frontalis	O: galea aponeurotica I: skin around eyes	raises eyebrows; surprised
epicranius:occipitalis	O: occipital bone I: galea aponeurotica	pulls scalp back; surprised
orbicularis oculi	O: maxillary & frontal bones I: eyelids	closes eyelids; blinking
orbicularis oris	O: muscle fibers around mouth I: skin around mouth	closes lips; kissing
buccinator	O: maxilla & mandible I: orbicularis oris	compresses cheek; whistling
platysma	O: fascia in upper chest I: mandible & corner of mouth	lowers mandible; opens mouth
mentalis	O: mandible I: skin of chin	protrudes lower lip; pouting
risorius	O: fascia on masseter muscle I: skin at corner of mouth	lateral movement of lips; grimacing
zygomaticus	O: zygomatic bone I: skin around mouth	raises edges of mouth; smiling
levator labii superioris	O: infraorbital margin of maxilla I: skin of upper lip	raises upper lip; as in disgust
depressor labii inferioris	O: mandible I: skin of lower lip	lowers lower lip
temporalis	O: parietal bone I: mandible	raises mandible; closes mouth
masseter	O: maxilla & zygomatic arch I: mandible	raises mandible; closes mouth
medial pterygoid	O: sphenoid & maxilla I: mandible	raises mandible; side- to-side mouth motion
lateral pterygoid	O: sphenoid I: mandible	raises mandible; side- to-side mouth motion
sternocleidomastoid	O: sternum & clavicle I: temporal bone	flexes & rotates head
splenius capitis	O: cervical & thoracic vertebrae I: temporal bone	rotates, bends, or extends head
semispinalis capitis	O: cervical & thoracic vertebrae I: occipital bone	rotates or extends head
longissimus	O: cervical & thoracic vertebrae I: temporal bone	rotates, bends, or extends head
omohyoid	O: scapula I: hyoid bone	depresses hyoid bone
sternohyoid	O: sternum & clavicle I: hyoid bone	depresses hyoid bone

■ Table 8 ■

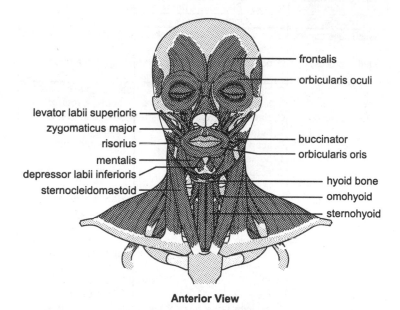

Anterior View

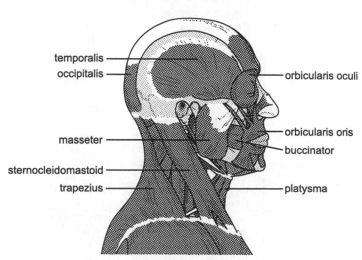

Lateral View

■ Figure 43 ■

Muscles of the Neck, Shoulder, Thorax, and Abdominal Wall		
Muscle	Origin/Insertion	Action
semispinalis capitis	O: cervical & thoracic vertebrae I: occipital bone	extends & rotates head
splenius capitis	O: occipital bone,c & t vertebrae I: occipital & temporal bone	extends & rotates head
deltoid	O: clavicle & scapula I: humerus	abducts, flexes, extends, & rotates arm
pectoralis major	O: clavicle, sternum, ribs I: humerus	flexes, adducts, & rotates arm
infraspinatus	O: scapula I: humerus	rotates humerus
teres major	O: scapula I: humerus	extends, rotates arm
latissimus dorsi	O: vertebrae, ribs, ilium I: humerus	extends, adducts, rotates arm
levator scapulae	O: cervical vertebrae I: scapula	elevates scapula
pectoralis minor	O: ribs I: scapula	stabilizes scapula, elevates ribs
serratus anterior	O: ribs I: scapula	stabilizes scapula, elevates ribs
trapezius	O: occipital bone & vertebrae I: scapula & clavicle	elevates, adducts, & rotates scapula
rhomboideus major rhomboideus minor	O: c & t vertebrae I: scapula	adducts & rotates scapula
rectus abdominis	O: pubic crest & symphysis I: xiphoid process & ribs	flexes vertebral column, compresses abdomen
external oblique	O: ribs I: linea alba, ilium	compresses abdomen, rotates trunk
transverse abdominis	O: ilium, ribs I: linea alba, xiphoid process	compresses abdomen
external intercostals	O: lower border of rib above I: upper border of rib below	elevates ribs, aids inspiration
internal intercostals	O: upper border of rib below I: lower border of rib above	pulls ribs together, aids expiration
diaphragm	O: lower ribs, sternum I: central tendon	aids inspiration
spinalis	O: lumbar & thoracic vertebrae I: thoracic & cervical vertebrae	extends vertebral column
longissimus	O: lumbar & cervical vertebrae I: temporal bone,vertebrae	extends vertebral column
iliocostalis	O: ilium, ribs I: ribs	extends vertebral column

■ Table 9 ■

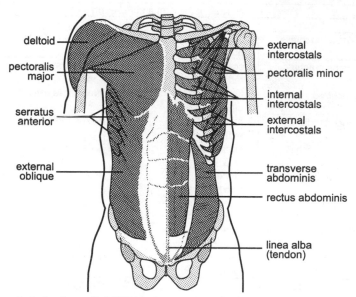

Anterior Superficial View   **Anterior Deep View**

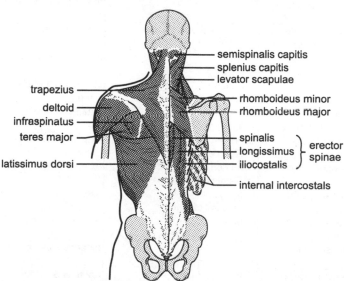

Posterior Superficial View   **Posterior Deep View**

■ Figure 44 ■

Muscles of the Arm and Forearm		
Muscle	Origin/Insertion	Action
coracobrachialis	O: scapula I: humerus	flexes & adducts arm
biceps brachii	O: scapula, glenoid cavity I: radius	flexes arm, rotates hand
brachialis	O: humerus I: ulna	flexes forearm
brachioradialis	O: humerus I: radius	flexes forearm
triceps brachii	O: humerus I: ulna	extends forearm
anconeus	O: humerus I: ulna	extends forearm
pronator teres	O: humerus, ulna I: radius	rotates forearm
pronator quadratus	O: ulna I: radius	rotates forearm
supinator	O: ulna I: radius	rotates forearm
flexor carpi radialis	O: humerus I: metacarpals	flexes & abducts wrist
flexor carpi ulnaris	O: humerus, ulna I: carpals, metacarpals	flexes & adducts wrist
flexor digitorum superficialis	O: humerus, ulna, radius I: phalanges	flexes fingers 2 - 5
flexor digitorum profundus	O: ulna I: phalanges	flexes distal fingers 2 - 5
palmaris longus	O: radius I: distal phalanx of thumb	flexes distal phalanx of thumb
extensor carpi radialis longus	O: humerus I: second metacarpal	extends & abducts wrist
extensor carpi ulnaris	O: humerus, ulna I: fifth metacarpal	extends & adducts wrist
extensor digitorum	O: humerus I: distal phalanges	extends fingers 2 - 5
extensor pollicis brevis	O: radius I: phalanx of thumb	extends thumb
extensor pollicis longus	O: ulna I: phalanx of thumb	extends thumb
extensor indicis	O: ulna I: index finger	extends index finger
abductor pollicis longus	O: radius & thumb I: first metacarpal	abducts & extends thumb

■ Table 10 ■

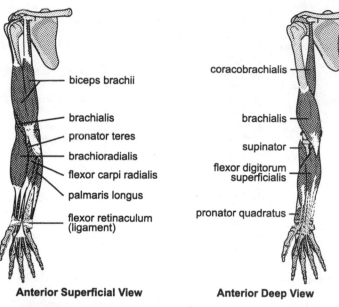

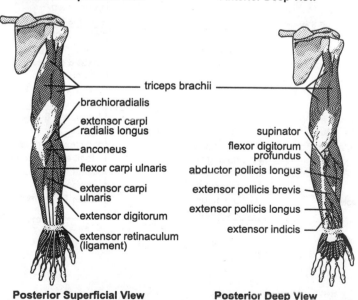

Anterior Superficial View

- biceps brachii
- brachialis
- pronator teres
- brachioradialis
- flexor carpi radialis
- palmaris longus
- flexor retinaculum (ligament)

Anterior Deep View

- coracobrachialis
- brachialis
- supinator
- flexor digitorum superficialis
- pronator quadratus

Posterior Superficial View

- triceps brachii
- brachioradialis
- extensor carpi radialis longus
- anconeus
- flexor carpi ulnaris
- extensor carpi ulnaris
- extensor digitorum
- extensor retinaculum (ligament)

Posterior Deep View

- triceps brachii
- supinator
- flexor digitorum profundus
- abductor pollicis longus
- extensor pollicis brevis
- extensor pollicis longus
- extensor indicis

■ Figure 45 ■

Muscles of the Thigh and Leg		
Muscle	Origin/Insertion	Action
gluteus maximus	O: ilium, sacrum, coccyx I: femur	extends & rotates thigh
gluteus medius	O: ilium I: femur	abducts & rotates thigh
pectineus	O: pubis I: femur	adducts & flexes thigh
adductor longus	O: pubis I: femur	adducts, flexes, & rotates thigh
adductor brevis	O: pubis I: femur	adducts, flexes, & rotates thigh
adductor magnus	O: pubis, ischium I: femur	adducts, flexes, & rotates thigh
gracilis	O: pubis I: tibia	adducts thigh & flexes leg
sartorius	O: ilium I: tibia	flexes & rotates thigh & flexes leg

quadriceps femoris:
  rectus femoris
  vastus lateralis
  vastus medialis
  vastus intermedius
	O: ilium, femur
	I: patella, tibia
		extends leg, flexes thigh
		extends leg
		extends leg
		extends leg

biceps femoris (hamstrings)	O: ischium, femur I: fibula, tibia	flexes & rotates leg, extends thigh
semitendinosus (hamstrings)	O: ischium I: tibia	flexes & rotates leg, extends thigh
semimembranosus	O: ischium I: tibia	flexes & rotates leg, extends thigh
tibialis anterior	O: tibia I: 1st metatarsal & cuneiform	dorsiflexes & inverts foot
extensor digitorum longus	O: tibia, fibula I: phalanges of toes	dorsiflexes & everts foot, extends toes
gastrocnemius	O: femur I: calcaneus	plantar flexes foot, flexes leg
soleus	O: tibia, fibula I: calcaneus	planter flexes foot

■ Table 11 ■

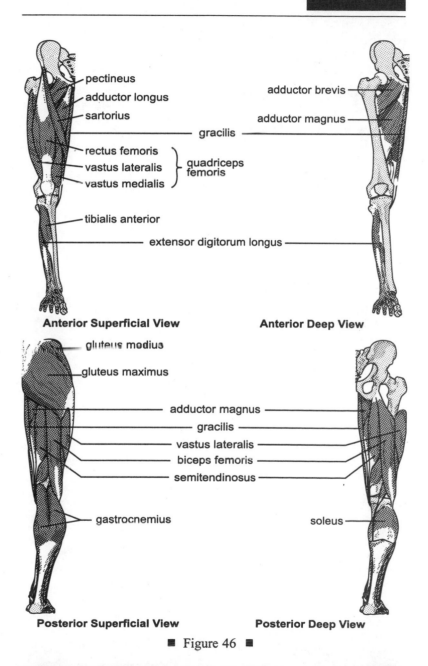

pectineus
adductor longus
sartorius
gracilis
rectus femoris
vastus lateralis } quadriceps femoris
vastus medialis
tibialis anterior
extensor digitorum longus

Anterior Superficial View

adductor brevis
adductor magnus

Anterior Deep View

gluteus medius
gluteus maximus
adductor magnus
gracilis
vastus lateralis
biceps femoris
semitendinosus
gastrocnemius
soleus

Posterior Superficial View

Posterior Deep View

■ Figure 46 ■

Nervous tissue consists of two kinds of **nerve cells**—neurons and neuroglia.

Neurons

A **neuron** is a cell that transmits nerve impulses. It consists of the following parts (Figure 47).

1. The **cell body (soma** or **perikaryon)** contains the nucleus and other cellular organelles.

2. **Nissl bodies (chromatophilic substance)** are clusters of rough endoplasmic reticulum, sites of protein synthesis.

3. The **dendrite** is typically a short, abundantly branched, slender process (extension) of the cell body that *receives* stimuli.

4. The **axon** is typically a long, slender process of the cell body that *sends* nerve impulses. It emerges from the cell body at the cone-shaped **axon hillock.** Nerve impulses arise in the **trigger zone,** generally located in the **initial segment,** an area just outside the axon hillock. The cytoplasm of the axon, the **axoplasm,** is surrounded by its plasma membrane, the **axolemma.** A few axons branch along their lengths to form **axon collaterals,** and these branches may return to merge with the main axon. At its end, each axon or axon collateral usually forms numerous branches (**telodendria**), with most branches terminating in bulb-shaped structures called **synaptic knobs (synaptic end bulbs).** The synaptic knobs contain **neurotransmitters,** chemicals that transmit nerve impulses to a muscle or another neuron.

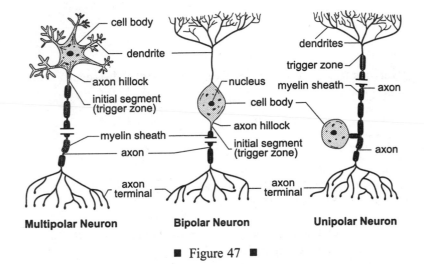

■ Figure 47 ■

Neurons can be classified by function or by structure. Functionally, they fall into three groups:

1. **Sensory neurons (afferent neurons)** transmit sensory impulses *from* the skin and other sensory organs or *from* various places within the body *toward* the central nervous system (CNS, or brain and spinal cord).

2. **Motor neurons (efferent neurons)** transmit nerve impulses *from* the CNS *toward* **effectors**, target cells that produce some kind of response. Effectors include muscles, sweat glands, and exocrine glands.

3. **Association neurons (interneurons)** are located in the CNS and transmit impulses from sensory neurons to motor neurons. More than 90% of the neurons of the body are association neurons.

Neurons are structurally classified into three groups (Figure 47).

1. **Multipolar neurons** have one axon and several to numerous dendrites. Most neurons are of this type.

2. **Bipolar neurons** have one axon and one dendrite. They emerge from opposite sides of the cell body. Bipolar neurons are found only as specialized sensory neurons in the eye, ear, or olfactory organs.

3. **Unipolar neurons** have one process emerging from the cell body that branches, T-fashion, into two processes. Both processes function together as a single axon. Dendrites emerge from one of the terminal ends of the axon. The trigger zone in a unipolar neuron is located at the junction of the axon and dendrites. Unipolar neurons are mostly sensory neurons.

The following terms apply to neurons and groups of neurons.

1. A **nerve fiber** is an axon or dendrite.

2. A **nerve** is a bundle of nerve fibers in the peripheral nervous system (PNS, or outside the CNS) held together with connective tissue. Most nerves contain both sensory and motor fibers. Cell bodies are usually grouped into separate bundles called **ganglia.**

3. A **nerve tract** is a bundle of nerve fibers in the CNS.

Neuroglia

Neuroglia (glia) are cells that support and protect neurons. The following four neuroglia are found in the CNS.

1. **Astrocytes** have numerous processes that give the cell a star-shaped appearance. Astrocytes maintain the ion balance around neurons and control the exchange of materials between blood vessels and neurons.

2. **Oligodendrocytes** have fewer processes than astrocytes. They wrap these cytoplasmic processes around neurons to create an insulating barrier called a **myelin sheath.**

3. **Microglia** are phagocytic macrophages that provide a protective function by engulfing microorganisms and cellular debris.

4. **Ependymal** cells line the fluid-filled cavities of the brain and spinal cord. Many are ciliated.

Two kinds of neuroglia are found in the PNS.

5. **Schwann cells (neurolemmocytes)** wrap around axons to produce an insulating myelin sheath. Schwann cells provide the same function in the PNS as oligodendrocytes provide in the CNS.

6. **Satellite cells** are located in ganglia where they surround the *cell bodies* of neurons.

Myelination

In the PNS, the **myelin sheath** is an insulation formed by Schwann cells around *axons* (Figure 47). Each Schwann cell tightly wraps around the axon numerous times to form a multilayered insulation. The last wrapping of the plasma membrane of the Schwann cell, the **neurilemma,** is loose and contains the nucleus, cytoplasm, and organelles of the Schwann cell.

The myelin sheath consists of numerous Schwann cell wrappings along the length of the axon. Spaces occur between adjacent Schwann cells, leaving uninsulated areas, or **neurofibral nodes (nodes of Ranvier)** along the axons. As an insulator, the Schwann cells interrupt the continuous conduction of a nerve impulse along the axon. In response, the nerve impulse jumps across each Schwann cell, from one neurofibral node to the next (**saltatory conduction**). In this fashion, the speed of the nerve impulse is significantly increased. In addition, the myelin sheath provides insulation between adjacent nerve fibers, preventing the crossover of one nerve impulse to an adjacent axon.

In the CNS, the *axons* of neurons are insulated by oligodendrocytes. The myelin sheath is formed when a process extended by the oligodendrocyte wraps around an axon. Many axons may be myelinated by multiple processes from a single oligodendrocyte. The oligodendrocyte does not form a neurilemma because its cell body does not wrap around any axons.

The white and gray matter of the brain and spinal cord are distinguished by the presence or absence of myelin sheaths.

1. **White matter** contains the myelinated axons of neurons. (The white color is from the myelin sheaths.)

2. **Gray matter** contains the unmyelinated portions of neurons (cell bodies, dendrites, and axon terminals), unmyelinated neurons, and neuroglia.

Transmission of Nerve Impulses

The transmission of a nerve impulse along a neuron from one end to the other occurs as a result of chemical changes across the membrane of the neuron. The membrane of an unstimulated neuron is **polarized;** that is, there is a difference in electrical charge between the outside and inside of the membrane. The *inside is negative* with respect to the outside. Polarization is established by maintaining an excess of sodium ions (**Na⁺**) on the outside and an excess of potassium ions (**K⁺**) on the inside. A certain amount of Na⁺ and K⁺ is always leaking across the membrane through **leakage channels,** but Na⁺/K⁺ pumps in the membrane actively restore the ions to the appropriate side. Other ions, such as large, negatively charged proteins and nucleic acids, reside within the cell. *It is these large, negatively charged ions that contribute to the overall negative charge on the inside of the cell membrane* as compared to the outside.

In addition to crossing the membrane through leakage channels, ions may also cross through **gated channels.** Gated channels open in response to neurotransmitters, changes in membrane potential, or other stimuli.

The following events characterize the transmission of a nerve impulse (Figure 48).

1. **Resting potential.** The resting potential describes the unstimulated, polarized state of a neuron (at about −70 millivolts).

2. **Graded potential.** A graded potential is a change in the resting potential of the plasma membrane in response to a stimulus. A graded potential occurs when the stimulus causes Na⁺ or K⁺ gated channels to open. If Na⁺ channels open, positive sodium ions enter, and the membrane **depolarizes** (becomes more positive). If the stimulus opens K⁺ channels, then positive potassium ions exit across the membrane and the membrane **hyperpolarizes** (becomes more negative). A graded potential is a local event that does not travel far from its origin. Graded potentials occur in *cell bodies* and *dendrites*. Light, heat, mechanical pressure, and chemicals such as neurotransmitters are examples of stimuli that may generate a graded potential (depending upon the neuron).

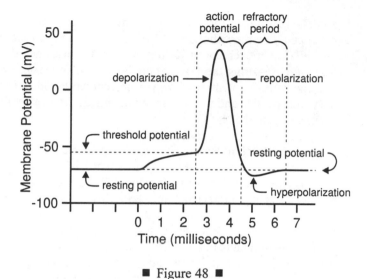

■ Figure 48 ■

3. **Action potential.** Unlike a graded potential, an action potential is capable of traveling long distances. If a depolarizing graded potential is sufficiently large, Na⁺ channels in the trigger zone open. In response, *Na⁺ on the outside of the membrane rush into the cell.* As the positively charged Na⁺ rush in, the cell membrane becomes **depolarized** (as in a graded potential). If the stimulus is strong enough, that is, if it is above a certain **threshold level,** additional Na⁺ gates open, increasing the inflow of Na⁺ even more, causing an **action potential,** or complete depolarization (from −70 to about +30 millivolts). This, in turn, stimulates neighboring Na⁺ gates, farther down the axon, to open. In this manner, the action potential travels down the length of the axon as opened Na⁺ gates stimulate neighboring Na⁺ gates to open. The action potential is an **all-or-nothing event:** when the stimulus fails to produce a depolarization that exceeds the threshold value, no action potential results, but when threshold potential is exceeded, complete depolarization occurs.

4. **Repolarization.** In response to the inflow of Na$^+$, K$^+$ channels open, this time allowing *K$^+$ on the inside to rush out of the cell.* The movement of K$^+$ out of the cell causes **repolarization** by restoring the original membrane polarization. Unlike the resting potential, however, in repolarization the K$^+$ are on the outside and the Na$^+$ are on the inside. Soon after the K$^+$ gates open, the Na$^+$ gates close.

5. **Hyperpolarization.** By the time the K$^+$ channels close, more K$^+$ have moved out of the cell than is actually necessary to establish the original polarized potential. Thus, the membrane becomes **hyperpolarized** (about -80 millivolts).

6. **Refractory period.** With the passage of the action potential, the cell membrane is in an unusual state of affairs. The membrane is polarized, but the Na$^+$ and K$^+$ are on the wrong sides of the membrane. During this **refractory period,** the axon will not respond to a new stimulus. To reestablish the original distribution of these ions, the Na$^+$ and K$^+$ are returned to their resting potential location by Na$^+$/K$^+$ pumps in the cell membrane. Once these ions are completely returned to their resting potential location, the neuron is ready for another stimulus.

The Synapse

A **synapse,** or **synaptic cleft,** is the gap that separates adjacent neurons or a neuron and a muscle. Transmission of an impulse across a synapse, from **presynaptic cell** to **postsynaptic cell,** may be electrical or chemical. In electrical synapses, the action potential travels along the membranes of **gap junctions,** small tubes of cytoplasm that allow the transfer of ions between adjacent cells. In chemical synapses, action potentials are transferred across the synapse by the diffusions of chemicals, as follows.

1. **Calcium (Ca^{2+}) gates open.** When an action potential reaches the end of an axon, the depolarization of the membrane causes gated channels to open that allow Ca^{2+} to enter.

2. **Synaptic vesicles release neurotransmitter.** The influx of Ca^{2+} into the terminal end of the axon causes **synaptic vesicles** to merge with the presynaptic membrane, releasing a **neurotransmitter** into the synaptic cleft.

3. **Neurotransmitter binds with postsynaptic receptors.** The neurotransmitter diffuses across the synaptic cleft and binds with specialized protein receptors on the postsynaptic membrane. Different proteins are receptors for different neurotransmitters.

4. **The postsynaptic membrane is excited or inhibited.** Depending upon the kind of neurotransmitter and the kind of membrane receptors, there are two possible outcomes for the postsynaptic membrane, both of which are graded potentials.

   - *If positive ion gates open (which allow more Na^+ and Ca^{2+} to enter than K^+ to exit),* the membrane becomes depolarized, which results in an **excitatory postsynaptic potential (EPSP)**. If the threshold potential is exceeded, an action potential is generated.

   - *If K^+ or chlorine ions (Cl^-) gates open (allowing K^+ to exit or Cl^- to enter),* the membrane becomes more polarized (hyperpolarized), which results in an **inhibitory postsynaptic potential (IPSP)**. As a result, it becomes more difficult to generate an action potential on this membrane.

5. **The neurotransmitter is degraded and recycled.** After the neurotransmitter binds to the postsynaptic membrane receptors, it is either transported back to and reabsorbed by the secreting neuron or it is broken down by enzymes in the syn-

aptic cleft. For example, the common neurotransmitter **acetylcholine** is broken down by **cholinesterase.** Reabsorbed and degraded neurotransmitters are recycled by the presynaptic cell.

Some of the common neurotransmitters and the kinds of activity they generate are summarized below.

1. **Acetylcholine (ACh)** is commonly secreted at **neuromuscular junctions,** the gaps between motor neurons and muscle cells, where it stimulates muscles to contract (by opening gated positive ion channels). At other kinds of junctions, it typically produces an inhibitory postsynaptic potential.

2. **Epinephrine, norepinephrine (NE), dopamine,** and **serotonin** are derived from amino acids and are secreted mostly between neurons of the CNS.

3. **Gamma aminobutyric acid (GABA)** is usually an inhibitory neurotransmitter (opening gated Cl^- channels) among neurons in the brain.

THE NERVOUS SYSTEM

Nervous System Organization

The **nervous system** consists of two parts, as follows (Figure 49).

1. The **central nervous system** (CNS) consists of the brain and spinal cord.

2. The **peripheral nervous system** (PNS) consists of nerves outside the CNS. Nerves of the PNS are classified in three ways. First, PNS nerves are classified by how they are connected to the CNS, as follows.

   - **Cranial nerves** originate from or terminate at the brain.

   - **Spinal nerves** originate from or terminate at the spinal cord.

   Second, nerves of the PNS are classified by the direction of nerve propagation, as follows.

   - **Sensory (afferent) neurons** transmit impulses *from* skin and other sensory organs or *from* various places within the body *to the CNS.*

   - **Motor (efferent) neurons** transmit impulses *from the CNS to effectors* (muscles or glands).

   Third, *motor neurons* are further classified according to the effectors they target, as follows.

   - The **somatic nervous system (SNS)** directs the contraction of skeletal muscles.

   - The **autonomic nervous system (ANS)** controls the activities of organs, glands, and various involuntary muscles, such as cardiac and smooth muscles.

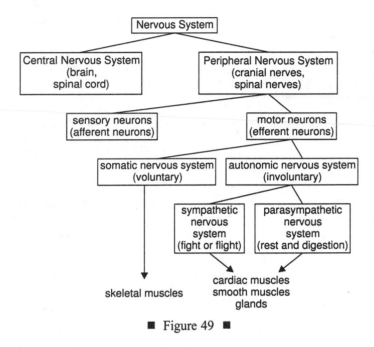

■ Figure 49 ■

There are two divisions of the autonomic nervous system.

1. The **sympathetic nervous system** is involved in the stimulation of activities that prepare the body for action, such as increasing the heart rate, increasing the release of sugar from the liver into the blood, and other activities generally considered as fight-or-flight responses (responses that serve to fight off or retreat from danger).

2. The **parasympathetic nervous system** activates tranquil functions, such as stimulating the secretion of saliva or digestive enzymes into the stomach.

Generally, both sympathetic and parasympathetic systems target the same organs but often work antagonistically. For example, the sympathetic system accelerates the heartbeat, while the parasympathetic slows the heartbeat. Each system is stimulated as is appropriate to maintain homeostasis.

Nervous System Terminology

The following terms are commonly used in descriptions of nervous system features.

1. A **nerve fiber** is an axon or dendrite. A **nerve** is a bundle of nerve fibers in the PNS. A **nerve tract** is a bundle of nerve fibers in the CNS.

2. **White matter** consists of myelinated axons of neurons in the CNS.

3. **Gray matter** consists of unmyelinated portions of neurons (cell bodies, dendrites, and axon terminals), unmyelinated neurons, and neuroglia in the CNS.

4. **Nuclei** are clusters of cell bodies in the CNS. **Ganglia** are clusters of cell bodies in the PNS (except the basal ganglia, which are more appropriately called basal nuclei).

5. **Vesicles** are fluid-filled cavities in the brain that form during early development. The tissues that form the vesicles divide to become the various components of the brain.

6. **Ventricles** are interconnected cavities in the mature brain that originate from the fluid-filled vesicles. Circulating fluid (cerebrospinal fluid) in the ventricles provides nourishment for nervous tissue.

7. **Peduncles** are large nerve tracts that emerge from certain regions of the brain. Their large size gives the appearance of supporting the structure from which they emerge (peduncle means "little foot").

The Brain

Three cavities, called the **primary brain vesicles,** form during the early embryonic development of the brain. These are the **forebrain (prosencephalon)**, the **midbrain (mesencephalon)**, and the **hindbrain (rhombencephalon)**.

During subsequent development, the three primary brain vesicles develop into five **secondary brain vesicles.** The names of these vesicles and the major adult structures that develop from the vesicles are given below (Table 12).

1. The **telencephalon** generates the **cerebrum** (which contains the cerebral cortex, white matter, and basal ganglia).

2. The **diencephalon** generates the **thalamus, hypothalamus,** and **pineal gland.**

3. The **mesencephalon** generates the midbrain portion of the **brain stem.**

4. The **metencephalon** generates the **pons** portion of the brain stem and the **cerebellum.**

5. The **myelencephalon** generates the **medulla oblongata** portion of the brain stem.

Primary Vesicles	Secondary Vesicles	Adult Structures	Important Components or Features	
prosen-cephalon (forebrain)	telen-cephalon	cerebrum (cerebral hemi-spheres)	cerebral cortex (gray matter)	motor areas
				sensory areas
				association areas
			cerebral white matter	association fibers
				commissural fibers
				projection fibers
			basal ganglia (gray matter)	caudate nucleus (& amygdala)
				putamen
				globus pallidus
	dien-cephalon	dien-cephalon	thalamus	relays sensory information
			hypothalamus	maintains body homeostasis
			mammillary bodies	relays sensations of smells to cerebrum
			optic chiasma	crossover of optic nerves
			infundibulum	stalk of pituitary gland
			pituitary gland	source of hormones
			epithalamus	pineal gland
mesen-cephalon (midbrain)	mesen-cephalon	brain stem	midbrain	cerebral peduncles
				sup. cerebellar peduncles
				corpora quadrigemina
				superior colliculi
rhomben-cephalon (hindbrain)	meten-cephalon	brain stem	pons	middle cerebellar peduncles
				pneumotaxic area
				apneustic area
		cere-bellum		sup. cerebellar peduncles
				middle cerebellar peduncles
				inferior cerebellar peduncles
	myelen-cephalon	brain stem	medulla oblongata	pyramids
				cardiovascular center
				respiratory center

■ Table 12 ■

A second method for classifying brain regions is by their organization in the adult brain. The following four divisions are recognized (Table 12, Figure 50).

1. The **cerebrum** consists of two **cerebral hemispheres** connected by a bundle of nerve fibers, the **corpus callosum.** The largest and most visible part of the brain, the cerebrum appears as folded ridges and grooves, called **convolutions.** The following terms are used to describe the convolutions.

   ▪ A **gyrus** (plural, **gyri**) is an elevated ridge among the convolutions.

   ▪ A **sulcus** (plural, **sulci**) is a *shallow* groove among the convolutions.

   ▪ A **fissure** is a *deep* groove among the convolutions.

   The deeper fissures divide the cerebrum into five lobes (most named after bordering skull bones)—the **frontal lobe,** the **parietal lobe,** the **temporal lobe,** the **occipital lobe,** and the **insula.** All but the insula are visible from the outside surface of the brain.

   A cross section of the cerebrum shows three distinct layers of nervous tissue.

   ▪ The **cerebral cortex** is a thin outer layer of gray matter. Such activities as speech, evaluation of stimuli, conscious thinking, and control of skeletal muscles occur here. These activities are grouped into **motor areas, sensory areas,** and **association areas** (Table 12).

   ▪ The **cerebral white matter** underlies the cerebral cortex. It contains mostly myelinated axons that connect cerebral hemispheres (**association fibers**), connect gyri within hemispheres (**commissural fibers**), or connect the cerebrum to the spinal cord (**projection fibers**). The corpus callosum is a major assemblage of association fibers that forms a nerve tract that connects the two cerebral hemispheres.

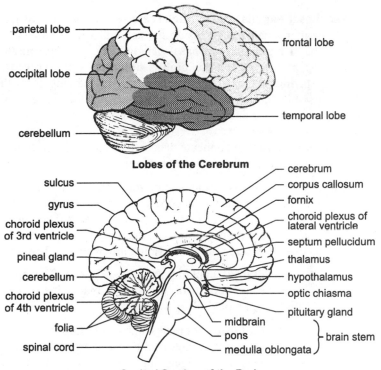

Lobes of the Cerebrum

parietal lobe

occipital lobe

cerebellum

frontal lobe

temporal lobe

sulcus

gyrus

choroid plexus
of 3rd ventricle

pineal gland

cerebellum

choroid plexus
of 4th ventricle

folia

spinal cord

cerebrum

corpus callosum

fornix

choroid plexus of
lateral ventricle

septum pellucidum

thalamus

hypothalamus

optic chiasma

pituitary gland

midbrain

pons

medulla oblongata

brain stem

Sagittal Section of the Brain

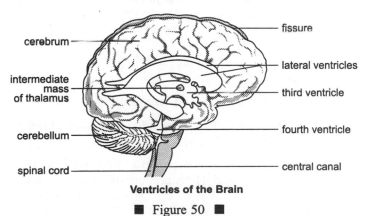

cerebrum

intermediate
mass
of thalamus

cerebellum

spinal cord

fissure

lateral ventricles

third ventricle

fourth ventricle

central canal

Ventricles of the Brain

■ Figure 50 ■

■ **Basal ganglia (basal nuclei)** are several pockets of gray matter located deep inside the cerebral white matter. The major regions in the basal ganglia—the **caudate nuclei,** the **putamen,** and the **globus pallidus**—are involved in relaying and modifying nerve impulses passing from the cerebral cortex to the spinal cord. Arm swinging while walking, for example, is controlled here.

2. The **diencephalon** connects the cerebrum to the brain stem. It consists of the following major regions.

■ The **thalamus** is a relay station for sensory nerve impulses traveling from the spinal cord to the cerebrum. Some nerve impulses are sorted and grouped here before being transmitted to the cerebrum. Certain sensory sensations, such as pain, pressure, and temperature are evaluated here also.

■ The **epithalamus** contains the **pineal gland.** The pineal gland secretes **melatonin,** a hormone that helps regulate the biological clock (sleep-wake cycles).

■ The **hypothalamus** regulates numerous important body activities. It controls the autonomic nervous system, regulates emotion, behavior, hunger, thirst, body temperature, and the biological clock. It also produces two hormones (ADH and oxytocin) and various releasing hormones that control hormone production in the anterior pituitary gland.

The following structures are either included or associated with the hypothalamus.

■ The **mammillary bodies** relay sensations of smell.

■ The **infundibulum** connects the **pituitary gland** to the hypothalamus.

■ The **optic chiasma** passes between the hypothalamus and the pituitary gland. Here, portions of the optic nerves from each eye cross over to the cerebral hemisphere on the opposite side of the brain.

3. The **brain stem** connects the diencephalon to the spinal cord. The brain stem resembles the spinal cord in that both consist of white matter fiber tracts surrounding a core of gray matter. The brain stem consists of the following four regions, all of which provide connections between various parts of the brain and between the brain and the spinal cord (some prominent structures are listed in Table 12 and illustrated in Figure 51).

- The **midbrain** is the uppermost part of the brain stem.

- The **pons** is the bulging region in the middle of the brain stem.

- The **medulla oblongata** (**medulla**) is the lower portion of the brain stem that merges with the spinal cord at the foramen magnum.

- The **reticular formation** consists of small clusters of gray matter interspersed within the white matter of the brain stem and certain regions of the spinal cord, diencephalon, and cerebellum. The **reticular activation system** (**RAS**), one component of the reticular formation, is responsible for maintaining wakefulness and alertness and for filtering out unimportant sensory information. Other components of the reticular formation are responsible for maintaining muscle tone and regulating visceral motor muscles.

4. The **cerebellum** consists of a central region, the **vermis,** and two winglike lobes, the **cerebellar hemispheres.** Like that of the cerebrum, the surface of the cerebellum is convoluted, but the gyri, called **folia,** are parallel and give a pleated appearance. The cerebellum evaluates and coordinates motor movements by comparing actual skeletal movements to the movement that was intended.

The **limbic system** is a network of neurons that extends over a wide range of areas of the brain. The limbic system imposes an emotional aspect to behaviors, experiences, and memories. Emotions such as pleasure, fear, anger, sorrow, and affection are imparted to events

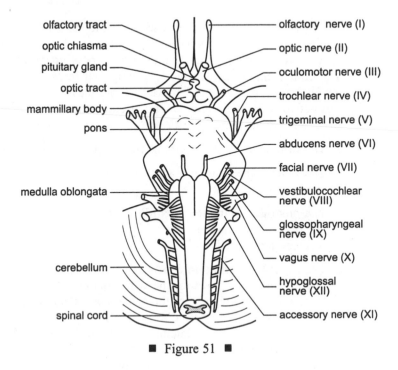

olfactory tract
optic chiasma
pituitary gland
optic tract
mammillary body
pons

olfactory nerve (I)
optic nerve (II)
oculomotor nerve (III)
trochlear nerve (IV)
trigeminal nerve (V)
abducens nerve (VI)
facial nerve (VII)
vestibulocochlear nerve (VIII)

medulla oblongata

glossopharyngeal nerve (IX)
vagus nerve (X)

cerebellum

hypoglossal nerve (XII)

spinal cord

accessory nerve (XI)

■ Figure 51 ■

and experiences. The limbic system accomplishes this by a system of fiber tracts (white matter) and gray matter that pervades the diencephalon and encircles the inside border of the cerebrum. The following components are included.

- The **hippocampus** (located in the cerebral hemisphere)

- The **dentate gyrus** (located in cerebral hemisphere)

- The **amygdala** (**amygdaloid body**) (an almond-shaped body associated with the caudate nucleus of the basal ganglia)

- The **mammillary bodies** (in the hypothalamus)

- The **anterior thalamic nuclei** (in the thalamus)

- The **fornix** (a bundle of fiber tracts that links components of the limbic system)

The Ventricles and Cerebrospinal Fluid

There are four cavities in the brain, called **ventricles**. The ventricles are filled with **cerebrospinal fluid (CSF)**, which provides the following functions.

1. Absorbs physical shocks to the brain

2. Distributes nutritive materials to and removes wastes from nervous tissue

3. Provides a chemically stable environment

There are four ventricles, as follows (Figure 50).

1. Each of two **lateral ventricles** occupies a cerebral hemisphere.

2. The **third ventricle** is connected by a passage (**interventricular foramen**) to each of the two lateral ventricles.

3. The **fourth ventricle** connects to the third ventricle (via the **cerebral aqueduct**) and to the **central canal** of the spinal cord (a narrow, central tube extending the length of the spinal cord). Additional openings in the fourth ventricle also allow CSF to flow into the subarachnoid space.

A network of capillaries called the **choroid plexuses** projects into each ventricle. Ependymal cells (a type of neuroglial cell) surround these capillaries. Blood plasma entering the ependymal cells from the capillaries is filtered as it passes into the ventrical, forming CSF. Any material passing from the capillaries to the ventricles of the brain must do so *through* the ependymal cells because tight junctions linking these cells prevent the passage of plasma *between* them. Thus, the ependymal cells maintain a **blood-CSF barrier** controlling the composition of the CSF.

The CSF circulates from the lateral ventricles (where most of the CSF is produced) to the third and then fourth ventricles. From the fourth ventricle, most of the CSF passes into the **subarachnoid space,** a space within the linings (meninges) of the brain (see below), although some CSF also passes into the central canal of the spinal cord. The CSF returns to the blood through the **arachnoid villi** located in the dural sinuses of the meninges (see below).

The Meninges

The **meninges** (singular, **meninx**) are protective coverings of the brain (**cranial meninges**) and spinal cord (**spinal meninges**). They consist of three layers of membranous connective tissue, as follows. (See Figure 53a for spinal meninges.)

1. The **dura mater** is the tough outer layer lying just inside the skull and vertebrae. Some characteristics follow.

   ▪ In the brain, there are channels within the dura mater, the **dural sinuses,** which contain venous blood returning from the brain to the jugular veins.

   ▪ In the spinal cord, the dura mater is often referred to as the **dural sheath.** A fat-filled space between the dura mater and the vertebrae, the **epidural space,** acts as a protective cushion to the spinal cord.

2. The **arachnoid (arachnoid mater)** is the middle meninx. Projections from the arachnoid, called **arachnoid villi,** protrude through the dura matter into the dural sinuses. The arachnoid villi transport the CSF from the subarachnoid space (see below) to the dural sinuses. Two cavities border the arachnoid.

   ▪ The **subdural space** occurs outside the arachnoid (between the arachnoid and the dura mater).

■ The **subarachnoid space** lies inside the arachnoid. This space contains blood vessels and circulates CSF. The fine threads of tissue that spread across this space resemble the web of a spider and give the arachnoid layer its name (arachnid means spider).

3. The **pia mater** is the innermost meninx layer. It tightly covers the brain (following its convolutions) and spinal cord and carries blood vessels that provide nourishment to these nervous tissues.

The Blood-Brain Barrier

Cells in the brain require a very stable environment to ensure controlled and selective stimulation of neurons. As a result, only certain materials are allowed to pass from blood vessels to the brain. Substances such as O_2, glucose, H_2O, CO_2, essential amino acids, and most lipid-soluble substances enter the brain readily. Other substances, such as creatine and urea (wastes transported in the blood), most ions (Na^+, K^+, Cl^-), proteins, and certain toxins either have limited access or are totally blocked from entering the brain. Unfortunately, most antibiotic drugs are equally blocked from entering, while other substances such as caffeine, alcohol, nicotine, and heroin readily enter the brain (because of their lipid solubility). This **blood-brain barrier** is established by the following.

1. Brain capillaries are less permeable than other capillaries because of tight junctions between the endothelial cells in the capillary walls.

2. The basal lamina (secreted by the endothelial cells) that surrounds the brain capillaries decreases capillary permeability. This layer is usually absent in capillaries found elsewhere.

---

3. Processes from astrocytes (a type of neuroglial cell) cover brain capillaries and are believed to influence capillary permeability in some way.

Cranial Nerves

Cranial nerves are nerves of the PNS which originate from or terminate in the brain. There are 12 pairs of cranial nerves, all of which pass through foramina of the skull. Cranial nerves are either **sensory nerves** (containing only or predominately sensory fibers) or **mixed nerves** (containing both sensory and motor fibers). Characteristics of the cranial nerves, which are numbered from anterior to posterior as they attach to the brain, are summarized in Table 13 and illustrated in Figure 51.

The Spinal Cord

The **spinal cord** has two functions.

1. **Transmission of nerve impulses.** Neurons in the white matter of the spinal cord transmit sensory signals from peripheral regions to the brain and motor signals from the brain to peripheral regions.

2. **Spinal reflexes.** Neurons in the gray matter of the spinal cord integrate incoming sensory information and respond with motor impulses that control muscles (skeletal, smooth, or cardiac) or glands.

The spinal cord is an extension of the brain stem that begins at the foramen magnum and continues down through the vertebral canal to the first lumbar vertebra (L_1). Here, the spinal cord comes to a

Cranial Nerve	Nerve Type	Major Functions
I Olfactory	sensory	smell
II Optic	sensory	vision
III Oculomotor	primarily motor	eyeball & eyelid movement; lens shape
IV Trochlear	primarily motor	eyeball movement; proprioception
V Trigeminal: ophthalmic branch maxillary branch mandibular branch	 sensory sensory mixed	sensations of touch & pain from facial skin, nose, mouth, teeth, & tongue; proprioception motor control of chewing
VI Abducens	primarily motor	eyeball movement; proprioception
VII Facial	mixed	movement of facial muscles; tear & saliva secretion; sense of taste & proprioception
VIII Vestibulocochlear: cochlear branch vestibular branch	 sensory sensory	 hearing sense of equilibrium
IX Glossopharyngeal	mixed	sensations of taste, touch & pain from tongue & pharynx; chemoreceptors (that monitor O_2 & CO_2), blood pressure receptors; movement of tongue & swallowing; secretion of saliva
X Vagus	mixed	parasympathetic sensations & motor control of smooth muscles associated with heart, lungs, viscera; secretion of digestive enzymes
XI Accessory	primarily motor	head movement, swallowing; proprioception
XII Hypoglossal	primarily motor	tongue movement, speech, & swallowing; proprioception

■ Table 13 ■

tapering point, the **conus medullaris.** The spinal cord is held in position at its inferior end by the **filum terminale,** an extension of the pia mater that attaches to the coccyx. Along its length, the spinal cord is held within the vertebral canal by **denticulate ligaments,** lateral extensions of the pia mater that attach to the dural sheath.

The following external features appear on the spinal cord (Figure 52).

1. **Spinal nerves** emerge in pairs, one from each side of the spinal cord along its length.

2. The **cervical enlargement** is a widening in the upper part of the spinal cord (C_4 to T_1). Nerves that extend into the upper limbs originate or terminate here.

3. The **lumbar enlargement** is a widening in the lower part of the spinal cord (T_9 to T_{12}). Nerves that extend into the lower limbs originate or terminate here.

4. The **anterior median fissure** and the **posterior median sulcus** are two grooves that run the length of the spinal cord on its anterior and posterior surfaces, respectively.

5. The **cauda equina** are nerves that attach to the end of the spinal cord and continue to run downward before turning laterally to other parts of the body.

A cross section of the spinal cord reveals the following features (Figure 53).

1. **Roots** are branches of the spinal nerve that connect to the spinal cord. Two major roots form, as follows.

   ■ A **ventral root** (**anterior** or **motor root**) is the branch of the nerve that enters the ventral side of the spinal cord. Ventral roots contain *motor nerve axons,* transmitting nerve impulses from the spinal cord to skeletal muscles.

   ■ A **dorsal root** (**posterior** or **sensory root**) is the branch of a nerve that enters the dorsal side of the spinal cord. Dorsal roots contain *sensory nerve fibers,* transmitting nerve impulses from peripheral regions to the spinal cord.

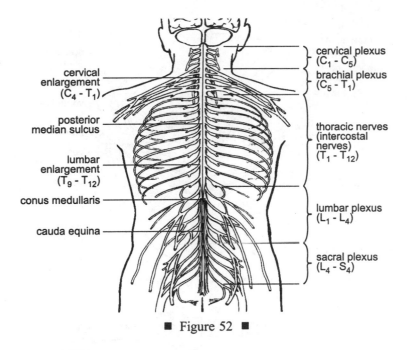

cervical plexus
(C_1 - C_5)

brachial plexus
(C_5 - T_1)

cervical
enlargement
(C_4 - T_1)

posterior
median sulcus

thoracic nerves
(intercostal
nerves)
(T_1 - T_{12})

lumbar
enlargement
(T_9 - T_{12})

conus medullaris

cauda equina

lumbar plexus
(L_1 - L_4)

sacral plexus
(L_4 - S_4)

■ Figure 52 ■

- **A dorsal root ganglion** is a cluster of cell bodies of a sensory nerve. It is located on the dorsal root.

2. Gray matter appears in the center of the spinal cord in the form of the letter H (or a pair of butterfly wings) when viewed in cross section.

- The **gray commissure** is the cross-bar of the H.

- The **anterior (ventral) horns** are gray matter areas at the front of each side of the H. Cell bodies of motor neurons that stimulate skeletal muscles are located here.

- The **posterior (dorsal) horns** are gray matter areas at the rear of each side of the H. These horns contain mostly interneurons that synapse with sensory neurons.

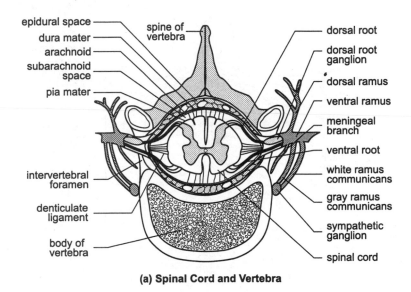

epidural space
dura mater
arachnoid
subarachnoid space
pia mater

spine of vertebra

dorsal root
dorsal root ganglion
dorsal ramus
ventral ramus
meningeal branch
ventral root
white ramus communicans
gray ramus communicans
sympathetic ganglion
spinal cord

intervertebral foramen
denticulate ligament
body of vertebra

(a) Spinal Cord and Vertebra

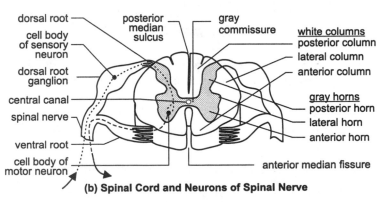

dorsal root
cell body of sensory neuron
dorsal root ganglion
central canal
spinal nerve
ventral root
cell body of motor neuron

posterior median sulcus

gray commissure

white columns
posterior column
lateral column
anterior column

gray horns
posterior horn
lateral horn
anterior horn

anterior median fissure

(b) Spinal Cord and Neurons of Spinal Nerve

■ Figure 53 ■

■ The **lateral horns** are small projections of gray matter at
the sides of the H. These horns are present only in the thoracic
and lumbar regions of the spinal cord. They contain cell
bodies of motor neurons in the sympathetic branch of the
autonomic nervous system.

- The **central canal** is a small hole in the center of the H cross-bar. It contains CSF and runs the length of the spinal cord and connects with the fourth ventricle of the brain.

3. **White columns (funiculi)** refer to six areas of the white matter, three on each side of the H. They are the **anterior (ventral) columns,** the **posterior (dorsal) columns,** and the **lateral columns.**

4. **Fasciculi** are bundles of nerve tracts within white columns containing neurons with common functions or destinations.

   - **Ascending (sensory) tracts** transmit sensory information from various parts of the body to the brain.

   - **Descending (motor) tracts** transmit nerve impulses from the brain to muscles and glands.

Spinal Nerves

There are 31 pairs of **spinal nerves** (62 total). The following discussion traces a spinal nerve as it emerges from the spinal column (Figure 53a).

1. A spinal nerve emerges at two points from the spinal cord, the ventral and dorsal roots.

2. The ventral and dorsal roots merge to form the whole spinal nerve.

3. The spinal nerve emerges from the spinal column through an opening (**intervertebral foramen**) between adjacent vertebrae. This is true for all spinal nerves except for the first spinal nerve (pair) which emerges between the occipital bone and the atlas (the first vertebra).

4. Outside the vertebral column, the nerve divides into the following branches.

- The **dorsal ramus** contains nerves that serve the dorsal portions of the trunk.

- The **ventral ramus** contains nerves that serve the remaining ventral parts of the trunk and the upper and lower limbs.

- The **meningeal branch** reenters the vertebral column and serves the meninges and blood vessels within.

- The **rami communicantes** contain autonomic nerves that serve visceral functions.

5. Some ventral rami merge with adjacent ventral rami to form a **plexus,** a network of interconnecting nerves. Nerves emerging from a plexus contain fibers from various spinal nerves which are now carried together to some target location.

An area of the skin that receives sensory stimuli that pass through a single spinal nerve is called a **dermatome.** Dermatomes are illustrated on a human figure with lines that mark the boundaries of the area where each spinal nerve receives stimuli.

Reflexes

A **reflex** is a rapid, involuntary response to a stimulus. A **reflex arc** is the pathway traveled by the nerve impulses during a reflex. Most reflexes are **spinal reflexes** with pathways that traverse only the spinal cord. During a spinal reflex, information may be transmitted to the brain, but it is the spinal cord, and not the brain, that is responsible for the integration of sensory information and a response transmitted to motor neurons. Some reflexes are **cranial reflexes** with pathways through cranial nerves and the brain stem.

A reflex arc involves the following components (Figure 54).

1. The **receptor** is that part of the neuron (usually a dendrite) that detects a stimulus.

2. The **sensory neuron** transmits the impulse to the spinal cord.

3. The **integration center** involves one synapse (**monosynaptic reflex arc**) or two or more synapses (**polysynaptic reflex arc**) in the gray matter of the spinal cord. In polysynaptic reflex arcs, one or more interneurons in the gray matter constitute the integration center.

4. A **motor neuron** transmits a nerve impulse from the spinal cord to a peripheral region.

5. An **effector** is a muscle or gland that receives the impulse from the motor neuron. In **somatic reflexes,** the effector is skeletal muscle. In **autonomic (visceral) reflexes,** the effector is smooth or cardiac muscle, or a gland.

Some examples of reflexes follow.

1. A **stretch reflex** is a monosynaptic reflex that is a response to a muscle that has been stretched (the knee jerk reflex is an example). When receptors in muscles, called **muscle spindles,** detect changes in muscle length, they stimulate, through a reflex arc, the contraction of a muscle. Stretch reflexes help maintain posture by stimulating muscles to regain normal body position.

2. A **flexor (withdrawal) reflex** is a polysynaptic reflex that causes a limb to be withdrawn when it encounters pain (Figure 54).

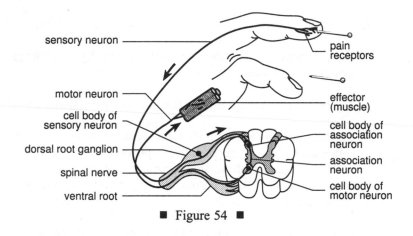

sensory neuron

pain
receptors

motor neuron

effector
(muscle)

cell body of
sensory neuron

cell body of
association
neuron

dorsal root ganglion

association
neuron

spinal nerve

cell body of
motor neuron

ventral root

■ Figure 54 ■

The Autonomic Nervous System

The peripheral nervous system consists of the somatic nervous system (SNS) and the **autonomic nervous system (ANS)**. The SNS consists of motor neurons that stimulate skeletal muscles. In contrast, the ANS consists of motor neurons that control smooth muscles, cardiac muscles, and glands. In addition, the ANS monitors visceral organs and blood vessels with sensory neurons which provide input information for the CNS.

The ANS is further divided into the **sympathetic nervous system** and the **parasympathetic nervous system.** Both of these systems can stimulate and inhibit effectors. However, the two systems work in opposition—where one system stimulates an organ, the other inhibits. Working in this fashion, each system prepares the body for a different kind of situation, as follows.

■ The *sympathetic nervous system* prepares the body for situations requiring alertness or strength or situations that arouse fear, anger, excitement, or embarrassment ("fight or flight" situations). In these kinds of situations, the sympathetic nervous system stimulates cardiac muscles to increase the heart rate, causes dilation of the bronchioles of the lungs (increasing oxygen intake), and causes dilation of blood vessels that supply the heart and skeletal muscles (increasing blood supply). The adrenal medulla is stimulated to release epinephrine (adrenalin) and norepinephrine (noradrenalin), which in turn increase the metabolic rate of cells and stimulate the liver to release glucose into the blood. Sweat glands are stimulated to produce sweat. In addition, the sympathetic nervous system reduces the activity of various "tranquil" body functions, such as digestion and kidney functioning.

- The *parasympathetic nervous system* is active during periods of digestion and rest. It stimulates the production of digestive enzymes and stimulates the processes of digestion, urination, and defecation. It reduces blood pressure and heart and respiratory rates and conserves energy through relaxation and rest.

In the SNS, a *single* motor neuron connects the CNS to its target skeletal muscle. In the ANS, the connection between the CNS and its effector consists of *two* neurons—the **preganglionic neuron** and the **postganglionic neuron.** The synapse between these two neurons lies outside the CNS, in an **autonomic ganglion.** The axon (preganglionic axon) of a preganglionic neuron enters the ganglion and forms a synapse with the dendrites of the postganglionic neuron. The axon (postganglionic axon) of the postganglionic neuron emerges from the ganglion and travels to the target organ (Figure 55). There are three kinds of autonomic ganglia, as follows.

1. The **sympathetic trunk,** or **chain,** contains *sympathetic* ganglia called **paravertebral ganglia.** There are two trunks, one on either side of the vertebral column along its entire length. Each trunk consists of ganglia connected by fibers, like a string of beads.

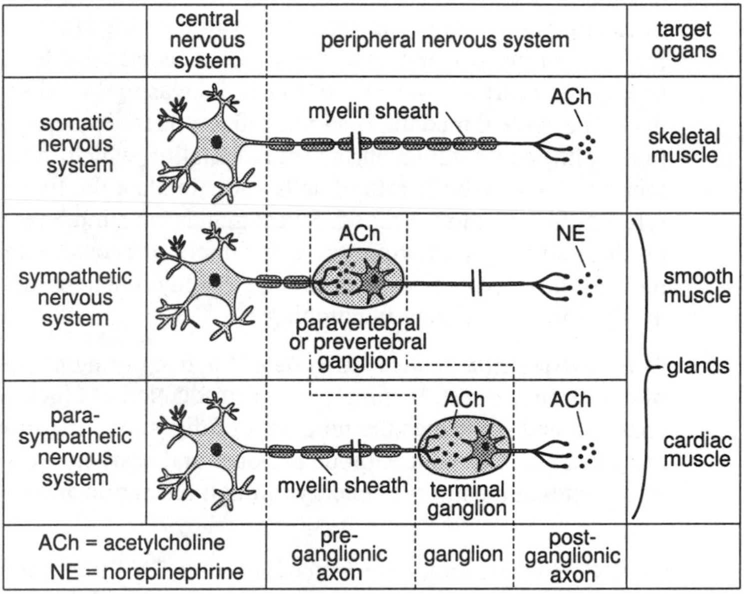

	central nervous system	peripheral nervous system			target organs
somatic nervous system		myelin sheath		ACh	skeletal muscle
sympathetic nervous system		ACh paravertebral or prevertebral ganglion		NE	smooth muscle glands
para-sympathetic nervous system		myelin sheath	ACh terminal ganglion	ACh	cardiac muscle
ACh = acetylcholine NE = norepinephrine		pre-ganglionic axon	ganglion	post-ganglionic axon	

■ Figure 55 ■

2. The **prevertebral (collateral) ganglia** also consist of *sympathetic* ganglia. Preganglionic sympathetic fibers that *pass through* the sympathetic trunk (without forming a synapse with a postganglionic neuron) synapse here. Prevertebral ganglia lie near the large abdominal arteries which the postganglionic fibers target.

3. **Terminal (intramural) ganglia** receive *parasympathetic* fibers. These ganglia occur near or within the target organ of the respective postganglionic fiber.

A comparison of the sympathetic and parasympathetic pathways follows (Figure 56).

- *Sympathetic nervous system.* Cell bodies of the preganglionic neurons occur in the lateral horns of gray matter of the 12 thoracic and first 2 lumbar segments of the spinal cord. (For this reason, the sympathetic system is also called the **thoracolumbar division.**) Preganglionic fibers leave the spinal cord within spinal nerves through the ventral roots (together with the PNS motor neurons). The preganglionic fibers then branch away from the nerve through **white rami (white rami communicantes)** that connect with the sympathetic trunk. White rami are white because they contain myelinated fibers. A preganglionic fiber that enters the trunk may synapse in the first ganglion it enters, travel up or down the trunk to synapse within another ganglion, or pass through the trunk and synapse outside the trunk. Postganglionic fibers that originate in ganglia within the sympathetic trunk leave the trunk through **gray rami (gray rami communicantes)** and return to the spinal nerve, which is followed until it reaches its target organ. Gray rami are gray because they contain unmyelinated fibers.

- *Parasympathetic nervous system.* Cell bodies of the preganglionic neurons occur in the gray matter of sacral segments S_2–S_4 and in the brain stem (with motor neurons of their associated cranial nerves III, VII, IX, and X). (For this reason, the parasympathetic system is also called the **craniosacral division** and the fibers arising from this division are called the **cranial outflow** or the **sacral outflow,** depending upon their origin.) Preganglionic fibers of the *cranial outflow* accompany the PNS motor neurons of *cranial nerves* and have terminal ganglia that lie near the target organ. Preganglionic fibers of the *sacral outflow* accompany the PNS motor neurons of *spinal nerves.* These nerves emerge through the ventral roots of the spinal cord and have terminal ganglia that lie near the target organ.

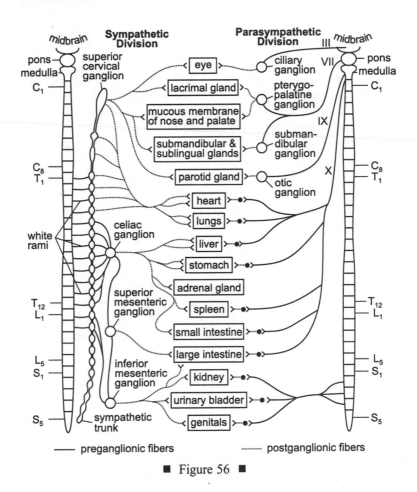

■ Figure 56 ■

Sensory Receptors

Sensory receptors are dendrites of sensory neurons specialized for receiving specific kinds of stimuli. Sensory receptors are classified by three methods, as follows.

1. *Classification by receptor complexity*

   - **Free nerve endings** are dendrites whose terminal ends have little or no physical specialization.

   - **Encapsulated nerve endings** are dendrites whose terminal ends are enclosed in a capsule of connective tissue.

   - **Sense organs** (such as the eyes and ears) consist of sensory neurons with receptors for the **special senses** (vision, hearing, smell, taste, and equilibrium) together with connective, epithelial, or other tissues.

2. *Classification by location*

   - **Exteroceptors** occur at or near the surface of the skin and are sensitive to stimuli occurring outside or on the surface of the body. These receptors include those for tactile sensations, such as touch, pain, and temperature, as well as those for vision, hearing, smell, and taste.

   - **Interoceptors (visceroceptors)** respond to stimuli occurring in the body from visceral organs and blood vessels. These receptors are the sensory neurons associated with the autonomic nervous system.

   - **Proprioceptors** respond to stimuli occurring in skeletal muscles, tendons, ligaments, and joints. These receptors collect information concerning body position and the physical conditions of these locations.

3. *Classification by type of stimulus detected*

- **Mechanoreceptors** respond to physical forces such as pressure (touch or blood pressure) and stretch.

- **Photoreceptors** respond to light.

- **Thermoreceptors** respond to temperature changes.

- **Chemoreceptors** respond to dissolved chemicals during sensations of taste and smell and to changes in internal body chemistry such as variations in O_2, CO_2, or H^+ in the blood.

- **Nociceptors** produce the sensation of pain in response to stimuli that may cause tissue damage.

The Somatic Senses

The **somatic (general) senses** collect information about **cutaneous sensations** (tactile sensations on the surface of the skin) and **proprioceptive sensations.** The following stimuli are detected.

1. **Tactile stimuli** are detected by mechanoreceptors and produce sensations of touch and pressure, as follows.

   - **Merkel discs** are receptors with free nerve endings that detect surface pressure (light touch). They are located at the bottom of the epidermis.

   - **Root hair plexuses** are receptors with free nerve endings that surround hair follicles and detect hair movement.

   - **Corpuscles of touch (Meissner's corpuscles)** are receptors with encapsulated nerve endings located in the dermal papillae (near the surface) of the skin that detect surface pressure (light touch).

   - **Pacinian corpuscles** are encapsulated nerve receptors that detect deep pressure and are located in the subcutaneous layer (below the skin).

2. **Thermal stimuli** are detected by free nerve ending thermoreceptors sensitive to heat or cold.

3. **Pain stimuli** are detected by free nerve ending nociceptors.

4. **Proprioceptive stimuli** are detected by the following receptors.

   - **Muscle spindles** are mechanoreceptors located in skeletal muscles. They consist of specialized skeletal muscle fibers enclosed in a spindle-shaped capsule made of connective tissue.

   - **Golgi tendon organs** are mechanoreceptors located at junctions of tendons and muscles.

   - **Joint kinesthetic receptors** are mechanoreceptors located in synovial joints.

Vision

The **eye** is supported by the following **accessory organs.**

1. The **eyebrows** shade the eyes and help keep perspiration that accumulates on the forehead from running into the eyes.

2. The **eyelids (palpebrae)** lubricate, protect, and shade the eyeballs. Contraction of the **levator palpebrae superioris** muscle raises the upper eyelid. Each eyelid is supported internally by a layer of connective tissue, the **tarsal plate. Tarsal (Meibomian) glands** embedded in the tarsal plate produce secretions that prevent the upper and lower eyelids from sticking together. The inner lining of the eyelid, the **conjunctiva,** is a mucous membrane that produces secretions that lubricate the eyeball. The conjunctiva continues beyond the eyelid, folding back to cover the white of the eye.

3. The **eyelashes,** on the borders of the eyelids, help protect the eyeball. Nerve endings at the base of the hairs initiate a reflex action that closes the eyelids when the eyelashes are disturbed.

4. The **lacrimal apparatus** produces and drains tears. Tears (**lacrimal fluid**) are produced by the **lacrimal glands,** which lie above each eye (toward the outer side). In each eye, tears flow across the eyeball and enter two openings (**lacrimal puncta**) into **lacrimal canals** that lead to the **lacrimal sac.** From here, the tears drain through the **nasolacrimal duct** into the nasal cavity. Tears contain antibodies and **lysozyme** (a bacteria-destroying enzyme).

5. Six **extrinsic eye muscles** provide fine motor control for the eyeballs. These are the **lateral, medial, superior,** and **inferior rectus muscles,** and the **inferior** and **superior oblique muscles.**

The **eyeball** is a hollow sphere whose wall consists of three tunics (layers), as follows (Figure 57).

1. The outer **fibrous tunic** consists of avascular connective tissue. The forward 1/6 portion of this tunic is the **cornea,** a transparent layer of collagen fibers that forms a window for entering light. The remainder of the fibrous tunic is the **sclera.** Consisting of tough connective tissue, the sclera maintains the shape of the eyeball and provides for the attachment of the eye muscles. The visible forward portion of the sclera is the white of the eye.

2. The middle **vascular tunic (uvea)** consists of three highly vascularized (as the name implies), pigmented parts.

   ■ The **iris** is the colored portion of the eye that opens and closes to control the size of its circular opening, the **pupil.** The size of the pupil regulates the amount of light entering the eye and helps bring objects into focus.

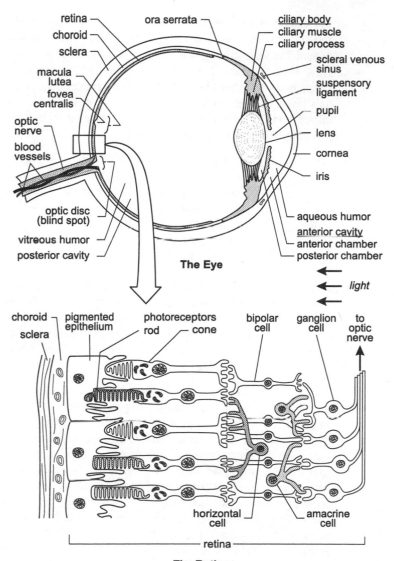

The Eye

The Retina

■ Figure 57 ■

■ The **ciliary body** lies between the iris and the choroid (the remainder of the vascular tunic). The **ciliary processes** that extend from the ciliary body secrete **aqueous humor,** the fluid that fills the forward chamber of the eye. The **suspensory ligament** between the ciliary processes and the lens holds the lens in place, while **ciliary muscles** (in the ciliary body) that pull on the suspensory ligament control the shape of the lens to focus images.

■ The **choroid** connects with the ciliary body at a jagged boundary, the **ora serrata,** and forms the remaining portion (5/6) of the vascular tunic. The choroid is dark brown, absorbing light and reducing reflection within the chamber of the eyeball that would otherwise blur images. The highly vascularized choroid provides nutrients to surrounding tissues, including the avascularized fibrous tunic.

3. The inner **nervous tunic** is the **retina.** The retina consists of an outer **pigmented epithelium** covered by nervous tissue (the **neural layer**) on the inside. The dark color of the pigmented epithelium absorbs light (as with the choroid) and stores vitamin A used by photoreceptor cells in the neural layer. There are two kinds of photoreceptors in the retina, as follows.

■ **Cones** are photoreceptor cells that respond to *bright light* and *color.* They transmit *sharp images.* The concentration of cones is low at the sides of the retina and increases as the cones approach the **macula lutea,** an oval region in the center of the rear portion of the retina. The center of the macula lutea, the **fovea centralis,** contains only cones; other retinal cells are absent, exposing the cones directly to incoming light. The high concentration of cones and direct exposure to light make the fovea centralis the site on the retina that provides the highest visual acuity. As a result, images that are viewed directly are focused upon the fovea centralis.

- **Rods** are photoreceptor cells that are more sensitive to light and more numerous than cones. As a result, rods provide vision in *dim light*. They are also more capable of *detecting movement*. However, rods cannot detect color, and dimly lit objects appear gray. Since the concentration of rods increases in areas farther away from the macula lutea, detecting a moving or dimly lit object can be more effectively achieved by looking slightly away from the object.

Within the nervous tunic, photoreceptor cells (rods and cones) form synapses with other nerve cells (Figure 57). When stimulated by light, rods and cones pass graded potentials to **bipolar cells,** which, in turn, pass graded potentials to the **ganglion cells.** The graded potentials may be modified by **horizontal cells** and **amacrine cells** that link adjacent photoreceptor or ganglion cells, respectively. *Action potentials* are ultimately generated by ganglion cells. The axons of all the ganglion cells gather at the **optic disc** and exit the nervous tunic through the optic disc as the optic nerve. The optic disc is a **blind spot** because photoreceptors are absent here.

The **lens** of the eye consists of tightly packed cells arranged in successive layers (as in an onion) and filled with transparent proteins called **crystallins.** The lens divides the interior of the eyeball into two cavities, as follows.

1. The **anterior cavity,** the area in front of the lens, is subdivided by the iris and ciliary body into the **anterior chamber** and the **posterior chamber.** Capillaries in the ciliary body produce a clear fluid, the aqueous humor, that flows into the posterior chamber, through the pupil, and into the anterior chamber. The aqueous humor then drains into veins through a channel (**scleral venous sinus,** or **canal of Schlemm**) that encircles the eye where the cornea and sclera join. The aqueous humor, which is continuously replaced, provides pressure

to maintain the shape of the forward portion of the eye and supplies O_2 and nutrients to the avascular lens and cornea.

2. The **posterior cavity,** the area behind the lens, is filled with a clear gel, the **vitreous humor.** The vitreous humor, which is produced during embryonic development and is not replaced, holds the lens and retina in position and maintains the shape of the eye.

The **process of sight** involves converting light energy to chemical energy. Features of the process follow.

1. The **outer segments** of rods and cones contain numerous folds that increase the surface area exposed to light.

2. **Photopigments** (visual pigments) in the outer segments respond to light by changing their chemical structure. Each visual photopigment consists of two parts—**retinal** (a vitamin A derivative) and **opsin** (a glycoprotein). There are four different kinds of photopigments because the opsin in each has a slightly different structure, enabling each photopigment to absorb a different range of light wavelengths (different colors)

3. There are three kinds of *cones,* each possessing a different photopigment, each sensitive to a different range of light wavelengths. A mixed stimulation of the three different cones (called red, green, and blue for their optimally absorbed wavelengths) provides for the perception of varied colors.

4. There is only one kind of *rod,* with a single kind of photopigment, **rhodopsin.**

5. When a photopigment absorbs light, retinal changes shape, causing it to separate from opsin. Because the product is colorless, the process is called bleaching.

6. Unlike most other neurons, photoreceptors continually secrete a neurotransmitter when in the resting (unstimulated), polarized condition. When a photoreceptor is stimulated, the freed opsin becomes chemically active and initiates a series of chemical reactions that close the Na^+ channels in the plasma membrane. Because the Na^+/K^+ pump continues to pump Na^+ out of the cell, the plasma membrane becomes hyperpolarized. Hyperpolarization stops the normal secretion of the neurotransmitter, which in turn stimulates a graded potential in the bipolar cells.

7. Photopigments are regenerated when opsin is enzymatically reattached to retinal. In bright light, the very light-sensitive rhodopsin in rods cannot be regenerated as fast as it is broken down, so most of the rhodopsin remains inactive. As a result, the less light-sensitive pigments in cones are active in normal daylight. When eyes move from bright conditions to dark conditions, the photopigments in cones are too insensitive to detect light, and the rhodopsin in rods is still bleached from its exposure to bright light. Vision returns as rhodopsin is regenerated, a process called **dark adaptation.** When eyes move from dark to bright conditions, the very light-sensitive rods are suddenly overwhelmed with stimulation, producing the sensation of glare. **Light adaptation** occurs as the rhodopsin in rods is completely bleached and the less light-sensitive cones resume activity.

When light reflected from an object enters the eye, the following processes occur.

1. *Light refraction.* When light rays pass from one substance to another substance of different density, the rays bend, or **refract.** The amount of bending depends upon the angle of incidence of the light ray and the degree to which the densities of the two substances differ. When *distant objects* are sighted, the normal curvature of the lens appropriately compensates

for the refraction of rays due to the differences in densities among the aqueous humor, the lens, and the vitreous humor.

2. *Lens accommodation.* Light rays from near objects enter the eyeball at more divergent angles than rays from distant objects. Thus, when *near objects* are sighted, muscles pull on the lens to increase its curvature so that the more divergent rays of the close object are properly refracted upon the retina.

3. *Pupil constriction.* One function of the pupil is to regulate the amount of light that enters the posterior cavity so that the retina receives the appropriate amount of stimulation. In addition, when *near objects* are sighted, the pupil constricts (**accommodation pupillary reflex**) to block the most divergent light rays that cannot be brought into focus by the accommodation of the lens. Reading under low levels of light may be difficult because the pupils are dilated to allow all available light to enter rather than constricted to improve focusing. Increasing the amount of light improves the ability to read because the surplus light permits the pupils to constrict and the lens to focus a more narrow beam of light rays.

4. *Eyeball convergence.* Both eyes point in the same direction when viewing a distant object. When *near objects* are sighted, the eyes must be directed medially to simultaneously view the object, a process called **convergence.**

Nerve impulses generated by visual stimuli travel along the axons of ganglion cells within the two optic nerves. Before entering the brain, axons representing the medial portions of the visual fields of each eye cross over at the **optic chiasma.** After the crossover, the axons, now forming the optic *tract*, enter the thalamus. Processed visual stimuli are then carried to visual areas of the occipital lobes of both cerebral hemispheres by nerve pathways called the **optic radiations.** Because of the partial crossover at the optic chiasma, each cerebral hemisphere receives the lateral portion of the visual field of the eye on the same side of the body as the cerebral hemisphere, but the medial portion of the visual field of the eye on the opposite side of the body. In addition, because of the action of the lens, the image that forms on the retina and that is sent to the brain is inverted and reversed right to left. The brain, however, interprets all of this seemingly disparate visual information into a coherent perception of the real world.

Hearing

The organ of **hearing,** the **ear,** consists of three major regions, as follows (Figure 58).

1. The **outer (external) ear** consists of the **auricle (pinna),** a flap of elastic cartilage that protrudes from the head, and the **external auditory canal (meatus),** a tube that enters the temporal bone. The canal is lined with **ceruminous glands** that secrete **cerumen (earwax),** a sticky substance that traps dirt and other foreign objects. The **eardrum (tympanic membrane),** at the internal end of the external auditory canal, vibrates in response to incident sound waves.

2. The **middle ear (tympanic cavity)** is an air-filled cavity within the temporal bone. It contains three small bones, the **auditory ossicles.** The bones, called the **malleus** (hammer), **incus** (anvil), and **stapes** (stirrup), act as a lever system that amplifies and transfers vibrations of the eardrum to the inner ear. The malleus at one end connects to the eardrum, while the stapes, at the other end, attaches with ligaments to the **oval window,** a small, membrane-covered opening into the inner ear. Synovial joints connect the incus, the center bone of the auditory ossicles, to the malleus and stapes on each side. A second membrane-covered opening to the inner ear, the **round window (secondary tympanic membrane),** lies just below the oval window. A third opening leads to the **auditory (Eustachian) tube** which connects the middle ear to the upper throat. The

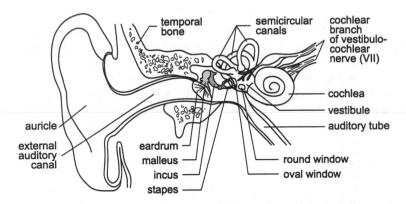

The Ear

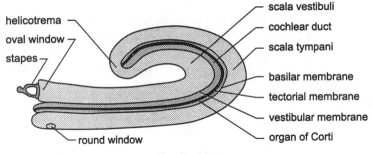

The Cochlea

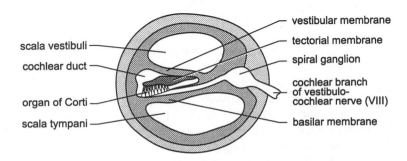

The Cochlea (Cross Section)

■ Figure 58 ■

auditory tube allows pressure differences between the middle and outer ear to equalize, thus reducing tension on the eardrum. Two muscles in the middle ear, the **tensor tympani** and the **stapedius,** connect to the malleus and stapes, respectively. Contraction of these two muscles restricts the movement of the eardrum and auditory ossicles, reducing damage that may occur when they are exposed to excessive vibration from loud noises.

3. The **inner (internal) ear,** also called the **labyrinth,** is a system of double-walled canals. The canals consist of an outer **bony (osseus) labyrinth** that encloses an inner **membranous labyrinth. Perilymph** fills the space between the two labyrinths, and **endolymph** fills the inner labyrinth. This double-layer labyrinth structure is found throughout the following inner ear structures.

   ■ Three **semicircular canals** contain receptor cells for determining angular movements of the head. This information is used for establishing equilibrium.

   ■ The **cochlea** is a coiled canal that contains receptor cells that respond to vibrations transferred from the middle ear. The interior of the cochlea is divided into three regions, or **scalas**—the **scala vestibuli,** the **scala tympani,** and the **cochlear duct (scala media).** The scalas are tubular channels that follow the coiled curvature of the cochlea. At the middle ear, the scala vestibuli and the scala tympani connect to the oval and round windows, respectively. At the other end of the cochlea, a region called the **helicotrema,** these two scalas join, allowing free movement of the perilymph within. The third scala, the cochlear duct, is separated from the scala vestibuli and the scala tympani by the **vestibular membrane** and the **basilar membrane**, respectively. The cochlear duct is filled with endolymph and internally lined with the **organ of Corti.** The organ of Corti contains numerous hair cells. The bases of the hair cells are attached to the basilar membrane, while hairlike microvilli called **stereocilia** project upwards into an overlying gel, the **tectorial membrane.** The stereocilia are receptors for vibrations that are produced when the underlying basal membrane moves relative to the overlying tectorial membrane.

■ The **vestibule** lies between the semicircular canals and the cochlea. It contains two bulblike sacs, the **saccule** and **utricle,** whose membranes are continuous with those of the cochlea and semicircular canals, respectively. The saccule and utricle contain receptors that help maintain equilibrium.

The **process of hearing** occurs as follows.

1. Sound waves, funneled into the outer ear by the auricle, cause the eardrum to vibrate.

2. Vibrations of the eardrum are amplified and transferred by the auditory ossicles to the oval window.

3. Vibrations on the oval window produce pressure waves in the perilymph of the scala vestibuli and the scala tympani. These vibrations are transferred to the basilar membrane.

4. Vibrations of the basilar membrane move the hair cells of the organ of Corti. The stereocilia of the hair cells bend when they move against the tectorial membrane. The bending generates a graded potential in the hair cell which causes the release of a neurotransmitter at its base. The neurotransmitter, in turn, generates an action potential in dendrites of the cochlear nerve. Cell bodies of the cochlear nerve assemble in the spiral ganglia, and its axons merge with the vestibulocochlear nerve.

5. Pressure waves in the perilymph of the scala tympani cause the round window to bulge into the middle ear. This allows vibrational movements of the perilymph (and indirectly the

endolymph) that, as an incompressible fluid, would not otherwise be able to vibrate within the surrounding rigid temporal bone.

Equilibrium

Equilibrium is maintained in response to two kinds of motion, as follows.

1. **Static equilibrium** maintains the position of the head in response to *linear motion* of the body, such as starting to walk or stopping.

2. **Dynamic equilibrium** maintains the position of the head in response to *rotational motion* of the body, such as rocking (as in a boat) or turning.

The perception of equilibrium occurs in the **vestibular apparatus,** which consists of the vestibule and the semicircular canals. Motion in these two structures is detected as follows.

1. The vestibule is the primary detector of changes in *static* equilibrium. A sensory receptor called a **macula** is located in the walls of the saccule and utricle, the two bulblike sacs of the vestibule. A macula contains numerous receptor cells called **hair cells,** from which numerous **stereocilia** (long microvilli) and a single **kinocilium** (a true cilium) extend into a glycoprotein gel, the **otolithic membrane.** Calcium carbonate crystals called **otoliths** pervade the otolithic membrane, increasing its density and thus responsiveness to changes in motion. Changes in linear motion cause the otolithic membrane to move forward and backward in the utricle or up and down in the saccule. The movement of the otolithic membrane causes similar movements in the embedded stereocilia of the hair cells, which in turn initiate graded potentials.

2. The semicircular canals are the primary detector of changes in *dynamic* equilibrium. The three canals, individually called the **anterior, posterior,** and **lateral canals,** are arranged at right angles to one another. The expanded base of each canal, called an **ampulla,** contains a sensory receptor, or **crista ampullaris.** Like the maculae of the vestibule, each crista contains numerous hair cells whose stereocilia and kinocilium protrude into a gelatinous matrix, the **cupula** (which is analogous to the otolithic membranes of the maculae). Changes in rotational motion cause the cupula and the embedded stereocilia to move, which stimulates the hair cell to generate a graded potential.

Graded potentials in the hair cells of the maculae and cristae result in changes in the amounts of neurotransmitter secreted. In response to these changes, action potentials are generated in the fibers of the vestibular nerve, which subsequently joins the vestibulocochlear nerve. From here, the nerve impulses travel to the pons and the cerebellum.

Smell

The **sense of smell,** or **olfactory sense,** occurs in **olfactory epithelium** that occupies a small area in the roof of the nasal cavity. The **olfactory receptor cells** are bipolar neurons whose dendrites have terminal knobs with hairlike cilia protruding beyond the epithelial surface. The cilia, or **olfactory hairs,** initiate an action potential when they react with a molecule from an inhaled vapor. However, molecules of the vapor must first dissolve in the mucus that covers the cilia before they can be detected. The action potential is transmitted along the axons of the olfactory receptor cells (which form the olfactory nerves) to the olfactory bulbs, where they synapse with sensory neurons of the olfactory tract.

Other cells of the olfactory epithelium include columnar **supporting cells** and **basal cells.** The basal cells continually divide to produce new olfactory receptor cells which, because of their short life, need regular replacement. The replacement of olfactory receptor cells is unusual because most other nerve cells cannot be replaced.

The mucus that lines the olfactory epithelium is produced by **olfactory (Bowman's) glands** that occupy the connective tissue above the olfactory epithelium.

Taste

The **sense of taste,** or **gustatory sense,** occurs in the taste buds. Located primarily on the tongue, taste buds reside in **papillae,** the bumps on the tongue that give it a rough texture. The taste bud consists of **supporting cells, basal cells,** and **gustatory (taste) receptor cells** arranged in the shape of a globe with an opening, or **taste pore,** to the outside located at the top. A long microvilli, or **gustatory hair,** from each gustatory receptor cell within the taste bud projects through the taste pore. Gustatory hairs generate action potentials when stimulated by chemicals that are dissolved in the saliva.

Basal cells are actively dividing epithelial cells. The daughter cells of basal cells develop into supporting cells which subsequently mature into gustatory receptor cells. Because they are easily damaged by the activities that occur in the mouth, gustatory receptor cells are short-lived and replaced about every ten days.

An individual gustatory receptor cell responds to only four taste sensations: sweet, bitter, sour, and salty. All other tastes arise from a mixture of these four tastes in combination with olfactory sensations associated with the substance tasted. Taste buds on certain areas of the tongue seem to specialize for certain tastes. For example, the sensation of sweetness is best detected at the front of the tongue, while bitterness is best detected at the back of the tongue.

The endocrine system produces **hormones** that are instrumental in maintaining homeostasis and regulating reproduction and development. A hormone is a chemical messenger produced by a cell that effects specific changes in the cellular activity of other cells (**target cells**). Unlike exocrine glands (that produce substances such as saliva, milk, stomach acid, and digestive enzymes), endocrine glands do not secrete substances into ducts (tubes). Instead, endocrine glands secrete their hormones directly into the surrounding extracellular space. The hormones then diffuse into nearby capillaries and are transported throughout the body in the blood.

The endocrine and nervous systems often work toward the same goal—both influence other cells with chemicals (hormones and neurotransmitters). However, they attain their goals differently. Neurotransmitters act *immediately* (within milliseconds) on *adjacent* muscle, gland, or other nervous cells, and their effect is *short-lived*. In contrast, hormones take *longer* to produce their intended effect (seconds to days), may affect *any cell*, nearby or distant, and produce effects that last *as long as they remain in the blood* (up to several hours).

Hormones

Hormones can be chemically classified into four groups, as follows.

1. **Amino acid-derived hormones** are modified amino acids.

2. **Polypeptide** and **protein hormones** are chains of amino acids of less than or more than about 100 amino acids, respectively. Some protein hormones are actually glycoproteins, containing glucose or other carbohydrate groups.

3. **Steroid hormones** are lipids that are synthesized from cholesterol. Steroids are characterized by four interlocking carbohydrate rings.

4. **Eicosanoids** are lipids that are synthesized from the fatty acid chains of phospholipids found in plasma membranes.

Mechanisms of Hormone Action

Hormones circulating in the blood diffuse into the interstitial fluids surrounding cells. Cells with specific receptors for a hormone respond with an action that is appropriate for the cell. Because of the specificity of hormone and target cell, the effects produced by a single hormone may vary among different kinds of target cells.

Hormones activate target cells by one of two methods, depending upon the chemical nature of the hormone.

1. **Lipid-soluble hormones** (steroid hormones and hormones of the thyroid gland) diffuse through the cell membranes of target cells. The lipid-soluble hormone then binds to a receptor protein that, in turn, activates a DNA segment that turns on specific genes. The proteins produced as a result of the transcription of the genes and subsequent translation of mRNA act as enzymes that regulate specific physiological cell activity.

2. **Water-soluble hormones** (polypeptide, protein, and most amino acid hormones) bind to a receptor protein on the plasma membrane of the cell. The receptor protein, in turn, stimulates the production of one of the following **second messengers.**

   ▪ **Cyclic AMP (cAMP)** is produced when the receptor protein activates another membrane-bound protein called a **G protein.** The G protein activates adenylate cyclase, the enzyme that catalyzes the production of cAMP from ATP. Cyclic AMP then triggers an enzyme that generates specific cellular changes.

- **Inositol triphosphate (IP$_3$)** is produced from membrane phospholipids. IP$_3$, in turn, triggers the release of Ca^{2+} from the endoplasmic reticulum that then activates enzymes that generate cellular changes.

Control of Hormone Production

Endocrine glands release hormones in response to one (or more) of the following stimuli.

1. Hormones from other endocrine glands.

2. Chemical characteristics of the blood (other than hormones).

3. Neural stimulation.

Most hormone production is regulated by a **negative feedback system.** The nervous system and certain endocrine tissues monitor various internal conditions of the body. If action is necessary to maintain homeostasis, hormones are released, either directly by an endocrine gland, or indirectly through the action of the hypothalamus of the brain, which stimulates other endocrine glands to release hormones. The hormones activate target cells, which initiate physiological changes that adjust body conditions. When normal conditions have been restored, the corrective action—the production of hormones—is discontinued. Thus, in negative feedback, when the original (abnormal) condition has been repaired, or negated, corrective actions *decrease* (or are discontinued). For example, the amount of glucose in the blood regulates the secretion of insulin and glucagon through negative feedback.

The production of some hormones is regulated by **positive feedback.** In such a system, hormones cause a condition to *intensify* (rather than decrease). As the condition intensifies, hormone production *in-*

creases. Such positive feedback is uncommon but does occur during childbirth (hormone levels build with increasingly intense labor contractions) and lactation (where hormone levels increase in response to nursing, which causes milk production to increase).

The Hypothalamus and Pituitary Glands

The **hypothalamus** makes up the lower region of the diencephalon and lies just above the brain stem. The **pituitary gland (hypophysis)** is attached to the bottom of the hypothalamus by a slender stalk called the **infundibulum.** The pituitary gland consists of two major regions—the **anterior pituitary gland (anterior lobe** or **adenohypophysis)** and the **posterior pituitary gland (posterior lobe** or **neurohypophysis).**

The hypothalamus oversees many internal body conditions. It receives nervous stimuli from receptors throughout the body and monitors chemical and physical characteristics of the blood, including temperature, blood pressure, and nutrient, hormone, and water content. When deviations from homeostasis occur or when certain developmental changes are required, the hypothalamus stimulates cellular activity in various parts of the body by directing the release of hormones from the anterior and posterior pituitary glands. The hypothalamus communicates directives to these glands by one of the following two pathways.

1. Communication between the hypothalamus and the *anterior pituitary* occurs through chemicals (**releasing hormones** and **inhibiting hormones**) that are produced by the hypothalamus and delivered to the anterior pituitary through blood vessels. The releasing and inhibiting hormones are produced by specialized neurons of the hypothalamus called **neurosecretory cells.** The hormones are released into a capillary network (**primary plexus**) and transported through veins (**hypophyseal portal veins**) to a second capillary network (**secondary plexus**) that supplies the anterior pituitary. The hormones then diffuse

from the secondary plexus into the anterior pituitary, where they initiate the production of specific hormones by the anterior pituitary. The releasing and inhibiting hormones secreted by the hypothalamus and the hormones produced in response by the anterior pituitary are listed in Table 14. Many of the hormones produced by the anterior pituitary are **tropic hormones (tropins)**, hormones that stimulate other endocrine glands to secrete their hormones.

2. Communication between the hypothalamus and the *posterior pituitary* occurs through neurosecretory cells that span the short distance between the hypothalamus and the posterior pituitary. Hormones produced by the cell bodies of the neurosecretory cells are packaged in vesicles and transported through the axon and stored in the axon terminals that lie in the posterior pituitary. When the neurosecretory cells are stimulated, the action potential generated triggers the release of the stored hormones from the axon terminals to a capillary network within the posterior pituitary. Two hormones, **oxytocin** and **antidiuretic hormone (ADH)**, are produced and released in this way. Their functions are summarized in Table 14.

Endocrine Organs and Tissues

A summary of the various endocrine organs, their hormones, and their functions is given in Table 14. Also listed are some organs whose major function is not the secretion of hormones but which, nonetheless, contain some specialized cells that produce hormones. These organs include the heart, the gastrointestinal tract, the placenta, the kidneys, and the skin.

In addition, all cells (except red blood cells) secrete a class of hormones called **eicosanoids.** These hormones are **paracrines,** or local hormones, that primarily affect neighboring cells. Two groups of eicosanoids, the **prostaglandins (PGs)** and the **leukotrienes (LTs)**, have a wide range of varying effects that depend upon the nature of

Source	Hormone (H), Releasing Hormone (RH), or Inhibiting Hormone (IH)	Chemical Form *	Target	Action
Hypothalamus	GHRH growth hormone RH	PP		stimulates release of hGH
	GHIH growth hormone IH (somatostatin)	PP		inhibits release of hGH
	TRH thyrotropin RH	PP		stimulates release of TSH and hGH
	GnRH gonadotropin RH	PP	anterior pituitary	stimulates release of LH and FSH
	PRH prolactin RH	PP		stimulates release of PRL
	PIH prolactin IH (dopamine)	PP		inhibits release of PRL
	CRH corticotropin RH	PP		stimulates release of ACTH
Anterior pituitary (tropic hormones)	TSH thyroid stimulating H (thyrotropin)	GP	thyroid	stimulates secretion of T_3 and T_4
	ACTH adrenocorticotropic hormone	PP	adrenal cortex	stimulates secretion of glucocorticoids
	FSH follicle stimulating hormone	GP	ovary, testes	regulates oogenesis & spermatogenesis
	LH luteinizing hormone	GP	ovary, testes	regulates oogenesis & spermatogenesis
Anterior pituitary (hormones)	PRL prolactin	PR	mammary glands	stimulates production of milk
	hGH human growth H (somatotropin)	PR	bone, muscle, various	stimulates growth
Posterior pituitary	OT oxytocin	PP	uterus, mammary glands	uterine contractions, release of milk
	ADH antidiuretic H (vasopressin)	PP	kidneys, sweat glands	increases water retention
Thyroid gland	T_4 thyroxine	AA	most body cells	increases rate of cellular metabolism
	T_3 triiodothyronine	AA	bone	increases rate of cellular metabolism
	calcitonin	PP	bone	decreases blood Ca^{2+}
Parathyroid gland	PTH parathyroid hormone	PP	bone, kidneys, intestine	increases blood Ca^{2+}
Adrenal medulla	epinephrine (adrenaline)	AA	blood vessels, liver, heart	increases blood sugar, constricts blood vessels (fight or flight response)
	NE norepinephrine (noradrenaline)	AA	heart	
Adrenal cortex	mineralocorticoids (e.g., aldosterone)	S	kidneys	increase reabsorption of Na^+, excretion of K^+
	glucocorticoids (e.g., cortisol)	S	most body cells	increase blood sugar
	androgens (e.g., DHEA)	S	general	stimulate onset of puberty, female sex drive

* Chemical forms are abbreviated AA (amino acid), E (eicosanoid), GP (glycoprotein), PP (polypeptide), PR (protein), and S (steroid).

Source		Hormone (H), Releasing Hormone (RH), or Inhibiting Hormone (IH)	Chemical Form *	Target	Action
Pancreas		glucagon (secreted by alpha cells)	PP	liver	increases blood glucose
		insulin (secreted by beta cells)	PP	liver, muscle, adipose	decreases blood glucose
		somatostatin (secreted by delta cells)	PP	alpha & beta cells	inhibits insulin & glucagon release
		pancreatic polypeptide (from F cells)	PP	delta cells	inhibits somatostatin & pancreatic enzymes
Ovaries		estrogen	S	uterus, general	menstrual cycle, secondary sex characteristics
		progesterone	S	uterus	regulates menstrual cycle, pregnancy
		relaxin	PP	pelvis, cervix	dilates cervix & birth canal
		inhibin	PR	anterior pituitary	inhibits FSH release
Testes		testosterone	S	testes, general	spermatogenesis, secondary sex characteristics
		inhibin	PR	anterior pituitary	inhibits FSH release
Pineal		melatonin	AA	various	regulates biological clock
Kidney		erythropoietin	GP	bone marrow	increases blood cell production
		calcitriol (Vitamin D)	S	intestine	increases Ca^{2+} absorption
Placenta		estrogen	S	uterus	maintains pregnancy, mammary glands
		progesterone	S	uterus	maintains pregnancy, mammary glands
		hCG	GP	ovary	stimulates release of estrogen & progesterone
		hCS	PR	mammary glands	prepares mammary glands for lactation
Gastrointestinal tract		gastrin	PP	stomach	stimulates HCl release
	GIP	gastrin inhibitory peptide	PP	stomach, pancreas	inhibits gastric juice release, increases insulin
		secretin	PP	pancreas, liver	stimulates release of enzymes & bile
	CCK	cholecystokinin	PP	pancreas, liver	stimulates release of enzymes & bile
		serotonin	AA	stomach	stimulates stomach muscle contraction
Heart	ANP	atrial natriuretic peptide	PP	kidney, adrenal cortex	decreases blood pressure
Most cells	PG	prostaglandins	E	all cells except red	various
	LT	leukotrienes	E	blood cells	various

■ Table 14 ■

* Chemical forms are abbreviated AA (amino acid), E (eicosanoid), GP (glycoprotein), PP (polypeptide), PR (protein), and S (steroid).

the target cell. Eicosanoid activity, for example, may impact blood pressure, blood clotting, immune and inflammatory responses, reproductive processes, and the contraction of smooth muscles.

Antagonistic Hormones

Maintaining homeostasis often requires conditions to be limited to a narrow range. When conditions exceed the *upper limit* of homeostasis, specific action, usually the production of a hormone, is triggered. When conditions return to normal, hormone production is discontinued. If conditions exceed the *lower limit* of homeostasis, a different action, usually the production of a second hormone, is triggered. Hormones that act to return body conditions to within acceptable limits from opposite extremes are called **antagonistic hormones**.

The regulation of blood glucose concentration (through negative feedback) illustrates how the endocrine system maintains homeostasis by the action of antagonistic hormones. Bundles of cells in the pancreas called the **islets of Langerhans** contain two kinds of cells, **alpha (α) cells** and **beta (β) cells.** These cells control blood glucose concentration by producing the antagonistic hormones **insulin** and **glucagon,** as follows.

1. *Beta cells secrete insulin.* When the concentration of blood glucose rises (after eating, for example), beta cells secrete insulin into the blood. Insulin stimulates the liver and most other body cells to absorb glucose. Liver and muscle cells convert the glucose to glycogen (for short-term storage), and adipose cells convert the glucose to fat. In response, glucose concentration decreases in the blood, and insulin secretion discontinues (through negative feedback from declining levels of glucose).

2. *Alpha cells secrete glucagon.* When the concentration of blood glucose drops (during exercise, for example), alpha cells secrete glucagon into the blood. Glucagon stimulates the liver to release glucose. The glucose in the liver originates from the breakdown of glycogen and the conversion of amino acids and fatty acids into glucose. When blood glucose levels return to normal, glucagon secretion discontinues (negative feedback).

Another example of antagonistic hormones occurs in the maintenance of Ca^{2+} concentration in the blood. **Parathyroid hormone (PTH)** from the parathyroid glands increases Ca^{2+} in the blood by increasing Ca^{2+} absorption in the intestines and reabsorption in the kidneys and stimulating Ca^{2+} release from bones. **Calcitonin (CT)** produces the opposite effect by inhibiting the breakdown of bone matrix and decreasing the release of calcium into the blood.

The **cardiovascular system** consists of the heart, blood vessels, and blood. There are three main functions of this system.

1. *Transport* of nutrients, oxygen, and hormones to cells throughout the body and removal of metabolic wastes (carbon dioxide, nitrogenous wastes, and heat).

2. *Protection* of the body by white blood cells, antibodies, and complement proteins that circulate in the blood and defend the body against foreign microbes and toxins. Clotting mechanisms are also present that protect the body from blood loss after injuries.

3. *Regulation* of body temperature, fluid *p*H and water content of cells.

The Blood

The **blood** consists of cells and cell fragments, called **formed elements,** and water with dissolved molecules, called **blood plasma.** These are discussed below (Table 15).

1. **Erythrocytes,** or **red blood cells (RBCs)**, transport oxygen (O_2) and carbon dioxide (CO_2) in the blood. Erythrocytes contain the protein hemoglobin to which both O_2 and CO_2 attach. Characteristics of erythrocytes are listed below.

   ■ Mature erythrocytes lack a nucleus and most cellular organelles, thereby maximizing the cell's volume and thus its ability to carry hemoglobin and to transport O_2.

Type	Constituent		Characteristics/Functions
Formed Elements (45%)	Erythrocytes (red blood cells) (98-99%)		anucleate, contain hemoglobin; O_2 & CO_2 transport
	Leukocytes (white blood cells) (0.1-0.3%)	Neutrophils (60-70%)	granulocytes, polymorphonuclear; phagocytosis, wound healing
		Eosinophils (2-4%)	granulocytes, bilobed nucleus; phagocytosis
		Basophils (0.5-1%)	granulocytes, 2-5 lobed nucleus; release histamine
		Lymphocytes (20-25%)	agranulocytes, circular nucleus, T cells, B cells; immune response, antibodies
		Monocytes (3-8%)	agranulocytes, large kidney-shaped nucleus; phagocytotic macrophages
	Thrombocytes (platelets) (1-2%)		anucleate, megakaryocyte fragments; blood clotting
Blood Plasma (55%)	Water (90%)		
	Plasma Proteins (8%)	Albumin (54%)	maintain osmotic pressure between blood & tissues
		Globulins (38%)	lipid and metal ion transporters, antibodies
		Fibrinogen (7%)	clotting factor
		Others (1%)	enzymes, hormones, clotting factors
	Electrolytes	Na^+, K^+, Ca^{2+}, Mg^{2+}	
		Cl^-, HCO_3^-, SO_4^{2-}, HPO_4^{2-}	
	Gases	O_2, CO_2, N_2	
	Nutrients	Glucose, other carbohydrates	sources of energy
		Amino acids	protein building blocks
		Lipids	fats, steroids, phospholipids
		Cholesterol	component of plasma membranes & steroid hormones
	Waste Products	Urea	from breakdown of proteins
		Creatinine	from breakdown of creatine phosphate (from muscles)
		Uric acid	from breakdown of nucleic acids
		Bilirubin	from breakdown of hemoglobin
	Hormones	Various	

■ Table 15 ■

- Erythrocytes are shaped like flattened donuts with a depressed center (rather than a donut hole). Their flattened shaped maximizes surface area for the exchange of O_2 and CO_2 and allows flexibility that permits their passage through narrow capillaries.

- **Hemoglobin** contains both a protein portion, called **globin,** and nonprotein **heme** groups. Globin consists of four polypeptide chains, each of which contains a heme group. The heme group is a red pigment that contains a single iron atom surrounded by a ring of nitrogen-containing carbon rings. One oxygen atom attaches to the iron of each heme group, allowing a single hemoglobin molecule to carry four oxygen atoms. Each erythrocyte contains about 250 million hemoglobin molecules.

- **Oxyhemoglobin (HbO$_2$)** forms in the lungs when erythrocytes are exposed to oxygen as they pass through the lungs. **Deoxyhemoglobin (HHb)** forms when oxygen detaches from the iron and diffuses into surrounding tissues.

- **Carbaminohemoglobin (HbCO$_2$)** forms when CO_2 attaches to amino acids of the globin part of the hemoglobin molecule. About 25% of the CO_2 transported from tissues to lungs is in this form.

- **Carbonic anhydrase,** an enzyme in erythrocytes, converts CO_2 and H_2O in the blood plasma to H^+ and HCO_3^-. About 65% of the CO_2 collected from tissues travels in the blood plasma as HCO_3^-.

Because they lack cellular organelles and thus the physiology to maintain themselves, erythrocytes survive for only about 120 days. Degenerated erythrocytes are broken down in the spleen and liver by macrophages (phagocytic white blood cells) as follows.

- The globin and heme parts of the hemoglobin are separated. The globin is reduced to amino acids, which are returned to the blood plasma.

- Iron is removed from the heme groups and bound to the proteins **ferritin** and **hemosiderin,** which store the iron for later use (because unbound iron is toxic). Iron is also attached to **transferrin,** which enters the bloodstream. Transferrin may be picked up by muscle or liver cells, where it may be stored (as ferritin or hemosiderin), or picked up by bone marrow, where the iron is used to produce new erythrocytes.

- The remainder of the heme group is broken down into **bilirubin** (a yellow-orange pigment), which enters the bloodstream and is picked up by the liver. Liver cells incorporate bilirubin into bile, which enters the small intestine during the digestion of fats. Bilirubin is then converted into **urobilinogen** by intestinal bacteria. Finally, most urobilinogen is converted to the brown pigment **stercobilin,** which is eliminated with the feces (and which gives feces their brown color). A small amount of urobilinogen is absorbed into the blood, converted to the yellow pigment **urobilin,** picked up by the kidneys, and eliminated with the urine (contributing to the yellow color of urine).

2. **Leukocytes,** or **white blood cells (WBCs),** are cells that protect the body from foreign microbes and toxins. Although all leukocytes can be found in the bloodstream, some permanently leave the bloodstream to enter tissues where they encounter microbes or toxins, while other kinds of leukocytes readily move in and out of the bloodstream. Leukocytes are classified into two groups, **granulocytes** and **agranulocytes,** based upon the presence or absence of granules in the cytoplasm and the shape of the nucleus.

Granulocytes contain numerous granules in the cytoplasm and have a nucleus that is irregularly shaped with lobes. Each of the three types of granulocytes is named after the bloodstains that its granules absorb.

- **Neutrophils,** the most numerous of granulocytes, have an S- or C-shaped nucleus with three to six lobes. Their granules, which are small and inconspicuous, poorly absorb both basic and acidic stains (*neutr*al pH preference), producing a pale, lilac color. Because the shape of the nucleus is so variable, neutrophils are referred to as **polymorpho-nuclear leukocytes (PMNs),** or **polys.** Young neutrophils, with immature nuclei that are shaped like rods, are called **band** neutrophils. Neutrophils are the first leukocytes to arrive at a site of infection, responding (by **chemotaxis**) to chemicals released by damaged cells. The neutrophils, by phagocytosis, actively engulf bacteria, which are then destroyed by the various antibiotic proteins (such as **defensins** and **lysozymes**) contained within the granules. The neutrophils, usually destroyed in the process, contribute, together with other dead tissue, to the formation of pus.

- **Eosinophils** have a bilobed nucleus (two lobes connected by a narrow strand of chromatin). Their granules, which stain red with acid (*eosin*) dyes, contain digestive enzymes and are considered lysosomes. Eosinophils actively phagocytize complexes formed by the action of antibodies on antigens (foreign substances). Numbers of eosinophils increase during parasitic infections and allergic reactions.

- **Basophils** have a U- or S-shaped nucleus with two to five lobes connected by a narrow strand of chromatin. Their granules, which stain blue-purple with *bas*ic dyes, contain histamine, serotonin, and heparin. Basophils release histamine in response to tissue damage and to pathogen invasion (as part of the inflammatory response). Basophils resemble **mast cells,** cells similar in appearance and function to basophils, but found only in connective tissues.

Agranulocytes, the second group of leukocytes, do not have visible granules in the cytoplasm and the nucleus is not lobed. There are two types of these leukocytes.

- **Lymphocytes,** often classified as small, medium, and large, have a roughly round nucleus surrounded by a small amount of blue-staining cytoplasm. Lymphocytes are the only leukocytes that return to the bloodstream, circulating among the bloodstream, tissue fluids, tissues, and lymph fluid. There are two major groups of lymphocytes which vary based upon their role in an immune response. **T lymphocytes (T cells),** which mature in the thymus gland, attack aberrant cells (such as tumor cells, organ transplant cells, or cells infected by viruses). **B lymphocytes (B cells),** which mature in the bone marrow, respond to circulating antigens (such as toxins, viruses, or bacteria) by dividing to produce **plasma cells,** which, in turn, produce antibodies.

- **Monocytes** have a large, kidney-shaped nucleus surrounded by ample blue-gray-staining cytoplasm. When monocytes leave the bloodstream and move into tissues, they enlarge and become **macrophages,** which engulf microbes and cellular debris.

3. **Platelets (thrombocytes)** are fragments of huge cells called megakaryocytes. Platelets lack a nucleus and consist of cytoplasm (with few organelles) surrounded by a plasma membrane. Platelets adhere to damaged blood vessel walls and release enzymes that activate **hemostasis,** the stoppage of bleeding.

4. **Plasma** is the straw-colored, liquid portion of the blood. It consists of the following.

- *Water* (90%).

- *Proteins* (8%). **Albumin,** the most common protein, is produced by the liver and serves to preserve osmotic pressure between blood and tissues. Other proteins include alpha and beta globulins (proteins that transport lipids and metal ions), gamma globulins (antibodies), fibrinogen and prothrombin (clotting proteins), and hormones.

- *Waste products* (urea, uric acid, creatinine, bilirubin, and others).

- *Nutrients* (absorbed from the digestive tract).

- *Electrolytes* (various ions such as sodium, calcium, chloride, and bicarbonate).

- *Respiratory gases* (O_2 and CO_2).

Serum is the liquid material remaining after blood clotting proteins have been removed from plasma as a result of clotting.

Blood Formation

Hemopoiesis (hematopoiesis) is the process that produces the formed elements of the blood. Hemopoiesis takes place in the red bone marrow found in the epiphyses of long bones (for example, the humerus and femur), flat bones (ribs and cranial bones), vertebrae, and the pelvis. Within the red bone marrow, **hemopoietic stem cells (hemocytoblasts)** divide to produce various "blast" cells. Each of these cells matures and becomes a particular formed element.

1. **Erythropoiesis,** the process of making erythrocytes, begins with the formation of **proerythroblasts** from hemopoietic stem cells. Over three to five days, several stages of development follow as ribosomes proliferate and hemoglobin is synthesized. Finally, the nucleus is ejected, producing the depression in the center of the cell. Young erythrocytes, called **reticulocytes,** still containing some ribosomes and endoplasmic reticulum, pass into the bloodstream and develop into mature erythrocytes after another one to two days.

Erythropoietin (EPO), a hormone produced mostly by the kidneys, stimulates bone marrow to produce erythrocytes. When inadequate amounts of oxygen are delivered to body cells, a condition called **hypoxia,** the kidneys increase EPO secretion, which, in turn, stimulates an increase in erythrocyte production.

The average production rate of erythrocytes in healthy individuals is two million cells per second. Normal production requires adequate amounts of iron and vitamins B_{12} and folic acid.

2. **Leukopoiesis,** the process of making leukocytes, is stimulated by various **colony-stimulating factors (CSFs),** hormones produced by mature white blood cells. The development of each kind of white blood cell begins with the division of hemopoietic stem cells into one of the following "blast" cells.

   ▪ **Myeloblasts** divide to form **eosinophilic, neutrophilic,** or **basophilic myelocytes,** which lead to the development of the three kinds of granulocytes.

   ▪ **Monoblasts** lead to the development of monocytes.

   ▪ **Lymphoblasts** lead to the development of lymphocytes.

3. **Thrombopoiesis,** the process of making platelets, begins with the formation of **megakaryoblasts** from hemopoietic stem cells. The megakaryoblasts divide without cytokinesis to become **megakaryocytes,** huge cells with a large, multilobed nucleus. The megakaryocytes then fragment into segments as the plasma membrane infolds into the cytoplasm.

Hemostasis

Hemostasis, the stoppage of bleeding, is accomplished through three steps, as follows.

1. A **vascular spasm,** a constriction of the damaged blood vessel, occurs at the site of injury. Vasoconstriction is initiated by the smooth muscle of the blood vessel in response to the injury and by nerve signals from pain receptors.

2. A **platelet plug** consisting of a mass of linked platelets fills the hole in the damaged blood vessel. Platelet plug formation follows these steps.

   ■ *Platelet adhesion.* Platelets adhere to the exposed collagen fibers in the damaged blood vessel wall.

   ■ *Platelet release.* Platelets release ADP (which attracts other platelets to the injury), serotonin (which stimulates vasoconstriction), and thromboxane A_2 (which attracts platelets and stimulates vasoconstriction). Cellular extensions from the platelets interconnect and form a loose mesh.

   ■ *Platelet aggregation.* Additional platelets arrive at the site of injury in response to the released ADP and expand the accumulation of platelets.

3. **Coagulation (blood clotting)** is a complex series of reactions that transform liquid blood into a gel (**clot**) that provides a secure patch to the injured blood vessel. Thirteen **coagulation factors** (numbered I through XIII in order of their discovery) are involved. Most of the factors are proteins released into the blood by the liver. Factor III is Ca^{2+}. Vitamin K is required for the synthesis of some of these factors. The coagulation process can be described in three major steps.

- *Formation of factor X and prothrombinase.* **Prothrombinase (prothrombin activator)** can form either intrinsically (inside the blood vessel) or extrinsically (outside the blood vessel). In the **intrinsic pathway,** the collagen of the damaged blood vessel initiates a cascade of reactions that activates factor X. In the **extrinsic pathway,** damaged tissues release **thromboplastin (tissue factor, TF),** which initiates a shorter and more rapid sequence of reactions to activate factor X. In *both* pathways, activated factor X combines with factor V (with Ca^{2+} present) to form prothrombinase.

- *Prothrombin is converted to thrombin.* In this **common pathway** that follows both the intrinsic and extrinsic pathways, prothrombinase (with Ca^{2+}) converts prothrombin to thrombin.

- *Fibrinogen is converted to fibrin.* The common pathway continues as thrombin (with Ca^{2+}) converts fibrinogen to fibrin. Fibrin forms long strands that bind the platelets together to form a dense web. Thrombin also activates factor XIII, which helps fibrin strands cohere to one another. The result is a clot.

Following its formation, a clot is further strengthened by a process called **clot retraction.** Platelets in the clot contract, pulling on the fibrin strands to which they are attached. The result is a more tightly sealed patch.

Fibrinolysis is the breakdown of the clot as the damaged blood vessel is repaired. During the formation of a clot, the plasma protein **plasminogen** is incorporated into the clot. The healthy endothelial tissue that replaces the damaged areas of the blood vessel secretes **tissue plasminogen activator (t-PA),** which converts plasminogen into its active form, **plasmin (fibrinolysin).** Plasmin, in turn, breaks down fibrin and leads to the dissolution of the clot.

Blood Groups

Various glycoproteins and lipoproteins are embedded in the surfaces of red blood cells. These proteins are inherited, and their structures may vary from one individual to another. If during a transfusion an individual receives blood containing RBCs with proteins that the individual does not carry, then these proteins may be recognized as **antigens** (foreign substances) by the immune system. If so, antibodies are produced that bind to the antigens and cause agglutination (clumping) and subsequent destruction of the foreign RBCs.

There are over 30 common groups of RBC proteins (referred to as antigens, **isoantigens,** or **agglutinogens**). Generally, each group is controlled by a single gene, and for each gene, two **alleles,** or forms, of the gene are inherited (one allele from each parent). Each blood group gene may have two or more different alleles in the population. Although not all blood group proteins stimulate the immune response, two important ones that do are described below.

1. **ABO blood group.** The gene responsible for this group has three alleles. One allele produces an "A" antigen, a second produces a "B" antigen, and a third produces no antigens ("O"). Since individuals inherit two alleles, individuals may be of the A blood type, inheriting two A alleles (*AA*) or an A and an O allele (*AO*), the B blood type (*BB* or *BO*), the AB blood type (*AB*), or the O blood type (*OO*). The immune response is activated when an individual receives a transfusion with blood carrying nonself antigens. For example, the immune system would respond if a person with A blood type (either *AA* or *AO*) receives blood of the B or AB blood types, but not of the O type (the O type does not carry any foreign antigens).

2. **Rh blood group.** This is a complex group defined by antigens produced by three different genes. Each gene has two (or rarely, three) alleles. Because of the close linkage of the genes (they are positioned close to one another on the same chromosome), the expression of the group can be evaluated as if it

were a single gene with two alleles, an Rh^+ allele (producing the Rh antigen) and an Rh^- allele (producing no Rh antigen). Thus, individuals are either Rh^+ if they inherit one or two Rh^+ alleles or Rh^- if they inherit two Rh^- alleles.

Circulatory Pathways

Blood is confined to a closed system of blood vessels and to the four chambers of the heart (essentially dilated vessels). Blood travels *away* from the heart through **arteries,** which branch into smaller vessels, the **arterioles.** Arterioles branch further into the smallest vessels, the **capillaries.** Gas, nutrient, and waste exchange occurs across the capillary walls. The blood *returns* to the heart as capillaries merge to form **venules,** which further merge to form larger **veins,** which connect to the heart. Blood circulates through the following two separate circuits.

1. In the **pulmonary circulation,** deoxygenated blood travels from the right side of the heart to each of the two lungs. Within the lungs, O_2 enters and CO_2 leaves the capillaries by diffusion. Oxygenated blood returns from the lungs to the left side of the heart.

2. In the **systemic circulation,** oxygenated blood travels from the left side of the heart to the various areas of the body. Gas, nutrient, and waste exchange occurs across the capillary walls into the interstitial fluids outside the capillaries and then into the surrounding cells. The deoxygenated blood returns to the right side of the heart.

The Heart

The **heart** is located in the **mediastinum**, the cavity between the lungs. The heart is tilted so that its pointed end, the **apex,** points downward toward the left hip, while the broad end, the **base,** faces upward toward the right shoulder. The heart is surrounded by the **pericardium,** a sac characterized by the following two layers.

1. The outer **fibrous pericardium** anchors the heart to the surrounding structures.

2. The inner **serous pericardium** consists of an outer **parietal layer** and an inner **visceral layer.** A thin layer of serous fluid, the **pericardial fluid,** lies between these two layers to provide a slippery surface for the movements of the heart.

The wall of the heart consists of three layers, as follows.

1. The **epicardium** is the visceral layer of the serous pericardium described above.

2. The **myocardium** is the muscular part of the heart that consists of contracting cardiac muscle and noncontracting Purkinje fibers that conduct nerve impulses.

3. The **endocardium** is the thin, smooth, endothelial, inner lining of the heart, which is continuous with the inner lining of the blood vessels.

As blood travels through the heart, it enters a total of four chambers and passes through four valves. The two upper chambers, the right and left **atria,** are separated longitudinally by the **interatrial septum.** The two lower chambers, the right and left **ventricles,** are the pumping machines of the heart and are separated longitudinally by the **interventricular septum.** A valve follows each chamber and prevents the blood from flowing backward into the chamber from which the blood originated.

Two prominent grooves are visible on the surface of the heart, as follows.

1. The **coronary sulcus (atrioventricular groove)** marks the junction of the atria and ventricles.

2. The **anterior interventricular sulcus** and **posterior interventricular sulcus** mark the junction of the ventricles on the front and back of the heart, respectively.

The pathway of blood through the chambers and valves of the heart is described below (Figure 59).

1. The **right atrium,** located in the upper right side of the heart, and a small appendage, the **right auricle,** act as a temporary storage chamber so that blood will be readily available for the right ventricle. *Deoxygenated* blood from the systemic circulation enters the right atrium through three veins, the **superior vena cava,** the **inferior vena cava,** and the **coronary sinus.** During the interval when the ventricles are not contracting, blood passes down through the **right atrioventricular (AV) valve** into the next chamber, the right ventricle. The AV valve is also called the **tricuspid valve** because it consists of three flexible cusps (flaps).

2. The **right ventricle** is the pumping chamber for the pulmonary circulation. The ventricle, with walls thicker and more muscular than those of the atrium, contracts and pumps deoxygenated blood through the three-cusped **pulmonary semilunar valve** and into a large artery, the **pulmonary trunk.** The pulmonary trunk immediately divides into two **pulmonary arteries,** which lead to the left and right lungs, respectively. The following events occur in the right ventricle.

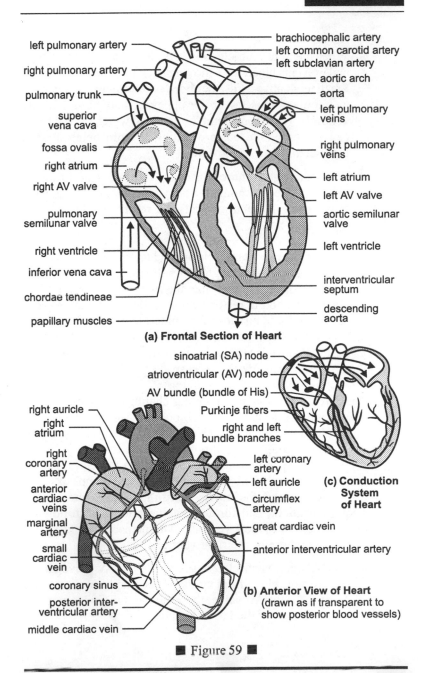

left pulmonary artery

brachiocephalic artery
left common carotid artery
left subclavian artery

right pulmonary artery

aortic arch

pulmonary trunk

aorta

superior vena cava

left pulmonary veins

fossa ovalis

right pulmonary veins

right atrium

right AV valve

left atrium

left AV valve

pulmonary semilunar valve

aortic semilunar valve

right ventricle

left ventricle

inferior vena cava

chordae tendineae

interventricular septum

papillary muscles

descending aorta

(a) Frontal Section of Heart

sinoatrial (SA) node
atrioventricular (AV) node
AV bundle (bundle of His)
Purkinje fibers
right and left bundle branches

right auricle
right atrium

left coronary artery

right coronary artery

left auricle

(c) Conduction System of Heart

anterior cardiac veins

circumflex artery

marginal artery

great cardiac vein

small cardiac vein

anterior interventricular artery

coronary sinus

posterior interventricular artery

(b) Anterior View of Heart
(drawn as if transparent to show posterior blood vessels)

middle cardiac vein

■ Figure 59 ■

- When the right ventricle *contracts,* the right AV valve closes and prevents blood from moving back into the right atrium. Small tendonlike cords, the **chordae tendineae,** are attached to **papillary muscles** at the opposite, bottom side of the ventricle. These cords limit the extent to which the AV valve can be forced closed, preventing it from being pushed through and into the atrium.

- When the right ventricle *relaxes,* the initial backflow of blood in the pulmonary artery closes the pulmonary semilunar valve and prevents the return of blood to the right ventricle.

3. The **left atrium** and its auricle appendage receive oxygenated blood from the lungs through four pulmonary veins (two from each lung). The left atrium, like the right atrium, is a holding chamber for blood in readiness for its flow into the left ventricle. When the ventricles relax, blood leaves the left atrium and passes through the **left AV valve** into the left ventricle. The left AV valve is also called the **mitral** or **bicuspid valve,** the only heart valve with two cusps.

4. The **left ventricle** is the pumping chamber for the systemic circulation. Because a greater blood pressure is required to pump blood through the much more extensive systemic circulation than through the pulmonary circulation, the left ventricle is larger and its walls are thicker than those of the right ventricle. When the left ventricle contracts, it pumps oxygenated blood through the **aortic semilunar valve,** into a large artery, the **aorta,** and throughout the body. The following events occur in the left ventricle, simultaneously and analogously with those of the right ventricle.

   - When the left ventricle *contracts,* the left AV valve closes and prevents blood from moving back into the right atrium. As in the right AV valve, the **chordae tendineae** prevent overextension of the left AV valve.

- When the left ventricle *relaxes,* the initial backflow of blood in the aorta closes the aortic semilunar valve and prevents the return of blood to the left ventricle.

Two additional passageways are present in the fetal heart.

1. The **foramen ovale** is an opening across the interatrial septum. It allows blood to bypass the right ventricle and the pulmonary circuit while the nonfunctional fetal lungs are still developing. The opening, which closes at birth, leaves a shallow depression called the **fossa ovalis** in the adult heart.

2. The **ductus arteriosus** is a connection between the pulmonary trunk and the aorta. Blood that enters the right ventricle is pumped out through the pulmonary trunk. Although some blood enters the pulmonary veins (to provide oxygen and nutrients to the fetal lungs), most of the blood moves directly into the aorta through the ductus arteriosus.

The **coronary circulation** consists of blood vessels that supply oxygen and nutrients to the tissues of the heart. Blood entering the chambers of the heart cannot provide this service because the endocardium is too thick for effective diffusion (and only the left side of the heart contains oxygenated blood). Instead, the following two arteries that arise from the aorta and encircle the heart in the atrioventricular groove provide this function.

1. The **left coronary artery** has the following two branches.

   - The **anterior interventricular artery (left anterior descending,** or **LAD,** artery)
   - The **circumflex artery**

2. The **right coronary artery** has the following two branches.

- The **posterior interventricular artery**
- The **marginal artery**

Blood from the coronary circulation returns to the right atrium by way of an enlarged blood vessel, the **coronary sinus.** Three veins, the **great cardiac vein,** the **middle cardiac vein,** and the **small cardiac vein,** feed the coronary sinus.

Cardiac Conduction

Unlike skeletal muscle fibers (cells), which are independent of one another, cardiac muscle fibers (**contractile muscle fibers**) are linked by **intercalated discs,** areas where the plasma membranes intermesh. (See Figure 27.) Within the intercalated discs, the adjacent cells are *structurally* connected by **desmosomes,** tight seals that weld the plasma membranes together, and *electrically* connected by **gap junctions,** ionic channels that allow the transmission of a depolarization event. As a result, the entire myocardium functions as a single unit with a single contraction of the atria followed by a single contraction of the ventricles.

Action potentials (electrical impulses) in the heart originate in specialized cardiac muscle cells called **autorhythmic cells.** These cells are self-excitable, able to generate an action potential without external stimulation by nerve cells. The autorhythmic cells serve as a **pacemaker** to initiate the cardiac cycle (pumping cycle of the heart) and provide a **conduction system** to coordinate the contraction of muscle cells throughout the heart. The autorhythmic cells are concentrated in the following areas (Figure 59c).

1. The **sinoatrial (SA) node,** located in the upper wall of the right atrium, initiates the cardiac cycle by generating an action potential that spreads through both atria through the gap junctions of the cardiac muscle fibers.

2. The **atrioventricular (AV) node,** located near the lower region of the interatrial septum, receives the action potential generated by the SA node. A slight delay of the electrical transmission occurs here, allowing the atria to fully contract before the action potential is passed on to the ventricles.

3. The **atrioventricular (AV) bundle (bundle of His)** receives the action potential from the AV node and transmits the impulse to the ventricles by way of the **right** and **left bundle branches.** Except for the AV bundle, which provides the only electrical connection, the atria are electrically insulated from the ventricles.

4. The **Purkinje fibers** are large-diameter fibers that conduct the action potential from the interventricular septum, down to the apex, and then upward through the ventricles.

Cardiac Muscle Contraction

The sarcolemma (plasma membrane) of an unstimulated muscle cell is polarized. That is, the inside of the sarcolemma is negatively charged with respect to the outside. The unstimulated state of the muscle cell, called the **resting potential,** is created by the presence of large, negatively charged proteins and nucleic acids inside the cell. A balance between K^+ inside the cell and Na^+ outside the cell contributes to the polarization. During an action potential, the balance of Na^+ and K^+ is upset, so that the cell becomes depolarized. The series of events that occurs during and following an action potential in contractile muscle fibers of the heart is similar to that in skeletal muscle. (See Figure 48.) These events are described below.

1. Rapid **depolarization** occurs when fast-opening Na^+ channels in the sarcolemma open and allow an influx of Na^+ ions into the cardiac muscle cell. The Na^+ channels rapidly close.

2. A **plateau** phase occurs during which Ca^+ enters the cytosol of the muscle cell. Ca^+ enters from the sarcoplasmic reticulum (endoplasmic reticulum) within the cell and also from outside the cell through slow-opening Ca^+ channels in the sarcolemma. Within the cell, Ca^+ binds to troponin, which, in turn, triggers the cross-bridge binding that leads to the sliding of actin filaments past myosin filaments. The sliding of the filaments produces cell contraction. At the same time that the Ca^+ channels open, K^+ channels, which normally leak small amounts of K^+ out of the cell, become more impermeable to K^+ leakage. The combined effects of the prolonged release of Ca^+ and the restricted leakage of K^+ lead to an extended depolarization that appears as a plateau when membrane potential is plotted against time.

3. **Repolarization** occurs as K^+ channels open and K^+ diffuses out of the cell. At the same time, Ca^+ channels close. These events restore the membrane to its original polarization, except that the positions of K^+ and Na^+ on each side of the sarcolemma are reversed.

4. A **refractory period** follows during which concentrations of K^+ and Na^+ are actively restored to their appropriate side of the sarcolemma by Na^+/K^+ pumps. The muscle cell cannot contract again until Na^+ and K^+ are restored to their resting potential state. The refractory period of cardiac muscle is dramatically longer than that of skeletal muscle. This prevents tetanus from occurring and insures that each contraction is followed by enough time to allow the heart chamber to refill with blood before the next contraction.

Electrocardiogram

Electrical currents generated by the heart during the cardiac cycle can be detected on the surface of the body by the electrodes of an **electro-**

cardiograph. A recording of these currents, called an **electrocardiogram** (**ECG** or **EKG**), represents a sum of all of the concurrent action potentials produced by the heart as detected by the 12 electrodes of the electrocardiograph. A single cardiac cycle produces a distinctive wave pattern, where peaks and valleys are indicated by the letters P, Q, R, S, and T (Figure 60a). An interpretation of the major characteristics of the ECG follows.

1. The **P wave** is a small wave that represents the depolarization of the atria. During this wave, the muscles of the atria are contracting.

2. The **QRS complex** is a rapid down-up-down movement. The upward movement produces a tall peak, indicated by R. The QRS complex represents the depolarization of the ventricles.

3. The **T wave** represents the repolarization of the ventricles. Electrical activity generated by the repolarization of the atria is concealed by the QRS complex.

The Cardiac Cycle

The **cardiac cycle** describes all the activities of the heart through one complete heartbeat, that is, through one contraction and relaxation of both the atria and ventricles. A contraction event (of either the atria or ventricles) is referred to as **systole,** and a relaxation event is referred to as **diastole.** The cardiac cycle includes a description of the systolic and diastolic activities of the atria and ventricles, the blood volume and pressure changes within the heart, and the action of the heart valves. A description of each period of the cardiac cycle follows (Figure 60c–60e).

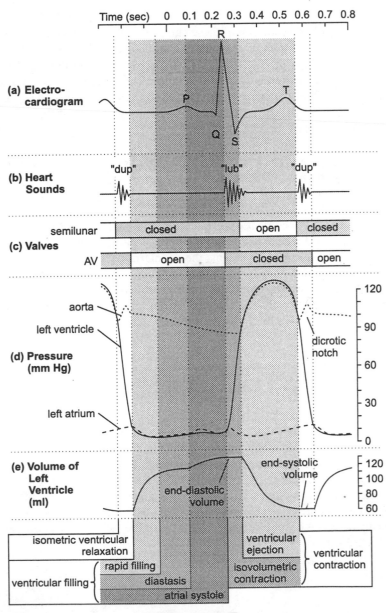

Figure 60

1. The **isovolumetric ventricular relaxation** is the period during which the ventricles are relaxed and both AV and semilunar valves are still closed. The volume of the ventricles remains unchanged (isovolumetric) during this period.

2. **Ventricular filling** begins as the AV valves open and blood fills the ventricles. The ventricles remain in diastole during this period. The filling of the ventricles can be described as three successive events, as follows.

   - **Rapid ventricular filling** occurs as blood flows into the empty and relaxed ventricles. Volume of the ventricles increases rapidly.

   - **Diastasis** is a slower filling event than that of the preceding because most of the volume of the ventricle is already occupied by blood.

   - **Atrial systole** (and the P wave of the ECG) occurs and forces the remaining blood from the atria into the ventricles. The blood volume at the end of this interval is called the **end-diastolic volume (EDV)**.

3. **Ventricular contraction** (ventricular systole) begins as the action potential from the AV node enters the ventricles, the ventricles depolarize, and the QRS complex is observed on the ECG. The following intervals during this phase are observed.

   - **Isovolumetric contraction** occurs when the AV valves are forced shut. During this brief period, while the semilunar valves are still closed, the volume of the ventricles remains unchanged.

   - **Ventricular ejection** occurs as the continuing contraction of the ventricles increases the pressure in the ventricles and forces the semilunar valves open. At this point, blood is forced out of the ventricles. This interval ends when the ventricles begin to relax, the blood in the aorta and pulmonary trunk begin to flow backward, and the semilunar valves, as a result, close. The closing of the semilunar valves causes a small increase in blood pressure visible as the **dicrotic notch** on a plot of blood pressure against time. The amount of blood remaining in the ventricles at this time is called the **end-systolic volume (ESV)**.

The **heart sounds** associated with the beating of the heart can be heard by auscultating (listening to) the thorax with a stethoscope. The two major heart sounds, described as "lub-dup," originate from blood turbulence generated by the closing of the AV valves and the semilunar valves, respectively (Figure 60b). Abnormal heart sounds called **murmurs** are usually caused by improperly functioning valves.

Cardiac Output

The following variables are measures of the capacity of the heart.

1. **Stroke volume (SV)** is the volume of blood ejected by each ventricle during a single contraction. The stroke volumes of the left and right ventricles are normally equal.

2. **Heart rate (HR)** is the number of heartbeats per minute.

3. **Cardiac output (CO)** is the volume of blood pumped out of the right or left ventricle per minute. $CO = SV \times HR$.

Cardiac output varies widely with the health of the individual and the state of activity at the time of measurement. Cardiac output in exercising athletes may exceed their resting cardiac output seven times. The ratio between the maximum and resting cardiac output of an individual is the **cardiac reserve.** Note that cardiac output changes when either stroke volume or heart rate changes.

Stroke volume is regulated by the following three factors.

1. **Preload** is the degree to which cardiac muscle cells are stretched by the blood entering the heart chambers. According to the **Frank-Starling law of the heart,** the more the chamber is stretched, the greater the force of its contraction. Since end-diastole volume (EDV) is a measure of how much blood enters the ventricles, the EDV is an indicator of ventricle preload.

2. **Contractility** is the degree to which cardiac muscle cells contract as a result of *extrinsic* influences. **Positive inotropic factors,** such as certain hormones (epinephrine or thyroxin), drugs (digitalis), or elevated levels of Ca^+, increase contractility, while **negative inotropic factors,** such as certain drugs (calcium channel blockers) or elevated levels of K^+, decrease contractility.

3. **Afterload** is a measure of the pressure that must be generated by the ventricles to force the semilunar valves open. The greater the afterload, the smaller the stroke volume. Arteriosclerosis (narrowing of the arteries) and high blood pressure increase afterload and reduce stroke volume.

Heart rate is regulated by the following three factors.

1. The *autonomous nervous system* may influence heart rate when the sympathetic nervous system stimulates cardiac muscle contractions or when the parasympathetic system inhibits cardiac muscle contractions.

2. *Chemicals* such as hormones and ions can influence heart rate. Epinephrine, secreted by the adrenal medulla, and thyroxin, secreted by the thyroid gland, increase heart rate. Abnormal blood concentrations of Na^+, K^+, and Ca^+ interfere with muscle contraction.

3. *Other factors* may also influence heart rate. These include age, gender, body temperature, and physical fitness.

Blood Vessels

The central opening of a **blood vessel,** the **lumen,** is surrounded by a wall consisting of three layers, as follows.

1. The **tunica intima** is the inner layer facing the blood. It is composed of an innermost layer of endothelium (simple squamous epithelium) surrounded by variable amounts of connective tissues.

2. The **tunica media,** the middle layer, is composed of smooth muscle with variable amounts of elastic fibers.

3. The **tunica adventitia,** the outer layer, is composed of connective tissue.

The cardiovascular system consists of three kinds of blood vessels that form a closed system of passageways.

1. **Arteries** carry blood *away* from the heart. The three kinds of arteries are categorized by size and function, as follows.

   ■ **Elastic arteries (conducting arteries)** are the largest arteries and include the aorta and other nearby branches. The tunica media of elastic arteries contains a large amount of elastic connective tissue, which enables the artery to expand as blood enters the lumen from the contracting heart. During relaxation of the heart, the elastic wall of the artery recoils to its original position, forcing blood forward and smoothing the jerky discharge of blood from the heart.

- **Muscular arteries (conducting arteries)** branch from elastic arteries and distribute blood to the various body regions. Abundant smooth muscle in the thick tunica media allows these arteries to regulate blood flow by **vasoconstriction** (narrowing of the lumen) or **vasodilation** (widening of the lumen). Most named arteries of the body are muscular arteries.

- **Arterioles** are small, nearly microscopic, blood vessels that branch from muscular arteries. Most arterioles have all three tunics present in their walls, with considerable smooth muscle in the tunica media. The smallest arterioles consist of endothelium surrounded by a single layer of smooth muscle. Arterioles regulate the flow of blood into capillaries by vasoconstriction and vasodilation.

2. **Capillaries** are microscopic blood vessels with extremely thin walls. Only the tunica intima is present in these walls, and some walls consist exclusively of a single layer of endothelium. Capillaries penetrate most body tissues with dense interweaving networks called **capillary beds.** The thin walls of capillaries allow the diffusion of oxygen and nutrients out of the capillaries, while allowing carbon dioxide and wastes into the capillaries.

- **Metarterioles (precapillaries)** are the blood vessels between arterioles and venules. Although metarterioles pass through capillary beds with capillaries, they are not true capillaries because metarterioles, like arterioles, have smooth muscle present in the tunica media. The smooth muscle of a metarteriole allows it to act as a shunt to regulate blood flow into the true capillaries that branch from it. The **thoroughfare channel,** the tail end of the metarteriole that connects to the venule, lacks smooth muscle.

- **True capillaries** form the bulk of the capillary bed. They branch away from a metarteriole at its arteriole end and return to merge with the metarteriole at its venule end (thoroughfare channel). Some true capillaries connect directly from an arteriole to a metarteriole or venule. Although the walls of true capillaries lack muscle fibers, they possess a ring of smooth muscle called a **precapillary sphincter** where they emerge from the metarteriole. The precapillary sphincter regulates blood flow through the capillary. There are three types of true capillaries, as follows.

- **Continuous capillaries** have continuous, unbroken walls consisting of cells that are connected by tight junctions. Most capillaries are of this type.

- **Fenestrated capillaries** have continuous walls between endothelial cells, but the cells have numerous pores (fenestrations) that increase their permeability. These capillaries are found in the kidneys, lining the small intestine, and in other areas where a high transfer rate of substances into or out of the capillary is required.

- **Sinusoidal capillaries (sinusoids)** have large gaps between endothelial cells that permit the passage of blood cells. These capillaries are found in the bone marrow, spleen, and liver.

3. **Veins** carry blood *toward* the heart. The three kinds of veins are listed here in the order that they merge to form increasingly larger blood vessels.

- **Postcapillary venules,** the smallest veins, form when capillaries merge as they exit a capillary bed. Much like capillaries, they are very porous but with scattered smooth muscle fibers in the tunica media.

- **Venules** form when postcapillary venules join. Although the walls of larger venules contain all three layers, they are still porous enough to allow white blood cells to pass.

- **Veins** have walls with all three layers, but the tunica intima and tunica media are much thinner than in similarly sized arteries. Few elastic or muscle fibers are present. The wall

consists primarily of a well-developed media adventitia. Many veins, especially those in the limbs, have **valves,** formed from folds of the tunica intima, that prevent the backflow of blood.

Many regions of the body receive blood supplies from two or more arteries. The points where these arteries merge are called **arterial anastomoses.** Arterial anastomoses allow tissues to receive blood even after one of the arteries supplying blood has been blocked.

Blood Pressure

Hydrostatic pressure created by the heart forces blood to move through the arteries. Systolic blood pressure, the pressure measured during contraction of the ventricles, averages about 120 mm Hg in arteries of the systemic circulation (for healthy, young adults). The diastolic blood pressure, measured during ventricle relaxation, is about 80 mm Hg in these arteries. As blood travels through the arterial system, resistance from the walls of the blood vessels reduces the pressure and velocity of the blood (Figure 61). Blood pressure drops sharply in the arterioles, and falls to between 40 and 20 mm Hg in the capillaries. Blood pressure descends further in the venules and approaches zero in the veins.

Because blood pressure is so low in venules and veins, two mechanisms assist the return of blood to the heart (**venous return**), as follows.

1. The **muscular pump** arises from contractions of skeletal muscles surrounding the veins. The contractions squeeze the veins, forcing the blood to move forward, the only direction it can move when valves in the veins close to prevent backflow.

2. The **respiratory pump** is created by the expansion and contraction of the lungs during breathing. During inspiration (inhaling), pressure in the abdominal region increases while

pressure in the thoracic cavity decreases. These pressures act upon the veins passing through these regions. As a result, blood flows toward the heart as it moves from regions of higher pressure (the abdomen) to those of lower pressure (the chest and right atrium). When the pressures are reversed during expiration (exhaling), backflow in the veins is prevented by valves.

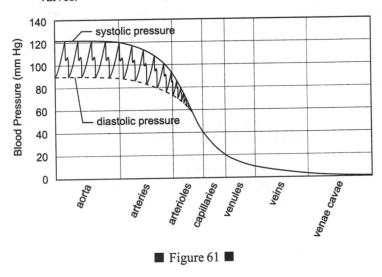

■ Figure 61 ■

Control of Blood Pressure

Changes in blood pressure are routinely made in order to direct appropriate amounts of oxygen and nutrients to specific parts of the body. For example, when exercise demands additional supplies of oxygen to skeletal muscles, blood delivery to the these muscles increases, while blood delivery to the digestive organs decreases. Adjustments in blood pressure are also required when forces are applied to our bodies, such as when starting or stopping in an elevator.

Blood pressure can be adjusted by producing changes in the following variables.

1. *Cardiac output* can be altered by changing stroke volume or heart rate.

2. *Resistance to blood flow* in the blood vessel is most often altered by changing the diameter of the vessel (vasodilation or vasoconstriction). Changes in blood viscosity (its ability to flow) or in the length of the blood vessels (which increases with weight gain) can also alter resistance to blood flow.

The following mechanisms help regulate blood pressure.

1. The **cardiovascular center** provides a *rapid, neural* mechanism for the regulation of blood pressure by managing *cardiac output* or by adjusting *blood vessel diameter.* Located in the medulla oblongata of the brain stem, it consists of three distinct regions, as follows.

   - The **cardiac center** *stimulates* cardiac output by increasing heart rate and contractility. These nerve impulses are transmitted over sympathetic cardiac nerves.

   - The **cardiac center** *inhibits* cardiac output by decreasing heart rate. These nerve impulses are transmitted over parasympathetic vagus nerves.

   - The **vasomotor center** regulates blood vessel diameter. Nerve impulses transmitted over sympathetic motor neurons called **vasomotor nerves** enervate smooth muscles in arterioles throughout the body to maintain **vasomotor tone,** a steady state of vasoconstriction appropriate to the region.

The cardiovascular center receives information about the state of the body through the following sources.

- **Baroreceptors** are sensory neurons that monitor arterial blood pressure. Major baroreceptors are located in the **carotid sinus** (an enlarged area of the carotid artery just above its separation from the aorta), the aortic arch, and the right atrium.

- **Chemoreceptors** are sensory neurons that monitor levels of CO_2, O_2, and H^+ (*pH*). These neurons alert the cardiovascular center when levels of O_2 drop or levels of CO_2 and H^+ rise. Chemoreceptors are found in **carotid bodies** and **aortic bodies** located near the carotid sinus and aortic arch.

- Higher brain regions, such as the cerebral cortex, hypothalamus, and limbic system, signal the cardiovascular center when conditions (stress, fight-or-flight response, hot or cold temperatures) require adjustments to the blood pressure.

2. The kidneys provide a *hormonal* mechanism for the regulation of blood pressure by managing *blood volume*.

- The **renin-angiotensin-aldosterone** system of the kidneys regulates blood volume. In response to rising blood pressure, the juxtaglomerular cells in the kidneys secrete renin into the blood. Renin converts the plasma protein angiotensinogen to angiotensin I, which, in turn, is converted to angiotensin II by the lungs. Angiotensin II activates two mechanisms that raise blood pressure.

  Angiotensin II constricts blood vessels throughout the body (raising blood pressure by increasing resistance to blood flow). Constricted blood vessels reduce the amount of blood delivered to the kidneys, which decreases the kidneys' potential to excrete water (raising blood pressure by increasing blood volume).

  Angiotensin II stimulates the adrenal cortex to secrete **aldosterone,** a hormone that reduces urine output by increasing retention of H_2O by the kidneys (increasing blood pressure by increasing blood volume).

3. Various substances influence blood pressure. Some important examples follow.

- **Epinephrine** and **norepinephrine**, hormones secreted by the adrenal medulla, increase blood pressure by increasing heart rate and the contractility of the heart muscles and by causing vasoconstriction of arteries and veins. These hormones are secreted as part of the fight-or-flight response.

- **Antidiuretic hormone (ADH)**, a hormone secreted by the hypothalamus, increases blood pressure by stimulating the kidneys to retain H_2O (increasing blood pressure by increasing blood volume).

- **Atrial natriuretic (ANP)**, a hormone secreted by the atria of the heart, decreases blood pressure by causing vasodilation and by stimulating the kidneys to excrete more water (decreasing blood pressure by reducing blood volume).

- **Nitric oxide (NO)**, secreted by endothelial cells, causes vasodilation.

- **Nicotine** in tobacco increases blood pressure by stimulating sympathetic neurons to increase vasoconstriction and by stimulating the adrenal medulla to increase secretion of epinephrine and norepinephrine.

- **Alcohol** decreases blood pressure by inhibiting the vasomotor center (causing vasodilation) and by inhibiting the release of ADH (increasing H_2O output, which decreases blood volume).

Blood Vessels of the Body

Figures 62 and 63 show the major arteries and veins of the body.

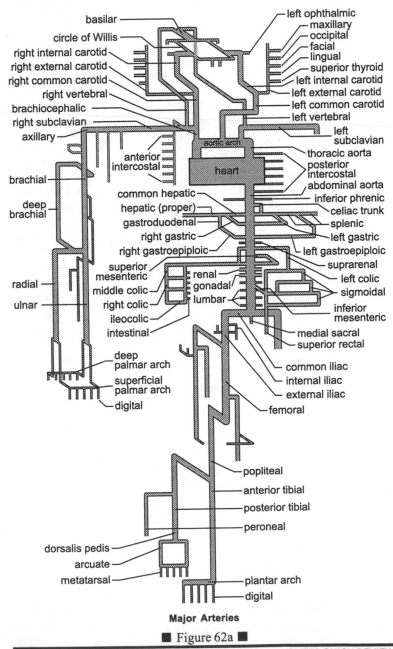

Major Arteries

■ Figure 62a ■

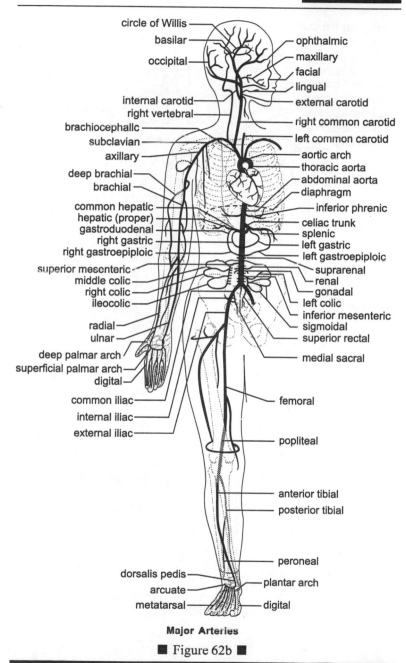

circle of Willis
basilar
occipital
ophthalmic
maxillary
facial
lingual
internal carotid
right vertebral
external carotid
brachiocephalic
subclavian
axillary
right common carotid
left common carotid
aortic arch
thoracic aorta
abdominal aorta
diaphragm
deep brachial
brachial
common hepatic
hepatic (proper)
gastroduodenal
right gastric
right gastroepiploic
inferior phrenic
celiac trunk
splenic
left gastric
left gastroepiploic
superior mesenteric
middle colic
right colic
ileocolic
suprarenal
renal
gonadal
left colic
inferior mesenteric
sigmoidal
superior rectal
radial
ulnar
deep palmar arch
superficial palmar arch
digital
medial sacral
common iliac
internal iliac
external iliac
femoral
popliteal
anterior tibial
posterior tibial
peroneal
dorsalis pedis
arcuate
metatarsal
plantar arch
digital

Major Arteries

■ Figure 62b ■

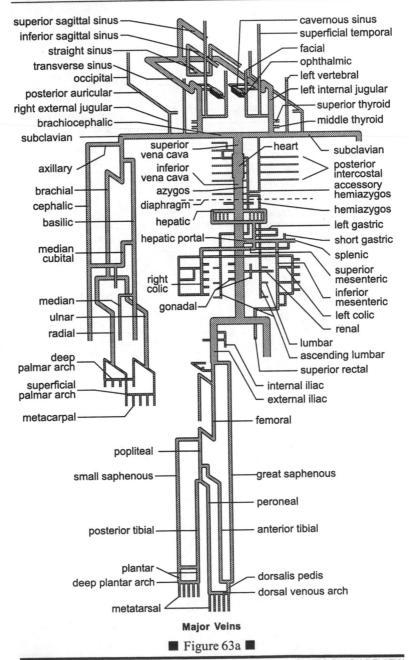

superior sagittal sinus — cavernous sinus
inferior sagittal sinus — superficial temporal
straight sinus — facial
transverse sinus — ophthalmic
occipital — left vertebral
posterior auricular — left internal jugular
right external jugular — superior thyroid
brachiocephalic — middle thyroid
subclavian — subclavian
axillary — superior vena cava — heart — posterior intercostal
brachial — inferior vena cava — accessory hemiazygos
cephalic — azygos — hemiazygos
basilic — diaphragm — left gastric
hepatic — short gastric
median cubital — hepatic portal — splenic
right colic — superior mesenteric
median — gonadal — inferior mesenteric
ulnar — left colic
radial — renal
deep palmar arch — lumbar
superficial palmar arch — ascending lumbar
— superior rectal
metacarpal — internal iliac
— external iliac
— femoral
popliteal
small saphenous — great saphenous
— peroneal
posterior tibial — anterior tibial
plantar — dorsalis pedis
deep plantar arch — dorsal venous arch
metatarsal —

Major Veins

■ Figure 63a ■

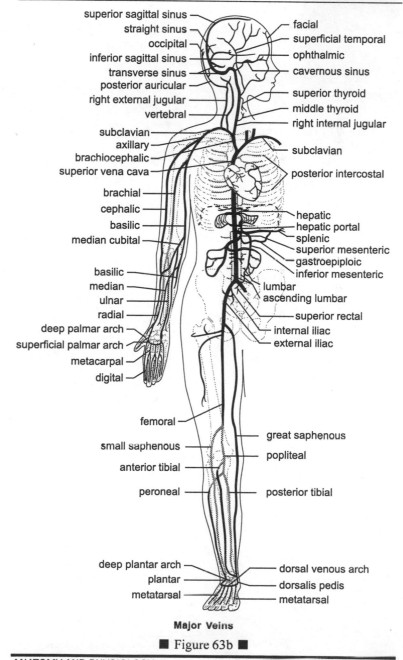

Major Veins

■ Figure 63b ■

The **lymphatic system** consists of lymphatic vessels, a fluid called **lymph, lymph nodes,** the **thymus,** and the **spleen.** This system supplements and extends the cardiovascular system in the following ways.

1. *The lymphatic system collects excess fluids and plasma proteins from surrounding tissues (interstitial fluids) and returns them to the blood circulation.* Because lymphatic capillaries are more porous than blood capillaries, they are able to collect fluids, plasma proteins, and blood cells that have escaped from the blood. Within lymphatic vessels, this collected material forms a usually colorless fluid called **lymph** which is transported to the neck, where it empties into the circulatory system.

2. *The lymphatic system absorbs lipids and fat-soluble materials from the digestive tract.*

3. *The lymphatic system filters the lymph by destroying pathogens, inactivating toxins, and removing particulate matter.* Lymph nodes, small bodies interspersed along lymphatic vessels, act as cleaning filters and as immune response centers that defend against infection.

The movement of lymph through lymphatic vessels is slow (3 liters/day) compared to blood flow (about 5 liters/minute). Lymph does not circulate like blood, but moves in one direction from its collection in tissues to its return to the blood. There are no lymphatic pumps. Instead, lymph, much like blood in veins, is propelled forward by the action of nearby skeletal muscles, the expansion and contraction of the lungs, and the contraction of smooth muscle fibers in the walls of the lymphatic vessels. Valves in the lymphatic vessels prevent the backward movement of lymph.

Lymphatic Vessels

Lymphatic vessels occur throughout the body alongside arteries (in the viscera) or veins (in the subcutaneous tissue). They are absent from the central nervous system, bone marrow, teeth, and avascular tissues.

1. **Lymph capillaries,** the smallest lymphatic vessels, begin as dead-end vessels. They resemble blood capillaries but are much more porous to surrounding fluids due to the following two features.

   - *Valvelike openings form at the juncture of adjacent endothelial cells.* Unlike the tightly joined endothelial cells that make up the walls of blood capillaries, those of lymph capillaries loosely overlap. When fluid pressure increases in surrounding regions, the overlapped cells separate, allowing fluids to enter the lymph capillary. When pressure inside the capillary exceeds the pressure outside, the spaces between the endothelial cells close, holding fluids inside the capillary.

   - *Anchoring filaments attach the endothelial cells of the lymphatic vessels to surrounding collagen.* When interstitial fluid pressure increases, the anchoring filaments prevent the endothelial cells from collapsing, keeping the spaces between the endothelial cells open.

2. **Lacteals** are specialized lymph capillaries that occur in the fingerlike projections (villi) that extend into the small intestine. Lacteals absorb lipids from the intestinal tract. The lymph within these capillaries, called **chyle,** has a creamy white color (rather than clear) due to the presence of fats.

3. **Lymphatic collecting vessels** form as lymph capillaries merge. Collecting vessels have the following characteristics.

- Valves are present to prevent the backward flow of lymph (as in veins).

- The walls of collecting vessels consist of the same three tunics (layers) that characterize veins, but the layers are thinner and poorly defined.

4. **Lymphatic trunks** form from the union of collecting vessels. The nine major trunks, draining lymph from regions for which they are named, are the **lumbar, jugular, subclavian,** and **bronchomediastinal trunks,** each of which occurs in pairs (left and right, for each side of the body), and a single **intestinal trunk.**

5. **Lymphatic ducts** are the largest lymphatic vessels. These two ducts drain lymph into veins in the neck (the right and left subclavian veins at their junctures with the internal jugular veins). Valves in the lymphatic ducts at their juncture with the veins prevent the entrance of blood into the lymphatic vessels.

- The **thoracic duct (left thoracic duct)** collects lymph from the left side of the body and regions of the right side of the body below the thorax. It begins at the **cisterna chyli,** an enlarged region of the lymphatic vessel that forms following the union of the intestinal trunk and right and left lumbar trunks.

- The **right thoracic duct** collects lymph from the upper right side of the body (right arm and right regions of thorax, neck, and head), a much smaller area than that serviced by the thoracic duct.

Lymphoid Cells

Lymphatic (lymphoid) tissue is a kind of connective tissue. It consists of the following types of cells.

1. **Lymphocytes** are white blood cells (**leukocytes**) that provide an immune response that attacks specific kinds of nonself cells and foreign substances (**antigens**). There are two major classes of lymphocytes, as follows.

   - **T cells (T lymphocytes)** originate in the *bone marrow* but mature in the *thymus gland*. T cells attack self cells that have been invaded by pathogens, abnormal self cells (such as cancerous cells), or nonself cells (such as those that might be introduced in an organ transplant).

   - **B cells (B lymphocytes)** originate *and* mature in the *bone marrow.* When B cells encounter an antigen (a toxin, virus, or bacterium), they produce **plasma cells** and **memory cells.** Plasma cells release antibodies that bind to the antigen and inactivate it. Memory cells circulate in the lymph and blood with the capacity to produce additional antigens for future encounters with the same antigen.

2. **Macrophages** are enlarged monocytes (white blood cells) that engulf microbes and cellular debris.

3. **Reticular cells** and their **reticular fibers** made from collagen and glycoproteins provide a network within which the lymphocytes and other cells reside.

Lymphatic Tissues and Organs

Lymphatic cells are organized into tissues and organs based upon how tightly the lymphatic cells are arranged and whether or not the tissue is encapsulated by a layer of connective tissue. Three general categories are described below.

1. *Diffuse, unencapsulated bundles of lymphatic cells.* This kind of lymphatic tissue consists of lymphocytes and macrophages associated with a reticular fiber network. It occurs in the lamina

propria (middle layer) of the mucus membranes (mucosae) that line the respiratory and gastrointestinal tracts.

2. *Discrete, unencapsulated bundles of lymphatic cells, called lymphatic **nodules** (**follicles**).* These bundles have clear boundaries that separate them from neighboring cells. Nodules occur within the lamina propria of the mucus membranes that line the gastrointestinal, respiratory, reproductive, and urinary tracts. They are referred to as **mucosa-associated lymphoid tissue (MALT)**. The nodules contain lymphocytes and macrophages that protect against bacteria and other pathogens that may enter these passages with food, air, or urine. Nodules occur as **solitary nodules** or they cluster as **patches** or **aggregates.** Major clusters of nodules are described below.

- **Peyer's patches** are clusters of lymphatic nodules that occur in the mucosa that lines the ileum of the small intestine.

- The **tonsils** are aggregates of lymphatic nodules that occur in the mucosa that lines the pharynx (throat). Each of seven tonsils that form a ring around the pharynx are named for their specific region: A single **pharyngeal tonsil** (**adenoid**) in the rear wall of the nasopharynx, two **palatine tonsils** on each side of the oral cavity at its entrance to the throat, two **lingual tonsils** at the base of the tongue, and two small **tubal tonsils** in the pharynx at the entrance to the auditory tubes.

- The **appendix,** a small, fingerlike attachment to the beginning of the large intestine, is lined with aggregates of nodules.

3. *Encapsulated organs contain lymphatic nodules and diffuse lymphatic cells surrounded by a capsule of dense connective tissue.* The following three lymphatic organs are discussed below in detail.

- **lymph nodes**
- **thymus**
- **spleen**

Lymph Nodes

Lymph nodes are small, oval or bean-shaped bodies that occur along lymphatic vessels. They are abundant where lymphatic vessels merge to form trunks, especially in the inguinal (groin), axillary (armpit), and mammary gland areas. Lymph flows into a node through **afferent lymphatic vessels** that enter the convex side of a node. It exits the node at the **hilus,** the indented region on the opposite, concave side of the node, through **efferent lymphatic vessels.** Efferent vessels contain valves that restrict lymph to movement in one direction out of the lymph node. The number of efferent vessels leaving the lymph node is fewer than the number of afferent vessels entering, slowing the flow of lymph through the node.

Lymph nodes perform three functions.

1. *They filter the lymph, preventing the spread of microorganisms and toxins that enter interstitial fluids.*

2. *They destroy bacteria, toxins, and particulate matter through the phagocytic action of macrophages.*

3. *They produce antibodies through the activity of B cells.*

The structure of a lymph node is characterized by the following features.

1. A **capsule** of dense connective tissue surrounds the lymph node.

2. **Trabeculae** are projections of the capsule that extend into the node forming compartments. The trabeculae support reticular fibers that form a network that supports lymphocytes.

3. The **cortex** is the dense, outer region of the node. It contains lymphatic nodules where B cells and macrophages proliferate.

4. The **medulla** is the center of the node. Less dense than the surrounding cortex, the medulla primarily contains T cells.

5. **Medullary cords** are strands of reticular fibers with lymphocytes and macrophages that extend from the cortex toward the hilus.

6. **Sinuses** are passageways through the cortex and medulla through which lymph moves toward the hilus.

Thymus

The **thymus** is a bilobed organ located in the upper chest region between the lungs. It grows during childhood and reaches its maximum size of 40 g at puberty. It then slowly decreases in size as it is replaced by adipose and areolar connective tissue. By age 65, it weighs about 6 g.

Each lobe of the thymus is surrounded by a capsule of connective tissue. Lobules produced by trabeculae (inward extensions of the capsule) are characterized by an outer cortex and inner medulla. The following cells are present.

- **Lymphocytes** consist almost entirely of T cells.

- **Epithelial-reticular cells** resemble reticular cells, but do not form reticular fibers. Instead, these star-shaped cells form a reticular network by interlocking their slender cellular processes (extensions). These processes are held together by desmosomes, cell junctions formed by protein fibers.

Epithelial-reticular cells produce thymosin and other hormones believed to promote the maturation of T cells.

- **Thymic (Hassall's) corpuscles** are dense, concentric layers of epithelial-reticular cells. Their function is unknown.

The function of the thymus is to promote the maturation of T lymphocytes. Immature T cells migrate through the blood from the red bone marrow to the thymus. Within the thymus, the immature T cells concentrate in the cortex where they continue their development. Mature T cells leave the thymus by way of blood vessels or efferent lymphatic vessels, migrating to other lymphatic tissues and organs where they become active (immunocompetent) in immune responses. The thymus does not provide a filtering function similar to lymph nodes (there are no afferent lymphatic vessels leading into the thymus), and unlike all other centers of lymphatic tissues, the thymus does not play a direct role in immune responses.

Blood vessels that permeate the thymus are surrounded by epithelial-reticular cells. These cells establish a protective **blood-thymus barrier** that prevents the entrance of antigens from the blood and into the thymus where T cells are maturing. Thus, an antigen-free environment is maintained for the development of T cells.

Spleen

Measuring about 12 cm (5 in) in length, the **spleen** is the largest lymphatic organ. It is located on the left side of the body between the diaphragm and stomach. Like other lymphatic organs, the spleen is surrounded by a capsule whose extensions into the spleen form trabeculae. The splenic artery, splenic vein, nerves, and efferent lymphatic vessels pass through the hilus of the thymus located on its slightly concave, upper surface. There are two distinct areas within the spleen.

1. **White pulp** consists of reticular fibers and lymphocytes in nodules that resemble the nodules of lymph nodes.

2. **Red pulp** consists of venous sinuses filled with blood. **Splenic cords** consisting of reticular connective tissue, macrophages, and lymphocytes form a mesh between the venous sinuses and act as a filter as blood passes between arterial vessels and the sinuses.

The functions of the spleen include the following.

1. *The spleen filters the blood.* Macrophages in the spleen remove bacteria and other pathogens, cellular debris, and aged blood cells. There are no afferent lymphatic vessels and, unlike lymph nodes, the spleen does not filter *lymph*.

2. *The spleen destroys old red blood cells and recycles their parts.* It removes the iron from heme groups and binds the iron to the storage protein ferritin.

3. *The spleen provides a reservoir of blood.* The diffuse nature of the red pulp retains large quantities of blood which can be directed to the circulation when necessary. One third of the blood platelets are stored in the spleen.

4. *The spleen is active in immune responses.* T cells proliferate in the white pulp before returning to the blood to attack nonself cells. B cells proliferate in the white pulp, producing plasma cells and antibodies that return to the blood to inactivate antigens.

5. *The spleen produces blood cells.* Red and white blood cells are produced in the spleen during fetal development.

The internal environment of the human body provides attractive conditions for the growth of bacteria, viruses, and other organisms. Although some of these organisms can live symbiotically within humans, many either cause destruction of cells or produce toxic chemicals. To protect against these foreign invaders, three lines of defense are employed—nonspecific barriers that deter the entrance of invaders and both nonspecific and specific defenses against invaders inside the body. A *nonspecific* defense is a rapid response to a wide range of pathogens. A *specific* defense, delivered by the **immune system,** takes several days to mount and targets specific invaders that escape the attack of the nonspecific defense.

Nonspecific Barriers

The **skin** and **mucous membranes** provide a *nonspecific first line of defense* against invaders entering through the skin or through openings into the body. The first line of defense features the following mechanisms.

1. **Skin** is a physical and hostile barrier covered with oily and acidic (*p*H from 3 to 5) secretions from sebaceous and sweat glands, respectively.

2. **Antimicrobial proteins** (such as **lysozyme,** which breaks down the cell walls of bacteria) are contained in saliva, tears, and other secretions found on mucous membranes.

3. **Cilia** that line the lungs serve to sweep invaders out of the lungs.

4. **Gastric juice** of the stomach, by the action of hydrochloric acid or enzymes, kills most microbes.

5. **Symbiotic bacteria** found in the digestive tract and the vagina outcompete many other organisms that could cause damage.

Nonspecific Defenses

The *second line of defense* consists of mechanisms or agents that indiscriminately challenge foreign invaders that are inside the body.

1. **Phagocytes** are white blood cells (leukocytes) that engulf pathogens by phagocytosis. They include **neutrophils, monocytes,** and **eosinophils.** Monocytes enlarge into large phagocytic cells called **macrophages.**

2. **Natural killer cells** (**NK** cells) are lymphocytes (white blood cells that mature in lymphoid tissues). NK cells kill pathogen-infected body cells or abnormal body cells (such as tumors).

3. **Complement** is a group of about 20 proteins that "complement" defense reactions. These proteins help attract phagocytes to foreign cells and help destroy foreign cells by promoting cell lysis (breaking open the cell).

4. **Interferons (IFNs)** are substances secreted by cells invaded by viruses and that stimulate neighboring cells to produce proteins that help them defend against the viruses. Certain IFNs (such as gamma-IFN) also amplify the activity of macrophages and natural killer cells.

5. The **inflammatory response** is a series of nonspecific events that occur in response to pathogens. The response typically produces *redness*, *swelling*, *heat*, and *pain* in the target area, and often the area is *disabled*. When skin is damaged, for example, and bacteria, other organisms, or toxic substances enter the body, the following events occur.

- A *chemical alarm* is generated in the injured area. Injured cells and nearby circulating cells release chemicals that initiate defensive actions and sound an alarm to other defense mechanisms. These chemicals include **histamine** (mostly secreted by **basophils,** white blood cells found in connective tissue), **kinins, prostaglandins (PGs)**, and complement.

- **Vasodilation** (dilation of blood vessels), stimulated by histamine and other chemicals, increases blood supply to the damaged area. This causes redness and an increase in local temperature. The increase in temperature stimulates white blood cells and makes the environment inhospitable to pathogens.

- **Vascular permeability** increases in response to alarm chemicals. As a result, white blood cells, clotting factors, and body fluids move more quickly through blood vessel walls and into the injured area. The increase in body fluids that results causes local edema (swelling). Edema may produce pain if nearby nerve endings experience pressure. Pain may also occur when nerve endings are exposed to bacterial toxins, kinins, and prostaglandins. (Aspirin reduces pain by inhibiting the production of prostaglandins.)

- **Phagocytes** arrive at the site of injury and engulf pathogens and damaged cells. Phagocytes find the site of injury by **chemotaxis,** the movement of cells in response to chemical gradients (provided here by alarm chemicals).

- **Complement** helps phagocytes engulf foreign cells, stimulates basophils to release histamine, and helps lyse foreign cells.

6. **Fever** is a total body response to infection characterized by elevated body temperature. An elevated temperature increases cellular metabolism (accelerating cellular repair), amplifies the effect of alarm chemicals, and creates a hostile environment for bacteria. An excessively high fever may cause the

breakdown of enzymes necessary for cellular metabolism, and death may result.

The Immune System

The **immune system** is the *third line of defense*. It consists of mechanisms and agents that target *specific* **antigens (Ags)**. An antigen is any molecule, usually a protein or polysaccharide, that can be identified as foreign or nonself. It may be a toxin (injected into the blood by the sting of an insect, for example), a part of the protein coat of a virus, or a molecule unique to the plasma membranes of bacteria, protozoa, pollen, or other foreign cells. Once the antigen is recognized, an agent is released that targets the specific antigen. In the process of mounting a successful defense, the immune system accomplishes five tasks, as follows.

1. *Recognition.* The antigen or cell is recognized as nonself. To differentiate self from nonself, unique molecules on the plasma membrane of cells called the **major histocompatibility complex (MHC)** are used as a means of identification.

2. *Lymphocyte selection.* The primary defending cells of the immune system are certain white blood cells called **lymphocytes.** The immune system potentially possesses billions of lymphocytes, each equipped to target a different antigen. When an antigen, or nonself cell, binds to a lymphocyte, the lymphocyte proliferates, producing numerous daughter cells, all identical copies of the parent cell. This process is called **clonal selection** because the lymphocyte to which the antigen effectively binds is "selected" and subsequently reproduces to make clones, or identical copies, of itself.

3. *Lymphocyte activation.* The binding of an antigen or foreign cell to a lymphocyte may activate the lymphocyte and initiate proliferation. In most cases, however, a costimulator is re-

quired before proliferation begins. Costimulators may be chemicals or other cells.

4. *Destruction of the foreign substance.* Lymphocytes and antibodies destroy or immobilize the foreign substance. Nonspecific defense mechanisms (phagocytes, NK cells) help eliminate the invader.

5. *Memorization.* Long-lived "memory" lymphocytes are produced that can quickly recognize and respond to future exposures to the antigen or foreign cell.

Major Histocompatibility Complex

The **major histocompatibility complex (MHC)** (also called **human leukocyte antigens, HLAs**) is the mechanism by which the immune system is able to differentiate between self and nonself cells. The MHC is a collection of glycoproteins (proteins with a carbohydrate) that exists on the plasma membranes of nearly all body cells. The proteins of a single individual are unique, originating from twenty genes, with more than 50 variations per gene between individuals. Thus, it is extremely unlikely that two people, except for identical twins, will possess cells with the same set of MHC molecules.

The immune system is able to identify nonself cells by aberrations in the MHC displayed on the plasma membrane. There are two groups of MHC molecules and each group generates different markings on the plasma membrane, as follows.

- **MHC-I** glycoproteins are produced by all body cells (except red blood cells). When a cell becomes cancerous or is invaded by a virus, unfamiliar proteins are synthesized in the cell. These proteins are **endogenous antigens,** that is, antigens produced inside the cell. Portions of these antigens are combined with MHC-I glycoproteins and, when displayed on the plasma membrane, indicate a nonself cell.

- **MHC-II** glycoproteins are produced only by **antigen-pre-senting cells (APCs)**—mostly macrophages and B cells. APCs actively ingest **exogenous antigens,** antigens that originate outside the cell. Exogenous antigens include viruses, toxins, pollen, or bacteria that are circulating in the blood, lymph, or body fluids. APCs break down the antigens and incorporate pieces of them with MHC-II proteins. This aberrant display of MHC markers is recognized as nonself.

Lymphocytes

The primary agents of the immune response are **lymphocytes,** white blood cells (leukocytes) that originate in the bone marrow (like all blood cells) but concentrate in lymphoid tissues such as the lymph nodes, the thymus gland, and the spleen. When lymphocytes mature, they become **immunocompetent,** or capable of binding with a specific antigen. An immunocompetent lymphocyte displays unique proteins on its plasma membrane that act as **antigen receptors** capable of binding to a specific antigen. Because all of the antigen receptors of an individual lymphocyte are identical, only a specific antigen can bind to an individual lymphocyte. The kind of antigen receptors displayed by a particular lymphocyte is determined by **somatic recombination,** a shuffling of gene segments during lymphocyte maturation. By mixing gene segments, more than one billion different antigen receptors can be generated.

The various kinds of lymphocytes are described below.

1. **B cells (B lymphocytes)** are lymphocytes that originate *and* mature in the *bone marrow*. The antigen receptors of B cells bind to *freely circulating antigens*. When B cells encounter antigens that bind to their antigen binding sites, the B cells proliferate, producing two kinds of daughter cells, plasma cells and memory cells.

- **Plasma cells** are daughter cells of B cells. Each plasma cell releases **antibodies,** proteins that have the same antigen binding capability as the antigen receptors of its parent B cell. Antibodies circulate through the body binding to the specific antigens that stimulated the proliferation of plasma cells.

- **Memory B cells** are long-lived daughter cells of B cells that, like plasma cells, produce antibodies. However, memory cells do not release their antibodies in response to the immediate antigen invasion. Instead, the memory cells circulate in the body and respond quickly to eliminate any *subsequent* invasion by the same antigen. This mechanism provides immunity to many diseases after the first occurrence of the disease.

2. **T cells (T lymphocytes)** are lymphocytes that originate in the bone marrow, but mature in the *thymus gland.* The antigen receptors of T cells bind to *self cells that display foreign antigens (with MHC proteins) on their plasma membrane.* When T cells bind to these aberrant self cells, they divide and produce the following kinds of daughter cells.

   - **Cytotoxic T cells (killer T cells)** are **activated** when they recognize antigens that are mixed with the *MHC-I* proteins of self cells. Following activation, cytotoxic cells proliferate and destroy the recognized cells by producing toxins that puncture them, thus causing them to lyse.

   - **Helper T cells** are activated when they recognize antigens that are mixed with the *MHC-II* proteins of self cells. Proliferation produces helper T cells that intensify antibody production of B cells. Helper T cells also secrete hormones called cytokines that stimulate the proliferation of B cells and T cells.

   - **Suppressor T cells** are believed to be involved in winding down a successful immune response and in preventing the attack of uninfected self cells.

- **Memory T cells** are long-lived cells possessing the same antigen receptors as their parent T cell. Like memory B cells, they provide a rapid defense to any *subsequent* invasion by the same antigen.

Antibodies

Antibodies are proteins that bind to specific antigens. B cells, located in lymphoid tissue, release the antibodies, which then circulate in the blood plasma, lymph, or extracellular fluids. Some antibodies migrate to other areas of the body, such as the respiratory tract or the placenta, or enter various body secretions, such as saliva, sweat, and milk. Additional properties of antibodies include the following.

- There are five classes of antibodies (or **immunoglobulins**): IgA, IgD, IgE, IgG, and IgM. Antibodies circulating in the blood are primarily IgG, IgA, and IgM. IgD and a second form of IgM antibodies are found on the plasma membranes of B cells where they act as antigen receptors. IgE antibodies attach to basophils and mast cells (both white blood cells found in connective tissue) and induce them to secrete histamine.

- The basic structure of an antibody is a Y-shaped protein that consists of constant and variable regions. The variable regions are sequences of amino acids that differ among antibodies and give them specificity to antigens.

- Antibodies inactivate antigens by binding to them and forming an **antigen-antibody complex.** Inactivation is followed by macrophage phagocytosis or lysis brought about by complement proteins. Inactivation may also cause **agglutination** (clumping) of antigens or foreign cells.

Costimulation

In some immune responses, a B cell or T cell becomes activated when an antigen or nonself cell binds to it. Activation then initiates proliferation. In most immune responses, however, activation requires the presence of a **costimulator.** That two signals, an antigen and a costimulator, are required to initiate the immune response insures that healthy self cells are not destroyed. Costimulation may occur in two ways, as follows.

1. *Cytokines, released by helper T cells and APCs, act as costimulators.* Cytokines are protein hormones that influence cell growth. When a helper T cell becomes activated or an APC engulfs an antigen, the helper T cell or APC secretes a cytokine called **interleukin.**

2. *Helper T cells and APCs act as costimulators.* Activated T cells or APCs that display antigens activate B cells or T cells when they temporarily bind to them.

Humoral and Cell-Mediated Immune Responses

The immune system distinguishes two groups of foreign substances. One group consists of antigens that are freely circulating in the body. These include molecules, viruses, and foreign cells. A second group consists of self cells that display aberrant MHC proteins. Aberrant MHC proteins can originate from antigens that have been engulfed and broken down (exogenous antigens) or from virus-infected and tumor cells that are actively synthesizing foreign proteins (endogenous antigens). Depending upon the kind of foreign invasion, two different immune responses occur, as follows.

1. The **humoral response** (or **antibody-mediated response**) involves *B cells that recognize antigens or pathogens that are circulating in the lymph or blood* ("humor" is a medieval term for body fluid). The response follows the following chain of events.

   - *Antigens bind to B cells.*

   - *Interleukins or helper T cells costimulate B cells.* In most cases both an antigen and a costimulator are required to activate a B cell and initiate B cell proliferation.

   - *B cells proliferate and produce plasma cells.* The plasma cells bear antibodies with the identical antigen specificity as the antigen receptors of the activated B cells. The antibodies are released and circulate through the body, binding to antigens.

   - *B cells produce memory cells.* Memory cells provide future immunity.

2. The **cell-mediated response** involves mostly *T cells* and responds to *any cell that displays aberrant MHC markers,* including cells invaded by pathogens, tumor cells, or transplanted cells. The following chain of events describes this immune response.

   - *Self cells or APCs displaying foreign antigens bind to T cells.*

   - *Interleukins (secreted by APCs or helper T cells) costimulate activation of T cells.*

   - *If MHC-I and endogenous antigens are displayed on the plasma membrane, T cells proliferate, producing cytotoxic T cells.* Cytotoxic T cells destroy cells displaying the antigens.

   - *If MHC-II and exogenous antigens are displayed on the plasma membrane, T cells proliferate, producing helper T cells.* Helper T cells release interleukins (and other cytokines) which stimulate B cells to produce antibodies that bind to the antigens and stimulate nonspecific agents (NK and macrophages) to destroy the antigens.

Supplements to the Immune Response

Three important agents are used in medicine to supplement the immune response, as follows.

1. **Antibiotics** are chemicals derived from bacteria or fungi that are harmful to other microorganisms.

2. **Vaccines** are substances that stimulate the production of memory cells. Inactivated viruses or fragments of viruses, bacteria, or other microorganisms are used as vaccines. Once memory cells are formed, the introduction of the live microorganism will stimulate a swift response by the immune system before any disease can become established.

3. **Passive immunity** is obtained by transferring antibodies from an individual who previously had a disease to a newly infected individual. Newborn infants are protected by passive immunity through the transfer of antibodies across the placenta and by antibodies in breast milk.

The function of the **respiratory system** is to deliver air to the lungs. Oxygen in the air diffuses out of the lungs and into the blood, while carbon dioxide diffuses in the opposite direction, out of the blood and into the lungs. **Respiration** includes the following processes.

1. **Pulmonary ventilation** is the process of breathing—**inspiration** (inhaling air) and **expiration** (exhaling air).

2. **External respiration** is the process of gas exchange between the lungs and the blood. Oxygen diffuses into the blood while CO_2 diffuses from the blood into the lungs.

3. **Gas transport,** carried out by the cardiovascular system, is the process of distributing the oxygen throughout the body and collecting CO_2 and returning it to the lungs.

4. **Internal respiration** is the process of gas exchange between the blood, the interstitial fluids (fluids surrounding the cells), and the cells. Inside the cell, **cellular respiration** generates energy (ATP), using O_2 and glucose and producing waste CO_2.

Structure of the Respiratory System

The respiratory system is represented by the following structures (Figure 64).

1. The **nose** consists of the visible **external nose** and the internal **nasal cavity.** The **nasal septum** divides the nasal cavity into right and left sides. Air enters two openings, the **external nares (nostrils;** singular, **naris),** and passes into the **vestibule** and through passages called **meatuses.** The bony walls of the meatuses, called **conchae,** are formed by facial bones (the infe-

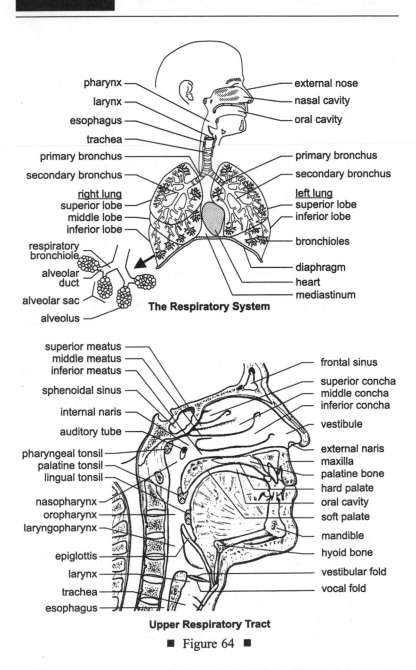

The Respiratory System

pharynx — external nose

larynx — nasal cavity

esophagus — oral cavity

trachea

primary bronchus — primary bronchus

secondary bronchus — secondary bronchus

right lung — **left lung**
superior lobe — superior lobe
middle lobe — inferior lobe
inferior lobe

respiratory bronchiole — bronchioles

alveolar duct — diaphragm

alveolar sac — heart

alveolus — mediastinum

superior meatus — frontal sinus
middle meatus
inferior meatus — superior concha
middle concha
sphenoidal sinus — inferior concha

internal naris — vestibule

auditory tube

pharyngeal tonsil — external naris
palatine tonsil — maxilla
lingual tonsil — palatine bone

hard palate

nasopharynx — oral cavity
oropharynx — soft palate
laryngopharynx

mandible

epiglottis — hyoid bone

larynx — vestibular fold

trachea — vocal fold

esophagus

Upper Respiratory Tract

■ Figure 64 ■

rior nasal conchae and the ethmoid bone). From the meatuses, air then funnels into two (left and right) **internal nares.** Hair, mucus, blood capillaries, and cilia that line the nasal cavity filter, moisten, warm, and eliminate debris from the passing air.

2. The **pharynx** (throat) consists of the following three regions, listed in the order through which incoming air passes.

   ■ The **nasopharynx** receives the incoming air from the two internal nares. The two auditory (Eustachian) tubes that equalize air pressure in the middle ear also enter here. The **pharyngeal tonsils (adenoids)** lie at the back of the nasopharynx.

   ■ The **oropharynx** receives air from the nasopharynx and food from the laryngopharynx. The **palatine** and **lingual tonsils** are located here.

   ■ The **laryngopharynx** passes food to the esophagus and air to the larynx.

3. The **larynx** receives air from the laryngopharynx. It consists of the following nine pieces of cartilage that are joined by membranes and ligaments (Figure 65).

   ■ The **epiglottis,** the first piece of cartilage of the larynx, is a flexible flap that covers the **glottis,** the upper region of the larynx, during swallowing to prevent the entrance of food.

   ■ The **thyroid cartilage** protects the front of the larynx. A forward projection of this cartilage appears as the **Adam's apple.**

   ■ The paired **arytenoid cartilages** in the rear are horizontally attached to the thyroid cartilage in the front by folds of mucous membranes. The upper **vestibular folds (false vocal cords)** contain muscle fibers that bring the folds together and allow the breath to be held during periods of muscular pressure on the thoracic cavity (straining while defecating or lifting a heavy object, for example). The lower **vocal folds (true vocal cords)** contain elastic ligaments that vibrate when skeletal muscles move them into the path of outgoing air. Various sounds, including speech, are produced in this manner.

- The **cricoid cartilage,** the paired **cuneiform cartilages,** and the paired **corniculate cartilages** are the remaining cartilages supporting the larynx.

4. The **trachea (windpipe)** is a flexible tube, 10 to 12 cm (4 inches) long and 2.5 cm (1 inch) in diameter, whose wall consists of four layers, as follows (Figure 65).

- The **mucosa** is the inner layer of the trachea. It contains mucus-producing goblet cells and pseudostratified ciliated epithelium. The movements of the cilia sweep debris away from the lungs toward the pharynx.

- The **submucosa** is a layer of areolar connective tissue that surrounds the mucosa.

- **Hyaline cartilage** forms 16 to 20 C-shaped rings that wrap around the submucosa. The rigid rings prevent the trachea from collapsing during inspiration.

- The **adventitia** is the outermost layer of the trachea. It consists of areolar connective tissue.

5. The **primary bronchi** are two tubes that branch from the trachea to the left and right lungs.

6. Inside the **lungs,** each primary bronchus divides repeatedly into branches of smaller diameters, forming **secondary (lobar) bronchi, tertiary (segmental) bronchi,** and numerous orders of **bronchioles** (1 mm or less in diameter), including **terminal bronchioles** (0.5 mm in diameter) and microscopic

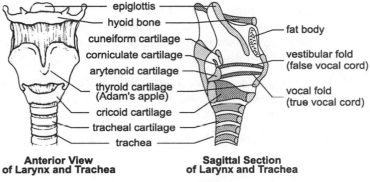

epiglottis

hyoid bone

cuneiform cartilage

corniculate cartilage

arytenoid cartilage

thyroid cartilage (Adam's apple)

cricoid cartilage

tracheal cartilage

trachea

fat body

vestibular fold (false vocal cord)

vocal fold (true vocal cord)

Anterior View of Larynx and Trachea

Sagittal Section of Larynx and Trachea

■ Figure 65 ■

respiratory bronchioles. The walls of the primary bronchi are constructed like the trachea, but as the branches of the tree get smaller, the cartilaginous rings and the mucosa are replaced by smooth muscle.

7. **Alveolar ducts** are the final branches of the bronchial tree. Each alveolar duct has enlarged, bubblelike swellings along its length. Each swelling is called an **alveolus,** and a cluster of adjoining alveoli is called an **alveolar sac.** Some adjacent alveoli are connected by **alveolar pores.**

8. The **respiratory membrane** consists of the alveolar and capillary walls. Gas exchange occurs across this membrane. Characteristics of this membrane follow.

   ■ **Type I cells** are thin, squamous epithelial cells that constitute the primary cell type of the alveolar wall. Oxygen diffusion occurs across these cells.

   ■ **Type II cells** are cuboidal epithelial cells that are interspersed among the type I cells. Type II cells secrete pulmonary **surfactant** (a phospholipid bound to a protein) that reduces the surface tension of the moisture that covers the alveolar walls. A reduction in surface tension permits oxygen to diffuse more easily into the moisture. A lower surface tension also prevents the moisture on opposite walls of an alveolus or alveolar duct from cohering and causing the minute airway to collapse.

- **Alveolar macrophages (dust cells)** wander among the other cells of the alveolar wall removing debris and microorganisms.

- A thin **epithelial basement membrane** forms the outer layer of the alveolar wall.

- A dense network of capillaries surrounds each alveolus. The capillary walls consist of endothelial cells surrounded by a thin basement membrane. The basement membranes of the alveolus and the capillary are often so close that they fuse.

Lungs

The lungs are a pair of cone-shaped bodies that occupy the thorax (Figure 64). The **mediastinum,** the cavity containing the heart, separates the two lungs. The left and right lungs are divided by **fissures** into two and three lobes, respectively. Each lobe of the lung is further divided into **bronchopulmonary segments** (each with a tertiary bronchiole), which are further divided into **lobules** (each with a terminal bronchiole). Blood vessels, lymphatic vessels, and nerves penetrate each lobule.

Each lung has the following superficial features.

1. The **apex** and **base** identify the top and bottom of the lung, respectively.

2. The **costal surface** of each lung borders the ribs (front and back).

3. On the **medial (mediastinal) surface,** where each lung faces the other lung, the bronchi, blood vessels, and lymphatic vessels enter the lung at the **hilus.**

The **pleura** is a double membrane consisting of an inner **pulmonary (visceral) pleura,** which surrounds each lung, and an outer **parietal pleura,** which lines the thoracic cavity. The narrow space between the two membranes, the **pleural cavity,** is filled with **pleural fluid,** a lubricant secreted by the pleura.

Mechanics of Breathing

Boyle's law describes the relationship between the pressure (P) and volume (V) of a gas. The law states that if the volume increases, then the pressure must decrease (or vice versa). This relationship is often written algebraically as PV = constant, or $P_1V_1 = P_2V_2$. Both equations state that the product of the pressure and volume remains the same. (The law applies only when the temperature does not change.)

Breathing occurs when the contraction or relaxation of muscles around the lungs changes the total volume of air within the air passages (bronchi, bronchioles) inside the lungs. When the volume of the lungs changes, the pressure of the air in the lungs changes in accordance with Boyle's law. If the pressure is greater in the lungs than outside the lungs, then air rushes out. If the opposite occurs, then air rushes in. The process is summarized below.

1. *Inspiration* occurs when the **inspiratory muscles,** that is, the **diaphragm** and the **external intercostal muscles,** contract. Contraction of the diaphragm (the skeletal muscle below the lungs) causes an increase in the size of the thoracic cavity while contraction of the external intercostal muscles elevates the ribs and sternum. Thus, both muscles cause the lungs to expand, increasing the volume of their internal air passages. In response, the air pressure inside the lungs decreases below

that of air outside the body. Because gases move from regions of high pressure to low pressure, air rushes into the lungs.

2. *Expiration* occurs when the diaphragm and external intercostal muscles relax. In response, the elastic fibers in lung tissue cause the lungs to recoil to their original volume. The pressure of the air inside the lungs then increases above the air pressure outside the body, and air rushes out. During high rates of ventilation, expiration is facilitated by contraction of the **expiratory muscles** (the **internal intercostal muscles** and the **abdominal muscles**).

Lung compliance is a measure of the ability of the lungs and thoracic cavity to expand. Due to the elasticity of lung tissue and the low surface tension of the moisture in the lungs (from the surfactant), the lungs normally have high compliance.

Lung Volumes and Capacities

The following terms describe the various **lung (respiratory) volumes.**

1. The **tidal volume (TV)**, about 500 ml, is the amount of air inspired during normal, relaxed breathing.

2. The **inspiratory reserve volume (IRV)**, about 3100 ml, is the *additional* air that can be forcibly *inhaled* after the inspiration of a normal tidal volume.

3. The **expiratory reserve volume (ERV)**, about 1200 ml, is the *additional* air that can be forcibly *exhaled* after the expiration of a normal tidal volume.

4. **Residual volume (RV)**, about 1200 ml, is the volume of air still *remaining* in the lungs after the expiratory reserve volume is exhaled.

Summing specific lung volumes produces the following **lung capacities.**

1. The **total lung capacity (TLC)**, about 6000 ml, is the maximum amount of air that can fill the lungs (TLC = TV + IRV + ERV + RV).

2. The **vital capacity (VC)**, about 4800 ml, is the total amount of air that can be expired after fully inhaling (VC = TV + IRV + ERV = approximately 80% TLC).

3. The **inspiratory capacity (IC)**, about 3600 ml, is the maximum amount of air that can be inspired (IC = TV + IRV).

4. The **functional residual capacity (FRC)**, about 2400 ml, is the amount of air remaining in the lungs after a normal expiration (FRC = RV + ERV).

Some of the air in the lungs does not participate in gas exchange. Such air is located in the **anatomical dead space** within bronchi and bronchioles (that is, outside the alveoli).

Gas Exchange

In a mixture of different gases, each gas contributes to the total pressure of the mixture. The contribution of each gas, called the **partial pressure,** is equal to the pressure that the gas would have if it were alone in the enclosure. **Dalton's law** states that the sum of the partial pressures of each gas in a mixture is equal to the total pressure of the mixture.

The following factors determine the degree to which a gas will dissolve in a liquid.

1. *The partial pressure of the gas.* According to **Henry's law,** the greater the partial pressure of a gas, the greater the diffusion of the gas into the liquid.

2. *The solubility of the gas.* The ability of a gas to dissolve in a liquid varies with the kind of gas and the liquid.

3. *The temperature of the liquid.* Solubility decreases with increasing temperature.

Gas exchange occurs in the lungs between alveoli and blood plasma and throughout the body between plasma and interstitial fluids. The following factors facilitate diffusion of O_2 and CO_2 at these sites.

1. *Partial pressures and solubilities.* Poor solubility can be offset by a high partial pressure (or vice versa). Compare the following characteristics of O_2 and CO_2:

   - *Oxygen.* The partial pressure of O_2 in the lungs is high (air is 21% O_2), but its solubility is poor.

   - *Carbon dioxide.* The partial pressure of CO_2 in air is extremely low (air is only 0.04% CO_2), but its solubility in plasma is about 24 times that of O_2.

2. *Partial pressure gradients.* A gradient is a change in some quantity from one region to another. Diffusion of a gas into a liquid (or the reverse) occurs *down* a partial pressure gradient—that is, from a region of higher partial pressure to a region of lower partial pressure. For example, the strong partial pressure gradient for O_2 (pO_2) from alveoli to deoxygenated blood (105 mm Hg in alveoli versus 40 mm Hg in blood) facilitates rapid diffusion.

3. *Surface area for gas exchange.* The expansive surface area of the lungs promotes extensive diffusion.

4. *Diffusion distance.* Thin alveolar and capillary walls increase the rate of diffusion.

Gas Transport

Oxygen is transported in the blood in two ways.

1. A small amount of O_2 (1.5%) is carried in the plasma as a dissolved gas.

2. Most oxygen (98.5%) carried in the blood is bound to the protein **hemoglobin** in red blood cells. A fully saturated **oxy-hemoglobin (HbO_2)** has four O_2 molecules attached. Without oxygen, the molecule is referred to as **deoxyhemoglobin (Hb)**.

The ability of hemoglobin to bind to O_2 is influenced by the partial pressure of oxygen. The greater the partial pressure of oxygen in the blood, the more readily oxygen binds to Hb. The oxygen-hemoglobin dissociation curve (Figure 66) shows that as pO_2 increases toward 100 mm Hg, Hb saturation approaches 100%. The following four factors *decrease* the **affinity,** or strength of attraction, of Hb for O_2 and result in a shift of the O_2-Hb dissociation curve to the right.

- *Increase in temperature.*

- *Increase in partial pressure of CO_2 (pCO_2).*

- *Increase in acidity* (decrease in pH). The decrease in affinity of Hb for O_2, called the **Bohr effect,** results when H^+ binds to Hb.

- *Increase in BPG* in red blood cells. BPG (bisphospho-glycerate) is generated in red blood cells when they produce energy from glucose.

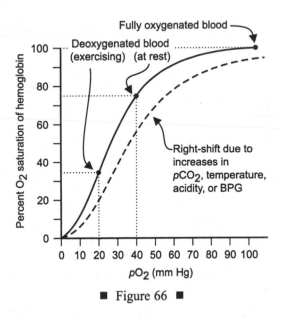

■ Figure 66 ■

Carbon dioxide is transported in the blood in the following ways.

1. A small amount of CO_2 (8%) is carried in the plasma as a dissolved gas.

2. Some CO_2 (25%) binds to Hb in red blood cells forming **carbaminohemoglobin** (**$HbCO_2$**). (The CO_2 binds to a place different from that of O_2.)

3. Most CO_2 (65%) is transported as dissolved bicarbonate ions (HCO_3^-) in the plasma. The formation of HCO_3^-, however, occurs in the red blood cells, where the formation of carbonic acid (H_2CO_3) is catalyzed by the enzyme **carbonic anhydrase,** as follows.

$$CO_2 + H_2O \leftrightarrow H_2CO_3 \leftrightarrow H^+ + HCO_3^-$$

Following their formation in the red blood cells, most H^+ bind to hemoglobin molecules (causing the Bohr effect) while the remaining H^+ diffuse back into the plasma, slightly decreasing the pH of the plasma. The HCO_3^- ions diffuse back into the plasma as well. To balance the overall increase in negative charges entering the plasma, chloride ions diffuse in the opposite direction, from the plasma to the red blood cells (**chloride shift**).

Control of Respiration

Respiration is controlled by three areas of the brain that stimulate the contraction of the diaphragm and the intercostal muscles. These areas, collectively called **respiratory centers,** are summarized below.

1. The **medullary inspiratory center,** located in the medulla oblongata, generates rhythmic nerve impulses that stimulate contraction of the **inspiratory muscles** (diaphragm and external intercostal muscles). Normally, expiration occurs when these muscles relax, but when breathing is rapid, the inspiratory center facilitates expiration by stimulating the **expiratory muscles** (internal intercostal muscles and abdominal muscles).

2. The **pneumotaxic area,** located in the pons, *inhibits* the inspiratory center, limiting the contraction of the inspiratory muscles, and preventing the lungs from overinflating.

3. The **apneustic area,** also located in the pons, *stimulates* the inspiratory center, prolonging the contraction of inspiratory muscles.

The respiratory centers are influenced by stimuli received from the following three groups of sensory neurons.

1. **Central chemoreceptors** (nerves of the *central* nervous system), located in the medulla oblongata, monitor the chemistry of cerebrospinal fluid. When CO_2 from the plasma enters the cerebrospinal fluid, it forms HCO_3^- and H^+, and the pH of the fluid drops (becomes more acidic). In response to the decrease in pH, the central chemoreceptors stimulate the respiratory center to increase the inspiratory rate.

2. **Peripheral chemoreceptors** (nerves of the *peripheral* nervous system), located in **aortic bodies** in the wall of the aortic arch and in **carotid bodies** in the walls of the carotid arteries, monitor the chemistry of the blood. An increase in pH or pCO_2, or decrease in pO_2, causes these receptors to stimulate the respiratory center.

3. **Stretch receptors** in the walls of bronchi and bronchioles are activated when the lungs expand to their physical limit. These receptors signal the respiratory center to discontinue stimulation of the inspiratory muscles, allowing expiration to begin. This response is called the **inflation (Hering-Breuer) reflex.**

The function of the digestive system is **digestion** and **absorption.** Digestion is the breakdown of food into small molecules which are then absorbed into the body. The digestive system is divided into two major parts, as follows.

1. The **gastrointestinal (GI) tract (alimentary canal)** is a continuous tube with two openings, the mouth and the anus. It includes the mouth, pharynx, esophagus, stomach, small intestine, and large intestine. Food passing through the internal cavity, or **lumen,** of the GI tract does not technically enter the body until it is absorbed through the walls of the GI tract and passes into blood or lymphatic vessels.

2. **Accessory organs** include the teeth and tongue, salivary glands, liver, gallbladder, and pancreas.

The treatment of food in the digestive system involves the following seven processes.

1. **Ingestion** is the process of eating.

2. **Propulsion** is the movement of food along the digestive tract. The major means of propulsion is **peristalsis,** a series of alternating contractions and relaxations of smooth muscle that lines the walls of the digestive organs and that forces food to move forward.

3. **Secretion** of digestive enzymes and other substances liquefies, adjusts the pH of, and chemically breaks down the food.

4. **Mechanical digestion** is the process of *physically* breaking down food into smaller pieces. This process begins with the chewing of food and continues with the muscular churning of

the stomach. Additional churning occurs in the small intestine through muscular constrictions of the intestinal wall. This process, called **segmentation,** is similar to peristalsis, except that the rhythmic timing of the muscle constrictions forces the food backward and forward rather than forward only.

5. **Chemical digestion** is the process of *chemically* breaking down food into simpler molecules. The process is carried out by enzymes in the stomach and small intestine.

6. **Absorption** is the movement of molecules (by passive diffusion or active transport) from the digestive tract to adjacent blood and lymphatic vessels. Absorption is the entrance of digested food into the body.

7. **Defecation** is the process of eliminating undigested material through the anus.

Structure of the GI Tract Wall

The digestive tract, from the esophagus to the anus, is characterized by a wall with four layers, or **tunics.** The layers are described below, from the inside of the tract to the outside.

1. The **mucosa** is a mucous membrane that lines the inside of the digestive tract from mouth to anus. Depending upon the section of the digestive tract, it *protects* the GI tract wall, *secretes* substances, and *absorbs* the end products of digestion. It is composed of three layers, as follows.

   ■ The **epithelium** is the innermost layer of the mucosa. It is composed of simple columnar epithelium or stratified squamous epithelium. Also present are goblet cells that secrete mucus that protects the epithelium from digestion and endocrine cells that secrete hormones into the blood.

- The **lamina propria** lies outside the epithelium. It is composed of areolar connective tissue. Blood vessels and lymphatic vessels present in this layer provide nutrients to the epithelial layer, distribute hormones produced in the epithelium, and absorb end products of digestion from the lumen. The lamina propria also contains the **mucosa-associated lymphoid tissue (MALT)**, nodules of lymphatic tissue bearing lymphocytes and macrophages that protect the GI tract wall from bacteria and other pathogens that may be mixed with food.

- The **muscularis mucosae,** the outer layer of the mucosa, is a thin layer of smooth muscle responsible for generating local movements. In the stomach and small intestine, the smooth muscle generates folds that increase the absorptive surface area of the mucosa.

2. The **submucosa** lies outside the mucosa. It consists of areolar connective tissue containing blood vessels, lymphatic vessels, and nerve fibers.

3. The **muscularis (muscularis externa)** is a layer of muscle. In the mouth and pharynx, it consists of skeletal muscle that aids in swallowing. In the rest of the GI tract, it consists of smooth muscle (three layers in the stomach, two layers in the small and large intestines) and associated nerve fibers. The smooth muscle is responsible for movement of food by peristalsis and mechanical digestion by segmentation. In some regions, the circular layer of smooth muscle enlarges to form **sphincters,** circular muscles that control the opening and closing of the lumen (such as between the stomach and small intestine).

4. The **serosa** is a serous membrane that lines the outside of an organ. The following serosae are associated with the digestive tract.

- The **adventitia** is the serous membrane that lines the esophagus.

- The **visceral peritoneum** is the serous membrane that lines the stomach, large intestine, and small intestine.

- The **mesentery** is an extension of the visceral peritoneum that attaches the small intestine to the rear abdominal wall.

- The **mesocolon** is an extension of the visceral peritoneum that attaches the large intestine to the rear abdominal wall.

- The **parietal peritoneum** lines the abdominopelvic cavity (abdominal and pelvic cavities). The abdominal cavity contains the stomach, small intestine, large intestine, liver, spleen, and pancreas. The pelvic cavity contains the urinary bladder, rectum, and internal reproductive organs.

Digestive Enzymes

During digestion, four different groups of molecules are commonly encountered. Each is broken down into its molecular components by specific enzymes, as follows.

1. **Complex carbohydrates,** or **polysaccharides,** (such as starches) are broken down into oligosaccharides (consisting of two to ten linked monosaccharides), disaccharides (such as maltose), or individual monosaccharides (such as glucose or fructose). Enzymes called **amylases** break down starch.

2. **Proteins** are broken down into short chains of amino acids (peptides) or individual amino acids by enzymes called **proteases.**

3. **Fats (lipids)** are broken down into glycerol and fatty acids by enzymes called **lipases.**

4. **Nucleic acids** are broken down into nucleotides by enzymes called **nucleases.**

A summary of enzymes and their substrates (substances upon which enzymes operate) is given in Table 16.

Source	Enzyme	Substrate	Products of Enzyme Activity
Saliva	salivary amylase	starches	maltose, oligosaccharides
Gastric Juice (chief cells of stomach)	pepsin	proteins	peptides
Pancreatic Juice (acinar cells of pancreas)	pancreatic amylase	starches	maltose, oligosaccharides
	trypsin	proteins	peptides
	chymotrypsin	proteins	peptides
	carboxypeptidase	proteins	peptides, amino acids
	pancreatic lipase	fats	fatty acids, monoglycerides
	nucleases	RNA & DNA	nucleotides
Brush Border (absorptive cells of small intestine)	dextrinase	oligo-saccharides	glucose
	maltase	maltose	glucose
	sucrase	sucrose	glucose & fructose
	lactase	lactose	glucose & galactose
	aminopeptidase	peptides	peptides, amino acids
	dipeptidase	dipeptides	amino acids
	nucleosidases	nucleotides	nitrogen bases, ribose,
	phosphatases	nucleotides	deoxyribose & phosphates

■ Table 16 ■

The Mouth

The **mouth (oral cavity, buccal cavity)** is where food enters the digestive tract. The following features are found in the mouth.

1. The **vestibule** is the narrow region between the cheeks and teeth and between the lips and teeth.

2. The **tongue** defines the lower boundary of the mouth. It helps position the food during **mastication** (chewing) and gathers the chewed food into a ball, or **bolus,** in preparation for swal-

lowing. The tongue is covered with **papillae,** small projections that help the tongue grip food. Many of the papillae bear taste buds.

3. The **palate** defines the upper boundary of the mouth. The forward portion is the **hard palate,** hard because bone (maxillae and palatine) lies above it. Further back in the mouth, the **soft palate** consists of muscle and lacks any bone support. A conical muscular projection, the **uvula,** is suspended from the rear of the soft palate.

4. **Saliva** contains water (99.5%), digestive enzymes, lysozyme (an enzyme that kills bacteria), proteins, antibodies (IgA), and various ions. Saliva lubricates the mouth, moistens food during chewing, protects the mouth against pathogens, and begins the chemical digestion of food. Chemical digestion is carried out by the digestive enzyme **salivary amylase,** which breaks down polysaccharides (starch and glycogen) into short chains of glucose, especially the disaccharide maltose (which consists of two glucose molecules). Saliva is produced by the following glands.

   - Three pairs of salivary glands, the **parotid, submandibular,** and **sublingual,** lie outside the mouth. They deliver their secretions to the mouth via ducts.

   - **Buccal glands** are located in the mucosa that lines the mouth.

5. The **teeth** are embedded within sockets of the upper and lower jawbones (maxillae and mandible). Each tooth is surrounded by **gum,** or **gingiva,** and held in its socket by a **periodontal ligament.** The 20 **deciduous teeth** (**baby teeth** or **milk teeth**) are eventually replaced by 32 **permanent teeth.** There are three types of teeth, based on shape and function, as follows.

   - **Incisors** have a chisel-shaped edge suitable for biting off food.

- **Canines (cuspids)** are pointed fangs and are used for tearing food.

- **Premolars (bicuspids)** and **molars** have flat surfaces used for grinding and crushing.

A tooth has the following structural features.

- **Dentin** is a calcified tissue (like bone) that composes the bulk of the tooth.

- The **crown** is the portion of the tooth that is visible outside the gum.

- The **root** is the portion of the tooth embedded in the bone.

- The **neck** is the region at the gum line where the crown and root meet.

- **Enamel** is the hard, nonliving material that covers the crown. Calcium compounds make the enamel the hardest substance in the body.

- **Cementum** is the bonelike substance that covers the root and binds it to the periodontal ligament.

- The **pulp cavity** is the central cavity inside the tooth. It contains blood vessels, nerves, and connective tissue (collectively called **pulp**).

The Pharynx

The **pharynx,** or throat, receives the food from the mouth during swallowing. From the mouth, it moves back and down into the oropharynx, then descends into the laryngopharynx. The food then passes into the esophagus.

The Esophagus

The **esophagus** is a 25 cm (10 inch) long tube that begins at the laryngopharynx and descends behind the trachea through the mediastinum (cavity between the lungs). It then passes through the diaphragm at an opening called the **esophageal hiatus** and connects to the stomach.

Food is forced through the esophagus toward the stomach by peristalsis. Two sphincter muscles, the **upper esophageal sphincter** at the top of the esophagus and the **cardiac sphincter (lower esophageal sphincter)** at the bottom of the esophagus, control the movement of food into and out of the esophagus.

Deglutition (Swallowing)

Swallowing, or **deglutition**, is divided into three phases, as follows.

1. The **buccal phase** occurs *voluntarily* in the mouth when the tongue forces the food bolus back into the pharynx.

2. The **pharyngeal phase** occurs *involuntarily* when food enters the pharynx, as follows.

   ■ The soft palate and uvula fold upward and cover the nasopharynx to prevent the passage of food up and into the nasal cavity.

   ■ The **epiglottis,** a flexible cartilaginous flap at the top of the larynx, folds down as the larynx rises. As a result, the opening to the larynx is covered, and food can pass only into the esophagus.

3. The **esophageal phase** occurs *involuntarily* in the esophagus. The esophageal sphincter, normally closed, opens to allow food to pass when the larynx rises during swallowing. When food

reaches the lower end of the esophagus, the cardiac sphincter opens to allow the food to enter the stomach.

The Stomach

The **stomach** is a J-shaped, baglike organ that expands to store food (Figure 67a). Typical of that of the entire digestive tract, the wall of the stomach contains four layers. However, the inner layer, the mucosa, is modified for the specialized functions of the stomach. In particular, the innermost layer of the mucosa (facing the lumen) contains a layer of simple columnar epithelium consisting of goblet cells. **Gastric pits** on the surface penetrate deep into the layer, forming ducts whose walls are lined with various **gastric glands.** A summary of the glands in the mucosa follows (Figure 67b).

1. **Mucous surface cells** are the goblet cells that make up the surface layer of the simple columnar epithelium. These cells secrete mucus which protects the mucosa from the action of acid and digestive enzymes.

2. **Mucous neck cells** line the upper walls ("necks") of the ducts. Like the mucous surface cells, they secrete mucus.

3. **Parietal (oxyntic) cells** are scattered along the neck and lower walls of the ducts. They secrete **hydrochloric acid (HCl)** and **intrinsic factor.** Intrinsic factor is necessary for the absorption of Vitamin B_{12} in the small intestine.

4. **Chief (zymogenic) cells** also line the lower walls of the ducts. They secrete **pepsinogen,** the inactive form of **pepsin.** Pepsin is a **protease,** an enzyme that breaks down proteins.

5. **Enteroendocrine cells** secrete various hormones that diffuse into nearby blood vessels. One important hormone, **gastrin,** stimulates other glands in the stomach to increase their output.

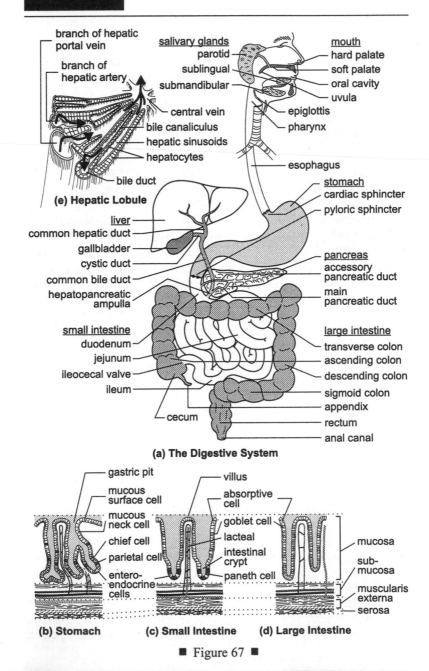

branch of hepatic portal vein

branch of hepatic artery

central vein
bile canaliculus
hepatic sinusoids
hepatocytes
bile duct

(e) Hepatic Lobule

salivary glands
parotid
sublingual
submandibular

mouth
hard palate
soft palate
oral cavity
uvula
epiglottis
pharynx

esophagus

stomach
cardiac sphincter
pyloric sphincter

liver
common hepatic duct
gallbladder
cystic duct
common bile duct
hepatopancreatic ampulla

pancreas
accessory pancreatic duct
main pancreatic duct

small intestine
duodenum
jejunum
ileocecal valve
ileum

cecum

large intestine
transverse colon
ascending colon
descending colon
sigmoid colon
appendix
rectum
anal canal

(a) The Digestive System

gastric pit
mucous surface cell
mucous neck cell
chief cell
parietal cell
entero-endocrine cells

villus
absorptive cell
goblet cell
lacteal
intestinal crypt
paneth cell

mucosa
sub-mucosa
muscularis externa
serosa

(b) Stomach   **(c) Small Intestine**   **(d) Large Intestine**

■ Figure 67 ■

The first four glands listed above are *exocrine* glands, whose secretions, collectively called **gastric juice,** enter the stomach and mix with food. The last gland is an *endocrine* gland, whose *hormone* secretions enter the blood supply.

The stomach serves a variety of functions, as follows.

- *Storage.* Because of its accordionlike folds (called **rugae**), the wall of the stomach can expand to store two to four liters of material. Temporary storage is important because we eat considerably faster than we can digest food and absorb its nutrients.

- *Mixing.* The stomach mixes the food with water and gastric juice to produce a creamy medium called **chyme.**

- *Physical breakdown.* Three layers of smooth muscles (rather than the usual two) in the muscularis externa churn the contents of the stomach, *physically* breaking food down into smaller particles. In addition, HCl denatures (or unfolds) proteins and loosens the cementing substances between cells (of the food). The HCl also kills most bacteria that may accompany the food.

- *Chemical breakdown. Proteins* are *chemically* broken down by the enzyme **pepsin.** Chief cells as well as other stomach cells, are protected from self-digestion because chief cells produce and secrete an inactive form of pepsin, **pepsinogen.** Pepsinogen is converted to pepsin by the HCl produced by the parietal cells. Only after pepsinogen is secreted into the stomach cavity can protein digestion begin. Once protein digestion begins, the stomach is protected by the layer of mucus secreted by the mucous cells.

- *Controlled release.* Movement of chyme into the small intestine is regulated by a valve at the end of the stomach, the **pyloric sphincter.**

Small Intestine

The **small intestine** (small in diameter compared to the large intestine) is divided into three sections, as follows (Figure 67a).

1. The **duodenum,** about 25 cm (10 in) long, receives chyme from the stomach through the pyloric sphincter. Ducts that empty into the duodenum deliver pancreatic juice and bile from the pancreas and liver, respectively.

2. The **jejunum,** about 2.5 m (8 ft) long, is the middle section of the small intestine.

3. The **ileum,** about 3.6 m (12 ft) long, is the last section of the small intestine. It ends with the **ileocecal valve (sphincter),** which regulates the movement of chyme into the large intestine and prevents backward movement of material from the large intestine.

The functions of the small intestine include the following.

1. *Mechanical digestion.* Segmentation mixes the chyme with enzymes from the small intestine and pancreas. Bile from the liver separates fat into smaller fat globules. Peristalsis moves the chyme through the small intestine.

2. *Chemical digestion.* Enzymes from the small intestine and pancreas break down all four groups of molecules found in food (polysaccharides, proteins, fats, and nucleic acids) into their component molecules (Table 16).

3. *Absorption.* The small intestine is the primary location in the GI tract for absorption of nutrients, as follows.

   - *Carbohydrates, proteins, nucleic acids, and water-soluble vitamins.* The components of these molecules (Table 16) are absorbed by facilitated diffusion or active transport. They are then passed to blood capillaries.

- *Vitamin B_{12}.* Vitamin B_{12} combines with intrinsic factor (produced in the stomach) and is absorbed by receptor-mediated endocytosis. It is then passed to the blood capillaries.

- *Lipids and fat-soluble vitamins.* Because fat-soluble vitamins and the components of lipids are insoluble in water, they are packaged and delivered to cells within water-soluble clusters of bile salts called **micelles.** They are then absorbed by simple diffusion and, once inside the cells, mix with cholesterol and protein to form **chylomicrons.** The chylomicrons are then passed to the *lymphatic capillaries.* When the lymph eventually empties into the blood, the chylomicrons are broken down by **lipoprotein lipase,** and the breakdown products, fatty acids and glycerol, pass through blood capillary walls to be absorbed by various cells.

- *Water and electrolytes.* About 90% of the water in chyme is absorbed, as well as various electrolytes (ions), including Na^+, K^+, Cl^-, nitrates, calcium, and iron.

Modifications of the mucosa for its various specialized functions in the small intestine include the following.

1. The **plicae circulares (circular folds)** are permanent ridges in the mucosa that encircle the inside of the small intestine. The ridges force the food to spiral forward. The spiral motion helps mix the chyme with the digestive juices.

2. **Villi** (singular, **villus**) are fingerlike projections that cover the surface of the mucosa, giving it a velvety appearance. They increase the surface area over which absorption and digestion occur. The spaces between adjacent villi lead to deep cavities at the bases of the villi called **intestinal crypts (crypts of**

Lieberkühn). Glands that empty into the cavities are called **intestinal glands,** and the secretions are collectively called **intestinal juice.**

3. **Microvilli** are microscopic extensions of the outer surface of the absorptive cells that line each villus. Because of their brushlike appearance (microscopically), the microvilli facing the lumen form the **brush border** of the small intestine. Like the villi, the microvilli increase the surface area over which digestion and absorption take place.

The villi of the mucosa have the following characteristics.

1. An outer epithelial layer (facing the lumen) consists of the following cell types (Figure 67c).

   ■ **Absorptive cells,** the primary cell type of the epithelial layer, synthesize digestive enzymes called **brush border enzymes** that become embedded in the plasma membranes around the microvilli. Various nutrients in the chyme that move over the microvilli are broken down by these brush border enzymes and subsequently absorbed. Table 16 lists these enzymes.

   ■ **Goblet cells,** located throughout the epithelial layer, secrete mucus that helps protect the epithelial layer from digestion.

   ■ **Enteroendocrine cells** secrete hormones into blood vessels that penetrate the villus.

   ■ **Paneth cells,** located in the epithelial layer facing the intestinal crypts, secrete lysozyme, an enzyme that destroys bacteria.

2. An inner core of lamina propria (connective tissue) contains blood capillaries and a small lymphatic capillary called a **lacteal.**

The submucosa that underlies the mucosa of the small intestine bears the following modifications.

1. **Brunner's (duodenal) glands,** found only in the submucosa of the duodenum, secrete an alkaline mucus that neutralizes the gastric acid in the incoming chyme.

2. **Peyer's patches (aggregated lymphatic nodules)**, found mostly in the submucosa of the ileum, are clusters of lymphatic nodules that provide a defensive barrier against bacteria.

Large Intestine

The **large intestine** is about 1.5 m (5 ft) long and is characterized by the following components (Figure 67a and 67d).

1. The **cecum** is a dead-end pouch at the beginning of the large intestine, just below the ileocecal valve.

2. The **appendix (vermiform appendix)** is an 8 cm (3 in) long fingerlike attachment to the cecum that contains lymphoid tissue and serves immunity functions.

3. The **colon,** representing the greater part of the large intestine, consists of four sections—the **ascending, transverse, descending,** and **sigmoid colons.** At regular distances along the colon, the smooth muscle of the muscularis layer causes the intestinal wall to gather, producing a series of pouches called **haustra.** The epithelium facing the lumen of the colon is covered with openings of tubular intestinal glands that penetrate deep into the thick mucosa. The glands consist of **absorptive cells** that absorb water and **goblet cells** that secrete mucus. The mucus lubricates the walls of the large intestine to smooth the passage of feces.

4. The **rectum** is the last 20 cm (8 in) of the large intestine. The mucosa in the rectum forms longitudinal folds called **anal columns.**

5. The **anal canal,** the last 3 cm (1 in) of the rectum, opens to the exterior at the **anus.** An involuntary (smooth) muscle, the **interior anal sphincter,** and a voluntary (skeletal) muscle, the **external anal sphincter,** control the release of feces through the anus.

The functions of the large intestine include the following.

1. *Mechanical digestion.* Rhythmic contractions of the large intestine produce a form of segmentation called haustral contractions in which food residues are mixed and forced to move from one haustrum to the next. Peristaltic contractions produce **mass movements** of larger amounts of material.

2. *Chemical digestion.* Digestion occurs as a result of bacteria that colonize the large intestine. They break down indigestible material by fermentation, releasing various gases. Vitamin K and certain B vitamins are also produced by bacterial activity.

3. *Absorption.* Vitamins B and K, some electrolytes (Na^+ and Cl^-) and most of the remaining water is absorbed by the large intestine.

4. *Defecation.* Mass movements of feces into the rectum stimulate a **defecation reflex** that opens the internal anal sphincter. Unless the external anal sphincter is voluntarily closed, feces are evacuated through the anus.

The Pancreas

The secretions of the **pancreas,** called **pancreatic juice,** include various enzymes, including **pancreatic amylase** (digestion of starch), **trypsin, carboxypeptidase,** and **chymotrypsin** (proteases), and **pancreatic lipase** (digestion of fats). Sodium bicarbonate is also produced, making the pancreatic juice alkaline. An alkaline solution neutralizes the HCl in the chyme and provides an optimal environment for the action of these enzymes.

Pancreatic juice is produced in clusters of *exocrine* cells called **acini.** The remaining cells in the pancreas (about 1% of the total) also form clusters (islets of Langerhans). These are the *endocrine* cells that produce the hormones insulin, glucagon, somatostatin, and pancreatic polypeptide.

Pancreatic juice collects in small ducts that merge to form two large ducts. The **main pancreatic duct (duct of Wirsung)** exits the pancreas and merges with the common bile duct from the liver and gallbladder. This combined duct, called the **hepatopancreatic ampulla (ampulla of Vater)** then enters the duodenum. A smaller, second duct that exits the pancreas, the **accessory pancreatic duct (duct of Santorini),** joins the duodenum directly.

The Liver and Gallbladder

The digestive function of the **liver** is to produce bile, which is then delivered to the duodenum to *emulsify* fats. Emulsification is the breaking up of fat globules into smaller fat droplets, increasing the surface area upon which fat-digesting enzymes (lipases) can operate. Since bile does not chemically change anything, it is not an enzyme. Bile is also alkaline, serving to help neutralize the HCl in the chyme.

Bile consists of bile salts, bile pigments, phospholipids (including lecithin), cholesterol, and various ions. The primary bile pigment, **bilirubin,** is an end product of the breakdown of hemoglobin from expended red blood cells. Although some of the bile is lost in the feces (bilirubin gives feces their brown color), much of the bile is reabsorbed by the small intestine and returned to the liver via the hepatic portal vein.

The liver performs numerous metabolic functions. Some of the most important are listed below.

1. Bile is produced.

2. Blood glucose is regulated. When blood glucose is high, the liver converts glucose to glycogen (**glycogenesis**) and stores the glycogen. When blood glucose is low, glycogen is broken down (**glycogenolysis**) and glucose is released into the blood.

3. Proteins (including plasma proteins) and certain amino acids are synthesized.

4. Ammonia (which is toxic) is converted to urea (less toxic) for elimination by the kidneys.

5. Bacteria and expended red and white blood cells are broken down. From the red blood cells, Fe and globin are recycled and bilirubin is secreted in the bile.

6. Vitamins (A, D, and B_{12}) and minerals (including Fe from expended red blood cells) are stored.

7. Toxic substances (drugs, poisons) and hormones are broken down.

The liver is composed of numerous functional units called **lobules** (Figure 67e). Within each lobule, epithelial cells called **hepatocytes** are arranged in layers that radiate out from a **central vein.** **Hepatic sinusoids** are spaces that lie between groups of layers, while smaller channels called **bile canaliculi** separate other layers. Each of (usually) six corners of the lobule are occupied by three vessels—one bile duct and two blood vessels (a **portal triad**). The blood vessels are branches from the **hepatic artery** (carrying oxygenated blood) and from the **hepatic portal vein** (carrying deoxygenated but nutrient-rich blood from the small intestine).

Blood enters the liver through the hepatic artery and hepatic portal vein and is distributed to lobules. Blood flows into each lobule by passing through the hepatic sinusoid and collecting in the central vein. The central veins of all the lobules merge and exit the liver through the **hepatic vein** (not the hepatic *portal* vein).

Within the sinusoids, phagocytes called **Kupffer cells (stellate reticuloendothelial cells)** destroy bacteria and break down expended red and white blood cells and other debris. Hepatocytes that border the sinusoids also screen the incoming blood. They remove various substances from the blood, including oxygen, nutrients, toxins, and waste materials. From these substances, they produce bile, which they secrete into the bile canaliculi, which empty into **bile ducts.** Bile ducts from the various lobules merge and exit the liver as a single **common hepatic duct.** The common hepatic duct merges with the **cystic duct** from the gallbladder to form the **common bile duct,** which, in turn, merges with the pancreatic duct to form the **hepatopancreatic ampulla.** This last duct delivers the bile to the duodenum.

The **gallbladder** stores excess bile. When food is in the duodenum, bile flows readily from the liver and gallbladder into the duodenum. When the duodenum is empty, a sphincter muscle (**sphincter of Oddi**) closes the hepatopancreatic ampulla, and bile backs up and fills the gallbladder.

Regulation of Digestion

The activities of the digestive system are regulated by both hormones and neural reflexes. Four important hormones and their effects upon target cells are described below.

1. **Gastrin** is produced by enteroendocrine cells of the *stomach* mucosa. Effects include the following.

- stimulation of gastric juice (especially HCl) secretion by gastric glands.

- stimulation of smooth muscle contraction in the stomach, small intestine, and large intestine, which increases gastric and intestinal motility.

- relaxation of the pyloric sphincter, which promotes gastric emptying into the small intestine.

2. **Secretin** is produced by the enteroendocrine cells of the *duodenal* mucosa. Effects include the following.

   - stimulation of bicarbonate secretion by the pancreas, which neutralizes the acidity of chyme when released into the duodenum.

   - stimulation of bile production by the liver.

   - inhibition of gastric juice secretions and gastric motility which, in turn, slows digestion in the stomach and retards gastric emptying.

3. **Cholecystokinin (CCK)** is produced by enteroendocrine cells of the *duodenal* mucosa. Effects include the following.

   - stimulation of bile release by the gallbladder.

   - stimulation of pancreatic juice secretion.

   - relaxation of the hepatopancreatic ampulla which allows flow of bile and pancreatic juices into the duodenum.

4. **Gastric inhibitory peptide (GIP)** is produced by enteroendocrine cells of the *duodenal* mucosa and causes the following effects.

   - inhibition of gastric juice secretions and gastric motility which, in turn, slows digestion in the stomach and retards gastric emptying.

The second regulatory agent of the digestive system is the nervous system. Stimuli that influence digestive activities may originate in the head, the stomach, or the small intestine. Based on these sites, there are three phases of digestive regulation, as follows.

1. The **cephalic phase** comprises those stimuli that originate from the head—sight, smell, taste, or thoughts of food, as well as emotional states. In response, the following reflexes are initiated.

   ■ *Neural response.* Stimuli that *arouse* digestion are relayed to the hypothalamus, which, in turn, initiates nerve impulses in the parasympathetic vagus nerve. These impulses innervate nerve networks of the GI tract (**enteric nervous system**) which promote contraction of smooth muscle (which causes peristalsis) and secretion of gastric juice. Stimuli that *repress* digestion (emotions of fear or anxiety, for example) innervate sympathetic fibers that suppress muscle contraction and secretion.

   ■ *General effects.* The stomach prepares for the digestion of proteins.

2. The **gastric phase** describes those stimuli that originate from the stomach. These stimuli include distention of the stomach (which activates stretch receptors), low acidity (high pH), and the presence of peptides. In response, the following reflexes are initiated.

   ■ *Neural response.* Gastric juice secretion and smooth muscle contraction are promoted.

   ■ *Hormonal response.* Gastrin production is promoted.

   ■ *General effects.* The stomach and small intestine prepare for the digestion of chyme, and gastric emptying is promoted.

3. The **intestinal phase** describes stimuli originating in the small intestine. These include distention of the duodenum, high acidity (low *p*H) and the presence of chyme (especially fatty acids and carbohydrates). In response, the following reflexes are initiated.

- *Neural response.* Gastric secretion and gastric motility are *inhibited* (**enterogastric reflex**). Intestinal secretions, smooth muscle contraction, and bile and pancreatic juice production are promoted.

- *Hormonal response.* Production of secretin, CCK, and GIP is promoted.

- *General effects.* Stomach emptying is retarded to allow adequate time for digestion (especially of fats) in the small intestine. Intestinal digestion and motility are promoted.

The **urinary system** helps maintain homeostasis by regulating water balance and by removing harmful substances from the blood. The blood is filtered by two **kidneys** which produce urine, a fluid containing toxic substances and waste products. From each kidney, the urine flows through a tube, the **ureter,** to the **urinary bladder,** where it is stored until it is expelled from the body through another tube, the **urethra.**

Anatomy of the Kidneys

The **kidneys** are surrounded by three layers of tissue, as follows.

1. The **renal fascia** is a thin, outer layer of fibrous connective tissue that surrounds each kidney (and the attached adrenal gland) and fastens it to surrounding structures.

2. The **adipose capsule** is a middle layer of adipose (fat) tissue that cushions the kidney.

3. The **renal capsule** is an inner fibrous membrane that prevents the entrance of infections.

Inside the kidney, three major regions are distinguished (Figure 68a and 68b).

1. The **renal cortex** borders the convex side.

2. The **renal medulla** lies adjacent to the renal cortex. It consists of striated, cone-shaped regions called **renal pyramids (medullary pyramids),** whose peaks, called **renal papillae,** face inward. The unstriated regions between the renal pyramids are called **renal columns.**

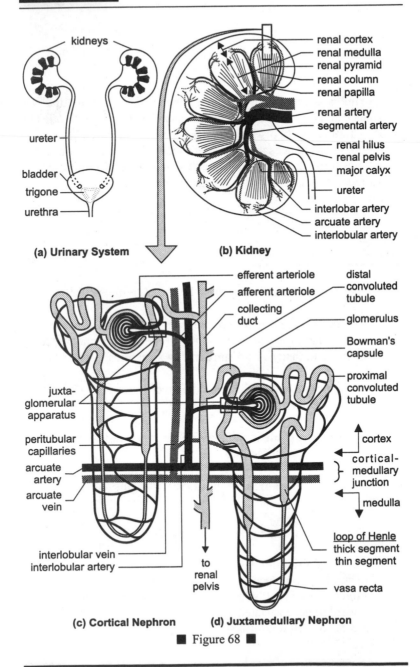

(a) Urinary System

(b) Kidney

(c) Cortical Nephron

(d) Juxtamedullary Nephron

■ Figure 68 ■

3. The **renal sinus** is a cavity that lies adjacent to the renal medulla. The other side of the renal sinus, bordering the concave surface of the kidney, opens to the outside through the **renal hilus.** The ureter, nerves, and blood and lymphatic vessels enter the kidney on the concave surface through the renal hilus. The renal sinus houses the **renal pelvis,** a funnel-shaped structure that merges with the ureter. The renal pelvis forms branches called **major** and **minor calyces** (singular, **calyx**) that extend into the renal medulla and abut the renal pyramids.

Blood and Nerve Supply

Because the major function of the kidneys is to filter the blood, a rich blood supply is delivered by the large **renal arteries.** The renal artery for each kidney enters the renal hilus and successively branches into **segmental arteries, lobar arteries,** and finally **interlobar arteries** that pass between the renal pyramids toward the renal cortex. The interlobar arteries then branch into the **arcuate arteries,** which curve as they pass along the junction of the renal medulla and cortex. Branches of the arcuate arteries, called **interlobular arteries,** penetrate the renal cortex, where they again branch into **afferent arterioles,** which enter the filtering mechanisms, or glomeruli, of the nephrons.

Blood leaving the nephrons exits the kidney through veins that trace the same path, in reverse, as the arteries that delivered the blood. **Interlobular, arcuate, interlobar,** and **segmental veins** successively merge and exit as a single **renal vein.**

Autonomic nerves from the **renal plexus** follow the renal artery into the kidney through the renal hilus. The nerve fibers follow the branching pattern of the renal artery and serve as vasomotor fibers that regulate blood volume. Sympathetic fibers constrict arterioles (decreasing urine output) while less numerous parasympathetic fibers dilate arterioles (increasing urine output).

The Nephron

The kidney consists of over a million individual filtering units called **nephrons.** Each nephron consists of a filtering body, the **renal corpuscle,** and a urine-collecting and concentrating tube, the **renal tubule.** The renal corpuscle is an assemblage of two structures, the **glomerulus** and the **Bowman's (glomerular) capsule.** Details follow (Figure 68c and 68d).

1. The **glomerulus** is a dense ball of capillaries (**glomerular capillaries**) that branches from the afferent arteriole that enters the nephron. Because blood in the glomerular capillaries is under high pressure, substances in the blood that are small enough to pass through the pores (**fenestrae,** or **endothelial fenestrations**) in the capillary walls are forced out and into the encircling Bowman's capsule. The glomerular capillaries merge, and the remaining blood exits the glomerulus through the efferent arteriole.

2. The **Bowman's capsule** is a cup-shaped body that encircles the glomerulus and collects the material (**filtrate**) that is forced out of the glomerular capillaries. The filtrate collects in the interior of the Bowman's capsule, the **capsular (Bowman's) space,** an area bounded by an inner visceral layer (that faces the glomerulus) and an outer parietal layer. The visceral layer consists of modified simple squamous epithelial cells called **podocytes** that project branches that bear fine processes called **pedicels.** The pedicels of adjacent podocytes mesh to form a dense network that envelops the glomerular capillaries. Spaces between the pedicels, called **filtration slits,** are openings into the capsular space that allow filtrate to enter the Bowman's capsule.

3. The **renal tubule** consists of three sections, as follows.

   ■ The first section, the **proximal convoluted tubule (PCT),** exits the Bowman's capsule as a winding tube in the renal cortex. The wall of the PCT consists of cuboidal cells containing numerous mitochondria and bearing a brush border of dense microvilli that face the lumen (interior cavity). The high-energy yield and large surface area of these cells support their functions of reabsorption and secretion.

- The middle of the tubule, the **loop of Henle,** is shaped like a hairpin and consists of a **descending limb** that drops into the renal medulla and an **ascending limb** that rises back into the renal cortex. As the loop descends, the tubule suddenly narrows, forming the **thin segment** of the loop. The loop subsequently widens in the ascending limb, forming the **thick segment** of the loop. Cells of the loop of Henle vary from simple squamous epithelium (descending limb and thin segment of ascending limb) to cuboidal and low columnar epithelium (thick segment of ascending limb) and almost entirely lack microvilli.

- The final section, the **distal convoluted tubule (DCT),** coils within the renal cortex and empties into the **collecting duct.** Cells here are cuboidal with few microvilli.

Renal tubules of neighboring nephrons empty urine into a single collecting duct. Here and in the final portions of the DCT, two types of cells are present. The more numerous **principal cells** respond to the hormones aldosterone and antidiuretic hormone (ADH) and **intercalated cells** secrete H^+.

Various collecting ducts within the medullary pyramids merge to form **papillary ducts** which drain into the minor calyces of the renal pelvis through the medullary papillae. Urine collects in the renal pelvis and drains out of the kidney through the ureter.

The efferent arteriole that carries blood away from the glomerulus branches to form **peritubular capillaries.** These capillaries weave around the portions of the renal tubule that lie in the renal cortex. In portions of the loop of Henle that descend deep into the renal medulla, the capillaries form loops, called **vasa recta,** that cross between the ascending and descending limbs. The peritubular capillaries collect water and nutrients from the filtrate in the tubule. They also release substances that are secreted into the tubule to combine with the filtrate in the formation of urine. The capillaries ultimately merge into an interlobular vein which transports blood out of the nephron. Note that the blood flow through the nephron actually passes through two separate capillary beds, the glomerulus and the capillary network surrounding the renal tubule.

There are two kinds of nephrons, as follows.

1. **Cortical nephrons,** representing 85% of the nephrons in the kidney, have loops of Henle that descend only slightly into the renal medulla (Figure 68c).

2. **Juxtamedullary nephrons** have long loops of Henle that descend deep into the renal medulla. Only juxtamedullary nephrons have vasa recta that traverse their loops of Henle (Figure 68d).

The **juxtaglomerular apparatus (JGA)** is an area of the nephron where the afferent arteriole and the initial portion of the distal convoluted tubule are in close contact. Here, specialized smooth muscle cells of the afferent arteriole, called **granular juxtaglomerular (JG) cells,** are mechanoreceptors that monitor blood pressure in the afferent arteriole. In the adjacent distal convoluted tubule, specialized cells, called **macula densa,** are chemoreceptors that monitor the concentration of Na^+ and Cl^- in the urine inside the tubule. Together, these cells help regulate blood pressure and the production of urine in the nephron.

Kidney Physiology

The operation of the human nephron consists of three processes, as follows.

1. *Glomerular filtration*
2. *Tubular reabsorption*
3. *Tubular secretion*

These three processes, which determine the quantity and quality of the urine, are discussed separately below.

Glomerular Filtration

When blood enters the glomerulus, water and solutes are forced into the Bowman's capsule. Passage of cells and certain molecules are restricted as follows.

1. The *fenestrae* (pores) of the capillary endothelium are large, permitting all components of blood plasma to pass except blood cells.

2. A *basement membrane* (consisting of extracellular material) that lies between the capillary endothelium and the visceral layer of the Bowman's capsule blocks the entrance of large proteins into the Bowman's capsule.

3. The *filtration slits* between the pedicels of the podocytes prevent the passage of medium-sized proteins into the Bowman's capsule.

The **net filtration pressure (NFP)** determines the quantity of filtrate that is forced into the Bowman's capsule. The NFP, estimated at about 10 mm Hg, is the sum of pressures that promote filtration less the sum of those that oppose filtration. The following contribute to the NFP.

1. The **glomerular hydrostatic pressure** (blood pressure in the glomerulus) promotes filtration.

2. The **glomerular osmotic pressure** inhibits filtration. This pressure is created as a result of the movement of water and solutes out of the glomerular capillaries while proteins and blood cells remain. This decreases the concentration of water

in the glomerulus and promotes the return of water to the glomerulus by osmosis.

3. The **capsular hydrostatic pressure** inhibits filtration. This pressure develops as water collects in the Bowman's capsule. The more water in the capsule, the greater the pressure.

The **glomerular filtration rate (GFR)** is the rate at which filtrate collectively accumulates in the Bowman's capsule of each nephron. The GFR, about 125 ml/min (180 liters/day), is regulated by the following.

1. *Renal autoregulation* is the ability of the kidney to maintain a constant GFR even when the body's blood pressure fluctuates. Autoregulation is accomplished by cells in the juxtaglomerular apparatus that decrease or increase secretion of a vasoconstrictor substance that dilates or constricts, respectively, the afferent arteriole.

2. *Neural regulation* of GFR occurs when vasoconstrictor fibers of the sympathetic nervous system constrict afferent arterioles. Such stimulation may occur during exercise, stress, or other fight-or-flight conditions and results in a decrease in urine production.

3. *Hormonal control* of GFR is accomplished by the **renin-angiotensinogen** mechanism. When cells of the juxtaglomerular apparatus detect a decrease in blood pressure in the afferent arteriole or a decrease in solute (Na^+ and Cl^-) concentrations in the distal tubule, they secrete the enzyme **renin.** Renin converts **angiotensinogen** (a plasma protein produced by the liver) to angiotensinogen I. Angiotensinogen I, in turn, is converted to angiotensinogen II by **angiotensin converting enzyme (ACE)**, an enzyme produced principally by capillary endothelium in the lungs. Angiotensinogen II circulates in the blood and increases GFR by

- constricting blood vessels throughout the body, causing the blood pressure to rise,

- constricting the afferent arterioles, and

- stimulating the adrenal cortex to secrete aldosterone, a hormone that increases blood pressure by decreasing water output by the kidneys.

Tubular Reabsorption

In healthy kidneys, nearly all of the desirable organic substances (proteins, amino acids, glucose) are reabsorbed by the cells that line the renal tube. These substances then move into the peritubular capillaries that surround the tubule. Most of the water (usually more than 99% of it) and many ions are reabsorbed as well, but the amounts are regulated so that blood volume, pressure, and ion concentration are maintained within required levels for homeostasis.

Reabsorbed substances move from the lumen of the renal tubule to the lumen of a peritubular capillary. Three membranes are traversed, as follows.

1. The **luminal membrane,** or the side of the tubule cells facing the tubule lumen.

2. The **basolateral membrane,** or the side of the tubule cells facing the interstitial fluids.

3. The **endothelium** of the capillaries.

Tight junctions between tubule cells prevent substances from leaking out between the cells. Movement of substances out of the tubule, then, must occur through the cells, either by active transport (requiring ATP) or by passive transport processes. Once outside the tubule and in the interstitial fluids, substances move into the peritubular capillaries or vasa recta by passive processes.

The reabsorption of most substances from the tubule to the interstitial fluids requires a membrane-bound transport protein that carries these substances across the tubule cell membrane by active transport. When all of the available transport proteins are being used, the rate of reabsorption reaches a **transport maximum (Tm)**, and substances that cannot be transported are lost in the urine.

The following mechanisms direct tubular reabsorption in the indicated regions.

1. *Active transport of Na^+ (PCT, DCT, collecting duct)*. Because Na^+ concentration is low inside tubular cells, Na^+ enters the tubular cells (across the luminal membrane) by passive diffusion. At the other side of the tubule cells, the basolateral membrane bears proteins that function as sodium-potassium (Na^+-K^+) pumps. These pumps use ATP to simultaneously export Na^+ while importing K^+. Thus, Na^+ in the tubule cells is transported out of the cells and into the interstitial fluid by active transport. The Na^+ in the interstitial fluid then enters the capillaries by passive diffusion. (The K^+ that is transported into the cell leaks back passively into the interstitial fluid.)

2. *Symporter transport (secondary active transport) of nutrients and ions (PCT, loop of Henle)*. Various nutrients, such as glucose and amino acids, and certain ions (K^+ and Cl^-) in the thick ascending limb of the loop of Henle are transported into the tubule cells by the action of Na^+ **symporters.** An Na^+ symporter is a transport protein that carries both Na^+ and another molecule, such as glucose, across a membrane in the *same* direction. Movement of glucose and other nutrients from the tubular lumen into tubule cells occurs in this fashion. The process requires a low concentration of Na^+ inside the cells, a condition maintained by the Na^+-K^+ pump operating on the basolateral membranes of the tubule cells. The movement of nutrients into cells by this mechanism is referred to as **secondary active transport,** because the ATP-requiring mechanism is the Na^+-K^+ pump and not the symporter itself. Once inside

the tubular cells, nutrients move into the interstitial fluid and into the capillaries by passive processes.

3. *Passive transport of H_2O by osmosis (PCT, DCT)*. The buildup of Na^+ in the peritubular capillaries creates a concentration gradient across which water passively moves, from tubule to capillaries, by osmosis. Thus, the reabsorption of Na^+ by active transport generates the subsequent reabsorption of H_2O by passive transport, a process called **obligatory H_2O reabsorption.**

4. *Passive transport of various solutes by diffusion (PCT, DCT, and collecting duct)*. As H_2O moves from the tubule to the capillaries, various solutes, such as K^+, Cl^-, HCO_3^-, and urea become more concentrated in the tubule. As a result, these solutes follow the water, moving by diffusion out of the tubule and into capillaries where their concentrations are lower, a process called **solvent drag.** Also, the accumulation of the positively charged Na^+ in the capillaries creates an electrical gradient that attracts (by diffusion) negatively charged ions (Cl^-, HCO_3^-).

5. *H_2O and solute transport regulated by hormones (DCT and collecting duct)*. The permeability of the DCT and collecting duct and the resultant reabsorption of H_2O and Na^+ are controlled by two hormones, as follows.

   - **Aldosterone** increases the reabsorption of Na^+ and H_2O by stimulating an increase in the number of Na^+-K^+ pump proteins in the **principal cells** that line the DCT and collecting duct.

   - **Antidiuretic hormone (ADH)** increases H_2O reabsorption by stimulating an increase in the number of H_2O-channel proteins in the principal cells of the collecting duct.

Tubular Secretion

In contrast to tubular reabsorption which *returns* substances to the blood, tubular secretion *removes* substances from the blood and secretes them into the filtrate. Secreted substances include H^+, K^+, NH_4^+ (ammonium ion), creatinine (a waste product of muscle contraction), and various other substances (including penicillin and other drugs). Secretion occurs in portions of the PCT, DCT, and collecting duct.

1. *Secretion of H^+.* Because a decrease in H^+ causes a rise in pH (a decrease in acidity), H^+ secretion into the renal tubule is a mechanism for raising blood pH. Various acids produced by cellular metabolism accumulate in the blood and require that their presence be neutralized by removing H^+. In addition, CO_2, also a metabolic by-product, combines with water (catalyzed by the enzyme **carbonic anhydrase**) to produce carbonic acid (H_2CO_3), which dissociates to produce H^+, as follows.

$$CO_2 + H_2O \leftrightarrow H_2CO_3 \leftrightarrow H^+ + HCO_3^-$$

This chemical reaction occurs in either direction (it is reversible) depending upon the concentration of the various reactants. As a result, if HCO_3^- increases in the blood, it acts as a buffer of H^+, combining with it (and effectively removing it) to produce CO_2 and H_2O. *An increase in acid levels in the blood, then, can be compensated for either by removing H^+ from the blood or by adding HCO_3^- to the blood to buffer H^+,* that is, to combine with the H^+ and neutralize its effect. In fact, renal secretion of H^+ accomplishes an increase in blood pH by this latter method.

CO_2 in tubular cells of the collecting duct combines with H_2O to form H^+ and HCO_3^-. The CO_2 may originate in the tubular cells or it may enter these cells by diffusion from the renal tubule, interstitial fluids, or peritubular capillaries. In the tubule cell, Na^+-H^+ **antiporters,** enzymes that move transported substances in *opposite* directions, transport H^+ across the luminal membrane into the tubule while importing Na^+. Inside the tubule, H^+ may combine with any of several buffers that entered the tubule as filtrate (HCO_3^-, NH_3, or HPO_4^{2-}). If HCO_3^- is the buffer, then H_2CO_3 is formed, producing H_2O and CO_2. The CO_2 then enters the tubular cell where it can combine with H_2O again. If H^+ combines with another buffer, it is excreted in the urine. Regardless of the fate of the H^+ in the tubule, the HCO_3^- produced in the first step is transported across the basolateral membrane by an HCO_3^--Cl^- antiporter. The HCO_3^- enters the peritubular capillaries where it combines with the H^+ in the blood and increases blood pH. Note that the blood pH is increased by adding HCO_3^- to the blood, not by removing H^+.

2. *Secretion of NH$_3$.* When amino acids are broken down, they produce toxic NH_3. The liver converts most NH_3 to urea, a less toxic substance. Both enter the filtrate during glomerular filtration and are excreted in the urine. However, when the blood is very acidic, the tubule cells break down the amino acid glutamate, producing NH_3 and HCO_3^-. The NH_3 combines with H^+, forming NH_4^+, which is transported across the luminal membrane by an Na^+ antiporter and excreted in the urine. The HCO_3^- moves to the blood (as discussed above for H^+ secretion) and increases blood pH.

3. *Secretion of K$^+$.* Nearly all of the K^+ in filtrate is reabsorbed during tubular reabsorption. When reabsorbed quantities exceed body requirements, excess K^+ is secreted back into the filtrate in the collecting duct and final regions of the DCT. Because aldosterone stimulates an increase in Na^+-K^+ pumps, K^+ secretion (as well as Na^+ reabsorption) increases with aldosterone.

Regulation of Urine Concentration

The loop of Henle of juxtamedullary nephrons is the apparatus that allows the nephron to concentrate urine. The loop is a **countercurrent multiplier system** in which fluids move in opposite directions through side-by-side, semipermeable tubes. Substances are transported horizontally, by passive or active mechanisms, from one tube to the other. The movement of the transported substances up and down the tubes results in a higher concentration of substances at the bottom of the tubes than at the tops of the tubes. Details of the process follow (Figure 69).

1. The descending limb of the loop of Henle is permeable to H_2O, so H_2O diffuses out into the surrounding fluids. Because the loop is impermeable to Na^+ and Cl^- and because these ions are not pumped out by active transport, Na^+ and Cl^- remain inside the loop.

2. As the fluid continues to travel down the descending limb of the loop, it becomes more and more concentrated, as water continues to diffuse out. Maximum concentration occurs at the bottom of the loop.

3. The ascending limb of the loop of Henle is impermeable to water, but Na^+ and Cl^- are pumped out into the surrounding fluids by active transport.

4. As fluid travels up the ascending limb, it becomes less and less concentrated because Na^+ and Cl^- are pumped out. At the top of the ascending limb, the fluid is only slightly less concentrated than at the top of the descending limb. In other words, there is little change in the concentration of the fluid in the tubule as a result of traversing the loop of Henle.

5. In the fluid surrounding the loop of Henle, however, a gradient of salt (Na^+, Cl^-) is established, increasing in concentration from the top to the bottom of the loop.

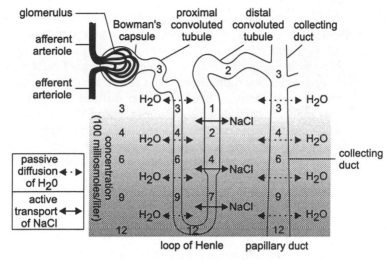

Regulation of Urine Concentration

■ Figure 69 ■

6. Fluid at the top of the collecting duct has a concentration of salts about equal to that at the beginning of the loop of Henle (some water is reabsorbed in the DCT). As the fluid descends the collecting duct, the fluid is exposed to the surrounding salt gradient established by the loop of Henle. Without ADH, the collecting duct is impermeable to H_2O. Two outcomes are possible.

   ■ If water conservation is necessary, ADH stimulates the opening of water channels in the collecting duct, allowing H_2O to diffuse out of the duct and into the surrounding fluids. The result is concentrated urine. This is illustrated in the collecting duct in Figure 69.

   ■ If water conservation is not necessary, ADH is not secreted and the duct remains impermeable to H_2O. The result is dilute urine.

7. The vasa recta delivers O_2 and nutrients to cells of the loop of Henle. The vasa recta, like other capillaries, is permeable to both H_2O and salts and could disrupt the salt gradient established by the loop of Henle. To avoid this, the vasa recta acts as a countercurrent multiplier system as well. As the vasa recta descends into the renal medulla, water diffuses out into the surrounding fluids and salts diffuse in. When the vasa recta ascends, the reverse occurs. As a result, the concentration of salts in the vasa recta is always about the same as that in the surrounding fluids, and the salt gradient established by the loop of Henle remains in place.

Ureters

The **ureters,** one from each kidney, deliver urine to the bladder. The ureters enter through the back of the bladder, entering at an angle such that when the bladder fills, the ureter openings are forced closed. A cross section of the ureter reveals three layers of tissue.

1. An inner **mucosa** consists of transitional epithelium covered by a lamina propria of connective tissue. Mucus secretions protect the ureter tissues from the urine.

2. A middle **muscularis** layer consists of longitudinal and circular layers of smooth muscle fibers. The muscle fibers force urine forward by peristalsis.

3. The outer **adventitia** consists of areolar connective tissue containing nerves, blood vessels, and lymphatic vessels.

Urinary Bladder

The **urinary bladder** is a muscular sac for storing urine. The triangular base of the bladder, the **trigone,** is defined by the two ureters that deliver the urine and the one urethra that drains the urine. When empty, the bladder collapses, and folds (called **rugae**) form in the bladder wall. As it fills, the folds become distended and the bladder becomes spherical. The wall of the bladder consists of three layers similar to those of the urethra—the mucosa, the muscularis (here called the **detrusor muscle**), and the adventitia. Circular smooth muscle fibers around the urethra form the **internal urethral sphincter.**

Urethra

The **urethra** drains urine from the bladder to an exterior opening of the body, the **external urethral orifice.** In females, the urethra is about 3-4 cm (1.5 in) long and opens to the outside of the body between the vagina and the clitoris. In males, the urethra is about 15-20 cm (6-8 in) long and passes through the prostate gland, the urogenital diaphragm, and the penis. In these regions, the urethra is called the **prostatic urethra, membranous urethra,** and spongy **(penile) urethra,** respectively. In both males and females, a skeletal muscle, the **external urethral sphincter,** surrounds the urethra as it passes through the urogenital diaphragm.

    Micturition, or urination, is the process of releasing urine from the bladder into the urethra. When the bladder fills to about 200 ml to 300 ml, stretch receptors in the bladder wall trigger a reflex arc. The signal stimulates the spinal cord which responds with a parasympathetic impulse that relaxes the internal urethral sphincter and contracts the detrusor muscle. Urine does not flow, however, until a voluntary nerve impulse relaxes the skeletal muscle of the external urethral sphincter.

Reproduction describes the production of eggs and sperm and the processes leading to fertilization. The **reproductive system** consists of the **primary sex organs,** or **gonads** (**testes** in males and **ovaries** in females), which secrete hormones and produce **gametes** (sperm and eggs). **Accessory reproductive organs** include ducts, glands, and the external genitalia.

The Male Reproductive System

The **male reproductive system** consists of the following structures (Figure 70).

1. The **scrotum** is a sac consisting of skin and superficial fascia that hangs from the base of the penis. A vertical septum divides the scrotum into left and right compartments, each of which encloses a testis. The external scrotum positions the testes outside the body in an environment about 3°C below that of the body cavity, a condition necessary for the development and storage of sperm. The following two muscles help maintain this temperature.

   - The **dartos muscle** is located in the superficial fascia of the scrotum and septum. Contraction of this smooth muscle creates wrinkles in the scrotum skin. The wrinkling thickens the skin, reducing heat loss when external temperatures are too cold.

   - The **cremaster muscles** extend from the internal oblique muscle to the scrotum. Contraction of these skeletal muscles lifts the scrotum closer to the body when external temperatures are too cold.

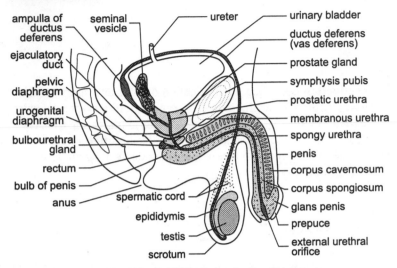

Sagittal View of Male Reproductive System

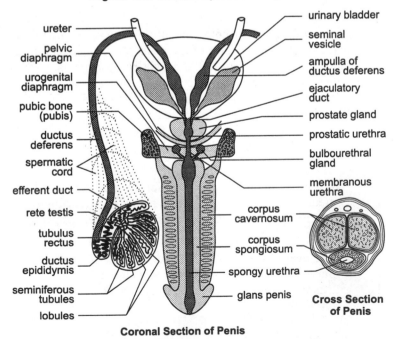

Coronal Section of Penis

Cross Section of Penis

■ Figure 70 ■

2. Each of the two **testes** (singular, **testis**) consists of the following structures.

- The **tunica vaginalis** is a two-layered outer serous membrane surrounding each testis.

- The **tunica albuginea** lies inside the tunica vaginalis and protrudes inward, dividing each testis into compartments called **lobules.**

- One to four tightly coiled tubes, the **seminiferous tubules,** lie inside each lobule. The seminiferous tubules are the sites of sperm production (**spermatogenesis**). The tubule is lined with **spermatogenic cells,** cells that form sperm, and **sustentacular cells (Sertoli cells),** cells that support the developing sperm. The coiled seminiferous tubules inside each lobule unite to form a straight tube, the **tubulus rectus.**

- The **rete testis** is a network of tubes formed by the merging of the tubulus recti from each lobule.

- The **efferent ducts** transport sperm out of the testis (from the rete testis) to the epididymis.

- **Interstitial cells (Leydig cells)** surrounding the seminiferous tubules secrete testosterone and other androgen hormones.

3. The **epididymis** is a comma-shaped organ that lies adjacent to each testis. Each of the two epididymides contains a tightly coiled tube, the **ductus epididymis.** Here sperm complete their maturation and are stored until ejaculation. During ejaculation smooth muscles encircling the epididymis contract, forcing mature sperm into the next tube, the ductus deferens. The walls of the ductus epididymis contain microvilli called **stereocilia** that nourish the sperm.

4. The **ductus deferens (vas deferens)** is the tube through which sperm travel when they leave the epididymis. Each of the two tubes enters the abdominal cavity, passes around the bladder

(see Figure 70), and together with the duct from the seminal vesicle, joins the ejaculatory duct. Before entering the ejaculatory duct, the ductus deferens enlarges, forming a region called the **ampulla.** Sperm are stored in the ductus deferens until peristaltic contractions of the smooth muscles surrounding the ductus force sperm forward during ejaculation.

5. The **ejaculatory ducts** are short tubes that connect each ductus deferens to the urethra.

6. The **urethra** is the passageway for urine and semen (sperm and associated secretions). Three regions of the urethra are distinguished.

   - The **prostatic urethra** passes through the prostate gland (discussed below).

   - The **membranous urethra** passes through the urogenital diaphragm (muscles associated with the pelvic region).

   - The **spongy (penile) urethra** passes through the penis.

   The urethra ends at the **external urethral orifice.**

7. The **spermatic cord** contains blood vessels, lymphatic vessels, nerves, the ductus deferens, and the cremaster muscle. It connects each testis to the body cavity, entering the abdominal wall through the **inguinal canal.**

8. The **accessory sex glands** are glands that secrete substances into the passageways that transport sperm. These substances contribute to the liquid portion of the semen.

   - The **seminal vesicles** secrete into the vas deferens an alkaline fluid (which neutralizes the acid in the vagina), fructose (which provides energy for the sperm), and prostaglandins (which increase sperm viability and stimulate female uterine contractions that help sperm move into the uterus).

- The **prostate gland** secretes a milky, slightly acidic fluid into the urethra. Various substances in the fluid increase sperm mobility and viability.

- The **bulbourethral (Cowper's) glands** secrete an alkaline fluid into the spongy urethra. The fluid neutralizes acidic urine in the urethra before ejaculation occurs.

9. The **penis** is a cylindrical organ that passes urine and delivers sperm. It consists of a **root** that attaches the penis to the perineum, a **body (shaft)** that makes up the bulk of the penis, and the **glans penis,** the enlarged end of the body. The glans penis is covered by a **prepuce (foreskin)**, which may be surgically removed by a procedure called **circumcision.** Internally, the penis consists of three cylindrical masses of tissue, each of which is surrounded by a thin layer of fibrous tissue, the **tunica albuginea.** The three cylindrical masses, which function as erectile bodies, are described below.

   - Two **corpora cavernosa** fill most of the volume of the penis. Their bases, called the **crura** (singular, **crus) of the penis,** attach to the urogenital diaphragm.

   - A single **corpus spongiosum** encloses the urethra and expands at the end to form the glans penis. The **bulb of the penis,** an enlargement at the base of the corpus spongiosum, attaches to the urogenital diaphragm.

During **erection,** *parasympathetic* neurons stimulate dilation of the arteries that deliver blood to the corpus cavernosa and spongiosum. As a result, blood collects in these blood vessels and causes the penis to enlarge and stiffen. **Ejaculation** occurs when *sympathetic* neurons stimulate the discharge of sperm and supporting fluids from their various sources. During ejaculation, the sphincter muscle at the base of the urinary bladder constricts, preventing the passage of urine.

Spermatogenesis

The cells that line the walls of the seminiferous tubules are collectively called spermatogenic cells. Those cells nearest the basement membrane are called **spermatogonia.** These cells are **stem cells;** that is, they are capable of continuous division and remain undifferentiated, never maturing into specialized cells. Extending from the spermatogonia toward the lumen of the tubule are cells at various levels of maturity, with the most mature cells—the sperm—facing the lumen.

Spermatogenesis begins at *puberty* within the seminiferous tubules of the testes. The spermatogonia, each of which contains 46 chromosomes, divide by mitosis repeatedly to produce **primary spermatocytes** (still diploid cells with 46 chromosomes each). The primary spermatocytes begin meiosis. During the first meiotic division (meiosis I, or the reduction division), each primary spermatocyte divides into two **secondary spermatocytes,** each with 23 chromosomes (haploid cells). During the second meiotic division (meiosis II, or the equatorial division), each secondary spermatocyte divides again, producing a total of four **spermatids.** Each spermatid still contains 23 chromosomes, but these chromosomes consist of only one chromatid (rather than the normal two chromatids).

Spermiogenesis describes the development of spermatids into mature sperm (sperm cells, or spermatozoa). At the end of this process each sperm cell bears the following structures.

1. The **head** of the sperm contains the haploid nucleus with 23 chromosomes. At the tip of the sperm head is the **acrosome,** a lysosome containing enzymes which are used to penetrate the egg. The acrosome originates from Golgi body vesicles that fuse to form a single lysosome.

2. The **midpiece** is the first part of the tail. Mitochondria spiral around the midpiece and produce energy (ATP) used to generate the whiplike movements of the tail that propel the sperm.

3. The **tail** is a flagellum consisting of the typical 9 + 2 microtubule array.

Hormonal Regulation of Spermatogenesis

The production of sperm is regulated by hormones, as follows (Figure 71a).

1. The hypothalamus begins secreting **gonadotropin releasing hormone (GnRH)** at puberty.

2. GnRH stimulates the anterior pituitary to secrete **follicle stimulating hormone (FSH)** and **luteinizing hormone (LH)**.

3. LH stimulates the interstitial cells in the testes to produce **testosterone** and other male sex hormones (androgens). (In males, LH is also called **interstitial cell stimulating hormone,** or **ICSH.**)

4. **Testosterone** produces the following effects.

   ■ Testosterone stimulates the final stages of sperm development in the nearby seminiferous tubules. It accumulates in these tissues because testosterone and FSH act together to stimulate sustentacular cells to release **androgen-binding protein (ABP).** ABP holds testosterone in these cells.

   ■ Testosterone entering the blood circulates throughout the body where it stimulates activity in the prostate gland, seminal vesicles, and various other target tissues.

   ■ Testosterone and other androgens stimulate the development of **secondary sex characteristics,** those characteristics not directly involved in reproduction. These include the distribution of muscle and fat typical in adult males, various body hair (facial and pubic hair, for example), and deepening of the voice.

Levels of testosterone are regulated by a negative-feedback mechanism with the hypothalamus. When the hypothalamus detects excessive amounts of testosterone in the blood, it reduces its secretion of GnRH. In response, the anterior pituitary reduces its production of LH and FSH, which results in a decrease in the production of testosterone by interstitial cells. GnRH secretion is also inhibited by **inhibin,** a hormone secreted by sustentacular cells in response to excessive levels of sperm production.

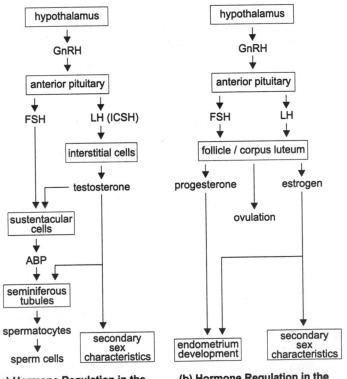

**(a) Hormone Regulation in the
Male Reproductive System**

**(b) Hormone Regulation in the
Female Reproductive System**

■ Figure 71 ■

The Female Reproductive System

The **female reproductive system** consists of the following structures
(Figure 72).

1. The **ovary** is the organ that produces **ova** (singular, **ovum**), or
   eggs. The two ovaries present in each female are held in place
   by the following ligaments.

   - The **mesovarium** is a fold of peritoneum that holds the
     ovary in place.

   - The **suspensory ligament** anchors the upper region of the
     ovary to the pelvic wall. Attached to this ligament are blood
     vessels and nerves which enter the ovary at the **hilus.**

   - The **broad ligament** is a section of the peritoneum that
     drapes over the ovaries and uterus. It includes both the meso-
     varium and suspensory ligament.

   - The **ovarian ligament** anchors the lower end of the ovary
     to the uterus.

   The following two tissues cover the outside of the ovary.

   - The **germinal epithelium** is an outer layer of simple epi-
     thelium.

   - The **tunica albuginea** is a fibrous layer inside the germi-
     nal epithelium.

   The inside of the ovary, or **stroma,** is divided into two indis-
   tinct regions, the outer **cortex** and the inner **medulla.** Embedded in the cortex are saclike bodies called **ovarian follicles.**
   Each ovarian follicle consists of an immature oocyte (egg)
   surrounded by one or more layers of cells that nourish the
   oocyte as it matures. The surrounding cells are called **follicular cells,** if they make up a single layer, or **granulosa cells,** if
   more than one layer is present.

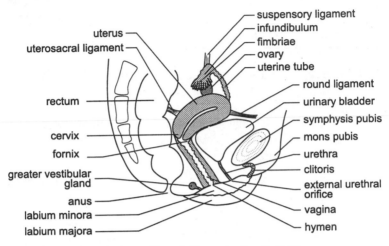

Sagittal View of Female Reproductive System

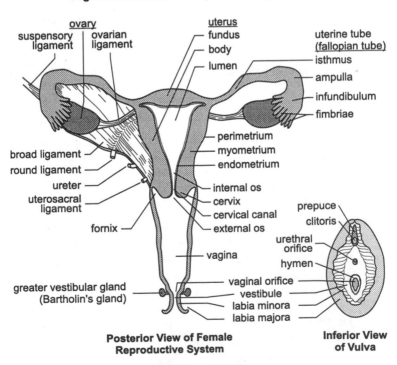

**Posterior View of Female
Reproductive System**

**Inferior View
of Vulva**

■ Figure 72 ■

2. The **uterine tubes (fallopian tubes,** or **oviducts)** transport the secondary oocytes away from the ovary and toward the uterus. The following regions characterize each of the two uterine tubes (one for each ovary).

- The **infundibulum** is a funnel-shaped region of the uterine tube that bears fingerlike projections called **fimbriae.** Pulsating cilia on the fimbriae draw the secondary oocyte into the uterine tube.

- The **ampulla** is the widest and longest region of the uterine tube. Fertilization of the oocyte by a sperm usually occurs here.

- The **isthmus** is a narrow region of the uterine tube whose terminus enters the uterus.

The wall of the uterine tube consists of the following three layers.

- The **serosa,** a serous membrane, lines the outside of the uterine tube.

- The middle **muscularis** consists of two layers of smooth muscle that generate peristaltic contractions that help propel the oocyte forward.

- The **inner mucosa** consists of ciliated columnar epithelial cells that help propel the oocyte forward and secretory cells that lubricate the tube and nourish the oocyte.

3. The **uterus (womb)** is a hollow organ within which fetal development occurs. The uterus is characterized by the following regions.

- The **fundus** is the upper region where the uterine ducts join the uterus.

- The **body** is the major, central portion of the uterus.

- The **isthmus** is the lower, narrow portion of the uterus.

- The **cervix** is a narrow region at the bottom of the uterus that leads into the vagina. The inside of the cervix, or **cervical canal,** opens to the uterus above through the **internal os** and to the vagina below through the **external os.** **Cervical mucus** secreted by the mucosa layer of the cervical canal serves to protect against bacteria entering the uterus from the vagina. If an oocyte is available for fertilization, the mucus is thin and slightly alkaline, attributes that promote the passage of sperm. At other times, the mucus is viscous and impedes the passage of sperm.

The uterus is held in place by the following ligaments.

- The **broad ligaments**
- The **uterosacral ligaments**
- The **round ligaments**
- The **cardinal (lateral cervical) ligaments**

The wall of the uterus consists of the following three layers.

- The **perimetrium** is a serous membrane that lines the outside of the uterus.

- The **myometrium** consists of several layers of smooth muscle and imparts the bulk of the uterine wall. Contractions of these muscles during childbirth help force the fetus out of the uterus.

- The **endometrium** is the highly vascularized mucosa that lines the inside of the uterus. If an oocyte has been fertilized by a sperm, the zygote (the fertilized egg) implants on this tissue. The endometrium itself consists of two layers. The **stratum functionalis (functional layer)** is the innermost layer (facing the uterine lumen) and is shed during menstruation. The outermost **stratum basalis (basal layer)** is permanent and generates each new stratum functionalis.

4. The **vagina** (**birth canal**) serves both as the passageway for a newborn infant and as a depository for semen during sexual intercourse. The upper region of the vagina surrounds the protruding cervix, creating a recess called the **fornix**. The lower region of the vagina opens to the outside at the **vaginal orifice**. A thin membrane called the **hymen** may cover the orifice. The vaginal wall consists of the following layers.

   ■ The outer **adventitia** holds the vagina in position.

   ■ The middle **muscularis** consists of two layers of smooth muscle that permit expansion of the vagina during childbirth and when the penis is inserted.

   ■ The inner **mucosa** has no glands. But bacterial action on glycogen stored in these cells produces an acid solution that lubricates the vagina and protects it against microbial infection. The acidic environment is also inhospitable to sperm. The mucosa bears transverse ridges called **rugae**.

5. The **vulvae** (**pudendum**) make up the external genitalia. The following structures are included.

   ■ The **mons pubis** is a region of adipose tissue above the vagina that is covered with hair.

   ■ The **labia majora** are two folds of adipose tissue that border each side of the vagina. Hair and sebaceous and sudoriferous glands are present. Developmentally, the labia majora are analogous to the male scrotum.

   ■ The **labia minora** are smaller folds of skin that lie inside the labia majora. Hair is absent.

   ■ The **vestibule** is the recess formed by the labia minora. It encloses the vaginal orifice, the urethral opening, and ducts from the greater vestibular glands whose mucus secretions lubricate the vestibule.

- The **clitoris** is a small mass of erectile and nervous tissues located above the vestibule. Extensions of the labia minora join to form the **prepuce of the clitoris,** a fold of skin covering the clitoris.

Mammary Glands

The **mammary glands** are sudoriferous (sweat) glands specialized for the production of milk. The milk-producing secretory cells form walls of bulb-shaped chambers called **alveoli** that join together with ducts, in grapelike fashion, to form clusters called **lobules.** Numerous lobules assemble to form a **lobe.** Each breast contains a single mammary gland consisting of 15 to 20 of these lobes. **Lactiferous ducts** leading away from the lobes widen into **lactiferous sinuses** that serve as temporary reservoirs for milk. The ducts narrow again as they lead through a protruding nipple. The nipple, whose texture is made coarse by the presence of sebaceous glands, is surrounded by a ring of pigmented skin called the **areola.** Contraction of **myoepithelial cells** surrounding the alveoli force milk toward the nipples.

The breasts begin to enlarge in females at the onset of puberty. Proliferating adipose (fat) tissue expands the breast while **suspensory ligaments (Cooper's ligaments)** attached to the underlying fascia provide support. In nonpregnant females (and males), the glands and ducts are not fully developed.

During pregnancy, estrogen and progesterone stimulate extensive development of the mammary glands and associated ducts. After childbirth, various hormones, especially prolactin from the anterior pituitary, initiate **lactation,** or milk production. When neurons are stimulated by the sucking of an infant, nerve impulses activate the posterior pituitary to secrete oxytocin which, in turn, stimulates contraction of the myoepithelial cells surrounding the alveoli. Milk is then forced toward the nipple (the **letdown reflex**).

Oogenesis

Oogenesis consists of the meiotic cell divisions that lead to the production of ova (eggs) in females. The process begins during *fetal development* within the fetal ovary. Diploid cells called **oogonia** divide by mitosis to produce **primary oocytes** (still diploid with 46 chromosomes). Each primary oocyte is encircled by one or more layers of cells. The oocyte and encircling cells together are called an **ovarian follicle.** The primary oocytes (within their follicles) begin meiosis, but division progresses only to prophase I. They remain at this stage until puberty.

The following stages in the development of an ovarian follicle are observed.

1. The **primordial follicle,** the initial fetal state of the follicle, encircles the oocyte with a single layer of cells called **follicular cells.**

2. The **primary follicle,** the next stage of follicular development, possesses two or more layers of encircling cells now called **granulosa cells.**

3. The **secondary follicle** is distinguished by the presence of the **antrum,** a fluid-filled, central cavity.

4. In a **mature (vesicular,** or **Graafian) follicle,** the primary oocyte has completed meiosis I. It is the stage of follicular development that precedes ejection of the oocyte from the ovary (ovulation). The following features are observed.

   - The **zona pellucida,** a clear layer of glycoprotein, surrounds the oocyte.

   - The **corona radiata,** a ring of granulosa cells, encircles the zona pellucida.

- The **theca folliculi,** the ovarian cells immediately surrounding the outer layers of granulosa cells, differentiate into an internal layer (facing the follicle) of secretory cells, the **theca interna,** and an external layer of connective tissue, the **theca externa.**

5. The **corpus luteum** is the remains of the follicle following ovulation. It remains functional, producing estrogen, progesterone, and inhibin, until it finally degenerates.

During each menstrual cycle, one primary oocyte, enclosed in its follicle, resumes meiosis I to produce two daughter cells (each haploid with 23 chromosomes). One daughter cell, the **secondary oocyte,** contains most of the cytoplasm, ensuring that adequate amounts of stored food, as well as mitochondria, ribosomes, and other cytoplasmic organelles, will be available for the developing embryo. The other daughter cell, a **first polar body,** is much smaller, and contains little cytoplasm and few, if any, organelles. The secondary oocyte then begins meiosis II (equatorial division) but again stops at prophase (this time prophase II). The first polar body may also begin meiosis II, but it will eventually degenerate.

Ovulation occurs when a secondary oocyte and its first polar body, surrounded by the zona pellucida and corona radiata, rupture from their mature follicle and are expelled from the surface of the ovary. The oocyte is then swept up into the uterine (fallopian) tube and advances toward the uterus. If a sperm cell penetrates the corona radiata and zona pellucida and enters the secondary oocyte, meiosis II resumes in the secondary oocyte producing an **ovum** and a **second polar body.** If a first polar body is present, it too may resume meiosis II, producing daughter polar bodies. Fertilization occurs when the nuclei of the sperm cell and ovum unite, forming a **zygote** (fertilized egg). Any polar bodies present ultimately degenerate.

Hormonal Regulation of Oogenesis and the Menstrual Cycle

The human female reproductive cycle is characterized by events in the ovary (**ovarian cycle**) and the uterus (**menstrual cycle**). The purpose of these cycles is to produce an egg and to prepare the uterus for the implantation of the egg, should it become fertilized. The **ovarian cycle** consists of three phases, as follows.

1. The **follicular phase** describes the development of the follicle, the meiotic stages of division leading to the formation of the secondary oocyte, and the secretion of estrogen from the follicle.

2. **Ovulation,** occurring at midcycle, is the ejection of the egg from the ovary.

3. The **luteal phase** describes the secretion of estrogen and progesterone from the corpus luteum (previously the follicle) after ovulation.

The **menstrual (uterine) cycle** consists of three phases, as follows.

1. The **proliferative phase** describes the thickening of the endometrium of the uterus, replacing tissues that were lost during the previous menstrual cycle.

2. The **secretory phase** follows ovulation and describes further thickening and vascularization of the endometrium in preparation for the implantation of a fertilized egg.

3. The **menstrual phase (menstruation, menses)** describes the shedding of the endometrium when implantation does not occur.

The activities of the ovary and the uterus are coordinated by negative and positive feedback responses involving **gonadotropin releasing hormone (GnRH)** from the hypothalamus, **follicle stimulating hormone (FSH)** and **luteinizing hormone (LH)** from the anterior pituitary, and the hormones **estrogen** and **progesterone** from the follicle and corpus luteum. A description of the events follows (Figures 71b and 73).

1. *The hypothalamus and anterior pituitary initiate the reproductive cycle.* The hypothalamus monitors the levels of estrogen and progesterone in the blood. In a *negative-feedback* fashion, low levels of these hormones stimulate the hypothalamus to secrete GnRH, which, in turn, stimulates the anterior pituitary to secrete FSH and LH.

2. *The follicle develops.* FSH stimulates the development of the follicle from primary through mature stages.

3. *The follicle secretes estrogen.* LH stimulates the cells of the theca interna and the granulosa cells of the follicle to secrete estrogen. Inhibin is also secreted by the granulosa cells.

4. *Ovulation occurs. Positive feedback* from rising levels of estrogen stimulate the anterior pituitary (through GnRH from the hypothalamus) to produce a sudden midcycle surge of LH. This high level of LH stimulates meiosis in the primary oocyte to progress toward prophase II and triggers ovulation.

5. *The corpus luteum secretes estrogen and progesterone.* After ovulation, the follicle, now transformed into the corpus luteum, continues to develop under the influence of LH and secretes both estrogen and progesterone.

6. *The endometrium thickens.* Estrogen and progesterone stimulate the development of the endometrium, the inside lining of the uterus. It thickens with nutrient-rich tissue and blood vessels in preparation for the implantation of a fertilized egg.

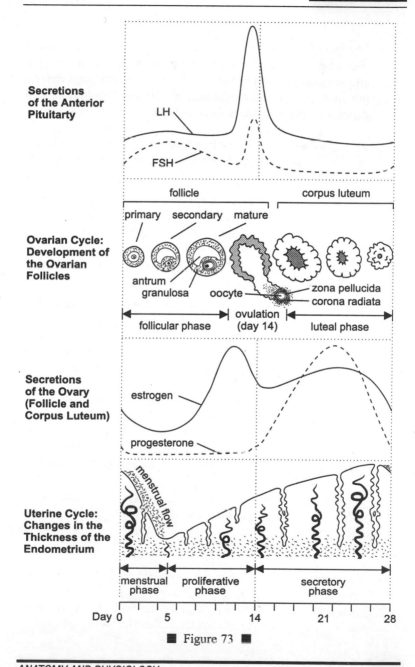

Secretions of the Anterior Pituitarty

Ovarian Cycle: Development of the Ovarian Follicles

Secretions of the Ovary (Follicle and Corpus Luteum)

Uterine Cycle: Changes in the Thickness of the Endometrium

LH

FSH

follicle

corpus luteum

primary   secondary   mature

antrum
granulosa

oocyte

zona pellucida
corona radiata

follicular phase

ovulation
(day 14)

luteal phase

estrogen

progesterone

menstrual flow

menstrual
phase

proliferative
phase

secretory
phase

Day 0   5   14   21   28

■ Figure 73 ■

7. *The hypothalamus and anterior pituitary terminate the reproductive cycle.* Negative feedback from high levels of estrogen and progesterone cause the anterior pituitary (through the hypothalamus) to abate production of FSH and LH. Inhibin also suppresses production of FSH and LH.

8. *The endometrium either disintegrates or is maintained, depending upon whether implantation of the fertilized egg occurs, as follows.*

   ▪ *Implantation does not occur.* In the absence of FSH and LH, the corpus luteum deteriorates. As a result, estrogen and progesterone production stops. Without estrogen and progesterone, growth of the endometrium is no longer supported, and it disintegrates, sloughing off during menstruation.

   ▪ *Implantation occurs.* The implanted embryo secretes human chorionic gonadotropin (hCG) to sustain the corpus luteum. The corpus luteum continues to produce estrogen and progesterone, maintaining the endometrium. (Pregnancy tests check for the presence of hCG in the urine.)

In addition to influencing the reproductive cycle, estrogen stimulates the development of secondary sex characteristics in females. These include the distribution of adipose tissue (to the breasts, hips, and mons pubis), bone development leading to a broadening of the pelvis, changes in voice quality, and growth of various body hair.

Think Quick

Now there are more Cliffs Quick Review® titles, providing help with more introductory level courses. Use Quick Reviews to increase your understanding of fundamental principles in a given subject, as well as to prepare for quizzes, midterms and finals.

Do better in the classroom, and on papers and tests with Cliffs Quick Reviews.